Out on a Limb

Short Plays by New Playwrights

edited by Kit Brennan

Signature EDITIONS

Cover design by Doowah Design.
This book was printed on Ancient Forest Friendly paper.
Printed and bound in Canada by Hignell Book Printing.

We acknowledge the support of the Canada Council for the Arts and the Manitoba Arts Council for our publishing program.

Library and Archives Canada Cataloguing in Publication

Out on a limb : short plays by new playwrights / edited by Kit Brennan.

ISBN 978-1-897109-55-7

1. Canadian drama (English)--21st century.
I. Brennan, Kit, 1957-

PS8315.1.O88 2011 C812'.608 C2011-907600-4

Signature Editions
P.O. Box 206, RPO Corydon, Winnipeg, Manitoba, R3M 3S7
www.signature-editions.com

Out on a Limb

Contents

Foreword

With this anthology of short plays by new writers, I was interested in taking the temperature of the times. Over the past several years, I've had the pleasure of teaching many smart, funny, insightful fledgling writers; I've also wanted to get to know the work of others studying at different schools. Consequently, a submission call went out across the country this past summer to university theatre departments and other professional theatre schools that offer courses in playwriting. I asked my colleagues to let their students know about the call, and many scripts flooded in. It was enjoyable reading, and I thank them all.

One of the pleasures of editing an anthology is finding a narrative for the book as a whole. This one speaks of love in its many guises. The dozen plays that lie within these pages are a kind of theatrical chocolate box: often funny, with dark centres.

The plays are more often than not about love, friendship, attraction, commitment — and about fear of these things. The characters range from the very young to the very old. They are witty, hilarious, loyal, and bewildered; they can also be devastatingly cruel or treacherous. They do what they do because they are searching — wishing to find perfect love, or the answer to life's profound mystery; to find release from a poisonous relationship, or a moment of transcendence through letting someone go. The point of view is youthful. Even the very oldest character is where she is because of a decision made in her twenties.

I coordinate the Major in Playwriting program at Concordia University, and a number of years ago, decided to fund a yearly playwriting award for work that comes out of the Theatre Department's writing courses. I enjoy discussions with the jurors later, and have found that comedy is hard but may seem deceptively easy, and it can be underestimated. Most of the plays in this volume exhibit a lively sense of humour, often with a sting or a dark slant or a quiet tragedy at their core, which makes them moving and memorable.

Twelve short scripts, twelve complete worlds. Cast size ranges from one to four actors. There are three one-woman plays, two plays for two men, one play for two women, four plays for one man and one woman, one play for one woman and one man and one other, and one play for two women and two men. Playing time in performance, for each of the scripts, is under one hour.

The book is organized in such a way that the plays might be chronological. The first has characters who are fifteen and sixteen; the final one features a feisty ninety-one-year-old nun. Several scripts in the centre of the volume are explorations of unexpected pregnancy and what happens to a relationship when under that pressure. There is new love which is afraid of itself, and old love that is opening the door to something new.

There are brothers and jealousy, a mother and daughter trying to change their lives, and the reworking of an old warning tale about little girls and temptation.

I've taught playwriting for many years, and often new writers choose cynicism and despair to augment their dramas. The writers in this volume, while still acknowledging that life is hard, make use of more complex observations. Life can be confusing, yes, but in moments such as those you'll encounter in these plays, it is very much worthwhile.

This anthology will interest those seeking short plays or scenes for young actors — whether you are a teacher, a young professional actor or director, or anyone else who is interested in new and exciting work by emerging writers.

Should you decide to produce any of these plays, please remember that these scripts are fully protected by copyright; see page 223, Information on Producing. I encourage you to contact the playwrights through the contact information on that page. I am sure they will be delighted to hear from you.

Kit Brennan
Theatre Department, Concordia University
Montreal, Quebec

Mature Young Adults

by Wesley J. Colford

About the playwright

Wesley J. Colford is an actor/playwright from Sydney, Nova Scotia. Having recently graduated from Sheridan College, he is currently studying acting at George Brown College in Toronto. In the past three years, Wesley has written four full-length plays (including two musicals), nine one-acts, and eight short plays for children. His most successful script to date, *Excuse Me, Would You Like to Buy a Bar?*, was the 2010 winner of Tarragon Theatre's "Under 20 by Under 20's Playwriting Competition," and received a brief workshop at Tarragon under the direction of Andrew Lamb. From there the play was expanded and later produced as part of the Paprika Festival at Tarragon, the success of which led to further expansion and a sold-out run at the 2011 Toronto Fringe Festival. Wesley's first full-length play, *Pizza Passion*, was produced in 2010 as part of the Cape Breton Stage Company's summer season to great artistic and financial acclaim. He has since had several plays produced by the CBSC, including *Too Too Sullied*, *The Collector*, *The Wakowski Brothers*, and his most recent one-act, *Shadowplay*. Wesley is currently in production with *Mature Young Adults* for the 2012 Paprika Festival, and has several other projects on the go, as well as attending occasional classes. Special thanks to everyone involved in the development and dramaturgy of *Mature Young Adults*, including Vaughn Harris, Nicole Power, Kent Nolan, Jono Logan, Scott Sharplin, Courtney Simpson, Renée Haché, Adriana Dimitri, and Mairi Mason.

Characters

BOY — 16
GIRL — 15

Setting

A park in Cape Breton, present.

Lights up on a small park in rural Cape Breton Island. There is a large bench and some shrubs or small trees. There should be an air of beauty, but the atmosphere is generally unkempt. Litter ornaments the scene, despite a garbage can prominent next to the bench.

It is late November and though it has been an unusually warm fall, the air is bitter and abrupt.

At lights up, a GIRL *is seated on the bench, huddled slightly to stay warm. She is wearing a fall sweater. She gets up, looks offstage, and begins pacing impatiently.*

After a minute, a BOY *enters.*

GIRL: And here he is!

BOY: Sorry!

GIRL: The long-awaited one!

BOY: Sorry!

GIRL: Where were you?

BOY: My bike was stolen!

GIRL: Really?

BOY: Not really. I got lost.

GIRL: You got lost?

BOY: I couldn't find the park!

GIRL: It's the only park.

BOY: Well, it's a small park!

GIRL: It's a small town!

BOY: I'm used to a small city.

GIRL: You could have asked someone!

BOY: What kind of adventure would that be?

GIRL: An adventure where I'm not waiting in the cold for half an hour!

BOY: It's not that cold.

GIRL: It's bloody freezing!

BOY: Don't say bloody, that's my word!

GIRL: After a half hour bloody waiting I'll say whatever I bloody want.

BOY: Oh, yeah?

GIRL: Bloody freezing…

BOY: Bloody word stealer…

GIRL: Bloody.

BOY: Hey.

GIRL: Hey.

They embrace sweetly. It is held slightly too long. They look at each other, staying close.

BOY: I missed you.

GIRL: Oh, really?

BOY: Yes.

GIRL: Despite the fact that you talked to me this morning?

BOY: That was three hours ago!

GIRL: And we chatted online until you had to leave?

BOY: Are you saying you didn't miss me?

GIRL: I didn't say that.

BOY: So what are you saying?

GIRL: I'm saying…I didn't not miss you.

BOY: You didn't not miss me?

GIRL: Right.

BOY: So you missed me.

GIRL: I didn't not say that.

BOY: You didn't not deny it.

GIRL: What?

BOY: I don't know. This is fun.

GIRL: Is it?

BOY: I like being here. Seeing you talk. Holding your hand.

He takes her hand. It's clear he's about to lean in to kiss her. She lets go of his hand and backs off slightly.

GIRL: I know, right?

He doesn't know how to take this. Beat.

BOY: I like your sweater.

GIRL: Do you?

BOY: A lot. It's really slimming. Not that you're not slim! You're so slim! If anything, it's not slimming. I mean, you're not fat enough for it to be slimming. Not that you're fat! I mean… You're fantastic. It just really makes your breasts look really… And now I'm talking about your breasts. Which are great. I mean, lovely. I mean… Wow. I am so… You just… You look beautiful.

Beat.

BOY: You look really beautiful.

GIRL: Do you really think that?

BOY: Yes.

Beat.

GIRL: You're crazy.

BOY: How long till you have to get back?

GIRL: Probably twenty more minutes…

BOY: I'm sorry I was so late.

GIRL: I can't believe you biked all the way here.

BOY: It's not that far.

GIRL: It's like an hour!

BOY: I would have walked.

She smiles.

BOY: You know, I really like you.

GIRL: Well...I really like you too.

BOY: Well...cool.

GIRL: Well, cool.

He kisses her hand. She smiles, but then pulls it away.

GIRL: You know my parents would kill me if they knew where I was.

BOY: You're not allowed in the park?

GIRL: Not with strange boys.

BOY: I'm not a strange boy.

GIRL: All boys are strange.

BOY: You'll to have to tell them eventually.

GIRL: Tell them what?

BOY: About us...

GIRL: What's there to tell?

BOY: Well...true.

GIRL: Exactly.

BOY: I mean, it's not like I've been unable to sleep for over a week because my heart won't stop racing and whenever I close my eyes all I can see is that picture of you smiling in the tree with the pink hat...

GIRL: Of course, and it's not like I've spent the last four English classes doodling little hearts in my notebook so the teacher won't notice that all I'm thinking about is how much I want class to be over so I can get home and you can call me...

BOY: Of course. (*beat*) You doodled little hearts?

GIRL: I said I *didn't* doodle little hearts.

BOY: Oh, of course.

GIRL: Indeed.

BOY: But seriously, I mean...I don't want you to get in trouble. I know your parents are...well...your parents.

GIRL: Well, I mean I'm allowed to have boys who are friends...I'm just not allowed to have a...you know...a boyfriend.

BOY: So that's what you consider me? A boy who's a friend?

GIRL: Well, yes. Aren't you?

BOY: Yes... But what about the fact that I'm completely and utterly crazy about you?

GIRL: That just means you're human.

BOY: So as long as I'm just a friend, you don't think your parents will mind?

GIRL: Well, I mean, technically, no. Why would they?

BOY: No reason.

GIRL: No reason at all.

BOY: So, we just have to be good.

GIRL: Yes.

BOY: Friends.

GIRL: Yes.

BOY: Which is good.

GIRL: Yes.

BOY: And…friendly.

GIRL: … Yes.

BOY: I mean, seeing you in person is infinitely preferable to the phone.

GIRL: Or online.

BOY: Or online.

He takes her hand again. Beat.

GIRL: So the only question is, can you behave yourself?

BOY: Oh, I think I can.

GIRL: Do you?

BOY: Yes. For the next twenty minutes we shall be merely two good friends out for a lovely tour of the park.

GIRL: Completely innocent.

BOY: Yes.

GIRL: Completely responsible.

BOY: Yes, two…mature young adults.

GIRL: Mature young adults.

BOY: Yes.

GIRL: Mature young adults… I like it.

BOY: Me too.

GIRL: I like you.

BOY: Me too.

GIRL: J'adore vous.

BOY: (*strained French*) Je ici.

GIRL: (*correcting*) Je aussi.

BOY: Aussi ici.

She smiles. He smiles.

BOY: So when you say I have to be good…

GIRL: Yes…

BOY: I suppose that means I'm not allowed to kiss you.

GIRL: That is correct.

BOY: (*obviously sarcastic*) Not that I'd want to.

GIRL: No.

BOY: I mean, gross.

GIRL: Gross.

BOY: So gross.

GIRL: Yeah, yucky.

BOY: Yucky?

GIRL: Yucky.

BOY: Well, I wouldn't say yucky…

GIRL: Well, no…

BOY: Who says yucky?

GIRL: I don't.

BOY: I don't.

GIRL: No. But gross.

BOY: Yes, gross.

GIRL: Really gross.

BOY: So gross. I would never want to do that…

GIRL: No…

BOY: Never.

GIRL: Never ever.

Beat.

BOY: But… If I did…

GIRL: Which you won't…

BOY: What would happen?

Beat.

GIRL: You can't.

BOY: I know, but what would happen?

GIRL: People would talk.

BOY: What people?

GIRL: People people!

BOY: But no one would see.

GIRL: Oh, people would see!

BOY: Really.

GIRL: Yes. People see everything.

BOY: Even one kiss?

GIRL: Especially one kiss. And then they would talk.

BOY: They would talk?

GIRL: About us.

BOY: Well, I better not kiss you.

GIRL: Better not, boy who's a friend.

She sticks her tongue out at him. Then she shivers.

BOY: Cold?

She nods.

BOY: Want my jacket?

GIRL: I'm tough.

BOY: Okay.

GIRL: Bloody freezing…

BOY: Don't use my word!

She sticks out her tongue again and hits him lightly. He lightly hits her back. She retaliates and they get in a minor, playful scuffle, ending with him holding her to keep her from hitting him. They suddenly realize how close they are and how close they are to kissing.

BOY: Well, I guess you're right.

GIRL: What?

BOY: About the kiss.

GIRL: Oh, yes, the kiss.

BOY: I mean, it would basically be the end of the world.

GIRL: Yes. Yes, it would.

BOY: I mean, like, the ground beneath us would start cracking and eroding…

GIRL: Earthquakes would be the least of our problems!

BOY: Well, the people!

GIRL: Yes, the people.

BOY: Once the people found out, it would be total pandemonium!

GIRL: Total! At least!

BOY: Mobs forming in the streets…

GIRL: People screaming for justice…

BOY: Mothers comforting their crying babes…

GIRL: They'd have to call in the army!

BOY: The air force!

GIRL: A flying squadron of ace fighter pilots would be sent to contain the mass global threat that had been initiated by your one little kiss.

BOY: Well. We'd have to go on the run.

GIRL: The run?

BOY: Yes.

GIRL: Where?

BOY: Spain.

GIRL: Spain?

BOY: Or Greece.

GIRL: I haven't had much luck with Spain…

BOY: Or Switzerland.

GIRL: What happened to Greece?

BOY: Okay, Greece.

GIRL: No, I like Switzerland.

BOY: Okay.

GIRL: Less obvious.

BOY: Very well. We shall run away to Switzerland.

GIRL: To avoid the army.

BOY: And air force.

GIRL: And what do we do when we get there?

BOY: … Eat cheese?

GIRL: Not very romantic.

BOY: Or make clocks…

GIRL: We shall ski.

BOY: Ski?

GIRL: Ski.

BOY: I'm not much of a skier person…

GIRL: Well, you better learn! 'Cause it's only a matter of time before they hunt us down!

BOY: And our only chance of escape is via ski hill?

GIRL: That's right! Over the hill!

BOY: And into Sweden!

GIRL: Sweden is not next to Switzerland.

BOY: It's a really big hill!

GIRL: But they're on to us!

BOY: No!

GIRL: They cut the power!

BOY: No!

GIRL: We're trapped in the ski lift! We're gonna have to jump!

BOY: It's all right, I'll catch you!

GIRL: You?

BOY: Me!

GIRL: My hero!

BOY: There's just one problem!

GIRL: What?

BOY: I broke my leg on the jump!

GIRL: It's all right, I'll carry you!

BOY: You?

GIRL: Me!

BOY: My hero!

GIRL: So we ski UP the hill!

BOY: Pursued by helicopters!

GIRL: Yes!

BOY: With grenades!

GIRL: Yes, yes! And bazookas!

BOY: Bazookas?

GIRL: Yes!

BOY: I don't think I've ever said the word "bazookas" before…

GIRL: Bazookas!

BOY: Bazookas!

GIRL: And we finally get to the top—

BOY: Thanks to your expert skiing slash carrying—

GIRL: But we're ambushed!

BOY: No!

GIRL: Surrounded!

BOY: No!

GIRL: By hundreds of machine-gun-toting robots slash Amazon warriors!

BOY: That's good…

GIRL: Thanks.

BOY: Well, this looks like the end…

GIRL: It looks that way…

BOY: There's only one thing that can defend against machine gun toting robots slash Amazon warriors…

GIRL: What?

BOY: The golden-throated yet hauntingly devastating melodies of my finely honed ancient Swiss yodelling!

He yodels. She cringes.

GIRL: But the yodelling's too loud!

BOY: Masterful though it is.

GIRL: The sound waves echo and start an avalanche!

BOY: Nooo!

GIRL: An all-encompassing blanket of snow and ice erupts down the mountain…

BOY: Crushing the machine-gun-toting robots slash Amazon warriors…

GIRL: But continuing down to bury all of Switzerland! Destroying all the cheese!

BOY: And clocks!

GIRL: And army knives!

BOY: And chalets!

GIRL: And THAT… (*realizing again how close they are*) …my good sir, is why you cannot kiss me.

Beat.

BOY: Right. For the sake of Switzerland.

GIRL: Right. And it is for that reason that we must be—

BOY: Mature young adults.

GIRL: Yes.

BOY: Yes.

Beat.

GIRL: Sorry.

BOY: Don't be.

GIRL: You know I want to, right?

BOY: Well, I would hope so.

GIRL: It's just—

BOY: Switzerland. No, I get it.

GIRL: Okay.

Beat.

BOY: It just sucks.

GIRL: I know.

BOY: Like, really sucks.

GIRL: I know.

Beat.

GIRL: Don't say sucks.

BOY: What?

GIRL: Don't say sucks! It's such a gross word.

BOY: What do you mean?

GIRL: It's so gross. It just sounds gross. Come on, say it.

BOY: Sucks.

GIRL: (*overemphasising the consonants*) S-uu-ckkk-ssss.

BOY: Sucks.

GIRL: See?

BOY: I guess.

GIRL: There are words that have within them the inherent capacity for grossness and other words that are inherently happy. I like happy words.

BOY: Happy words?

GIRL: Yeah. Like "teacup."

BOY: Teacup?

GIRL: Teacup. You can't say teacup without feeling just a little bit happier. Say it. Teacup.

BOY: Teacup.

GIRL: See? Because it's a happy word.

BOY: Teacup…

GIRL: See? Say gross words, you'll feel gross. Say happy words, you'll feel happy.

BOY: This is ridiculous.

GIRL: But it's true, right? Teacup.

BOY: Teacup.

GIRL: Doesn't that just sound happy?

BOY: Yeah…I guess…

GIRL: You know I'm right. Teacup.

BOY: Teacup.

She smiles. He smiles.

BOY: I love you.

Long beat.

BOY: You don't have to… But I wanted you to know.

GIRL: I know.

BOY: Okay. You don't have to—

GIRL: I want to.

BOY: Okay.

GIRL: It's just…

BOY: Yeah.

GIRL: Those words—

BOY: It's okay. I get it.

GIRL: J'adore vous…

BOY: J'adore vous.

GIRL: … Je t'aime.

BOY: Je t'aime vous.

She shivers.

BOY: You're freezing.

GIRL: … No…

BOY: Come here.

He holds her close, trying to warm her up.

BOY: Better?

GIRL: Yeah. Thanks.

BOY: My pleasure.

They stay still for a moment.

BOY: Plus, that's not the worst thing that could happen.

GIRL: What?

BOY: I mean, Switzerland.

GIRL: What?

BOY: If we kissed.

GIRL: No?

BOY: Not at all. (*beat*) You could like it.

GIRL: The kiss?

BOY: Yes.

GIRL: Never!

BOY: You could!

GIRL: Impossible!

BOY: You would!

GIRL: Nuh uh.

BOY: And then you'd start wanting more!

GIRL: Now you're just being crazy!

BOY: And you'd like it so much, I'd have to bike here all the time.

GIRL: Uh huh?

BOY: Just to kiss you.

GIRL: Yeah, right.

BOY: Every day.

GIRL: Whatever.

BOY: And then eventually, you'd miss me kissing you so much, you'd ask me to stay here all the time.

GIRL: Uh huh?

BOY: All night.

GIRL: Oh, you wish!

BOY: *You* wish! And I'd just hold you. And kiss you. And keep you safe in my arms. And you'd fall asleep with your head on my shoulder and I'd kiss your forehead and keep you warm… And just fall asleep with you smiling in my arms…

GIRL: … Yeah?

BOY: Yeah. And then in the morning you'd wake up and I'd have breakfast all ready for you. And you'd be all groggy and sleepy-looking and do that cute little thing with your nose when you yawn.

GIRL: What thing?

BOY: That cute thing you do when you yawn.

GIRL: I don't do any cute thing.

BOY: Yawn.

GIRL: I can't just yawn!

BOY: Yawn!

She yawns.

BOY: That thing.

GIRL: What am I doing?

BOY: I don't know, but it's cute!

GIRL: (*like a bad comeback*) *You're* cute.

BOY: What?

GIRL: I don't know…

BOY: (*smiling*) And you'd say adorable things like that.

GIRL: Leave me alone…

BOY: And you'd be happy. And I'd be happy. I'd be so happy.

She smiles.

BOY: And we could spend as much time as we wanted together. And we'd be nice and warm. And we wouldn't be bloody freezing… And we could just… spend our whole lives together. And I would tell you how beautiful you are every day. Every morning and every night. Even when you're not…

She gives him a look.

BOY: Which will never happen because you always are! And I'd make sure that every night, the last thing you see is me. And the last thing I see is your smile. And I'd look after you. And take care of you. And no matter what happened during the day, we'd always have each other to come home to. And we'd always have each other to hold and cry. And we wouldn't have to be mature. Or grown-up. Or bloody freezing. We could just be happy. We could just be in love.

Beat. They're sooo close.

GIRL: I want to kiss you so bad right now.

BOY: Then do it.

She stops smiling. So does he. They separate.

BOY: I know.

GIRL: I'm sorry.

BOY: No, don't be.

GIRL: I'm sorry.

Beat. He is clearly heartbroken.

GIRL: Teacup?

Beat.

BOY: (*reluctantly*) Teacup…

GIRL: Teacup.

At first he is just humouring her, but eventually she is able to make him genuinely smile.

BOY: Teacup…

GIRL: Teacup!

BOY: Teacup.

GIRL: Teacup!

He smiles.

BOY: Teacup.

GIRL: Teacup!

BOY: Teacup!

GIRL: Teacup!

BOY: (*jokingly suggestive…*) Teacup!

GIRL: (*suggestive back*) Teacup!

Getting closer, no longer joking…

BOY: Teacup…

GIRL: Teacup…

They are so close to kissing! Long beat!

GIRL: We have to be mature young adults now.

They don't move.

BOY: Why?

GIRL: Because.

BOY: We don't have to.

GIRL: Yes, we do.

BOY: Why?

GIRL: Because.

BOY: Why do we have to be mature and responsible?

GIRL: Because—

BOY: Why can't we be irresponsible teenagers?

GIRL: Because…

BOY: People?

GIRL: Yes, people.

BOY: People will say things?

GIRL: That's not the only—

BOY: I love you. I love you so much.

GIRL: I know.

BOY: And for once I don't want to think! I don't want to worry about a million things and the future and everything else. I just want to love you. And kiss you. And be with you here right now. And do what we both want to do, what we both should be able to do. Why can't we? Really, why can't we?

GIRL: Because!

BOY: Because what?

GIRL: The people!

BOY: Screw the people!

GIRL: And Switzerland!

BOY: Screw Switzerland!

GIRL: And my parents!

BOY: Would they really care?

GIRL: Yes.

BOY: If they knew—

GIRL: And because…

BOY: Because… ?

GIRL: Because if we kiss…

BOY: Yes?

GIRL: If I kiss you…

BOY: Yes?

GIRL: If we—

BOY: Yes?

GIRL: I'll never stop!

Beat.

GIRL: If you kiss me now, I will never let go. And I will never be able to leave you. And we will have to come back here. Every day. And I'll kiss you and kiss you.

BOY: Okay!

GIRL: No. And you'll be so good. And you'll be so romantic. And I'll want to do other things. And I'll let you do other things.

BOY: No, that's not—

GIRL: And I'll let you do other things. Right here. In the bloody cold. And eventually someone will see us. Or if they don't, they'll assume. And they'll talk.

BOY: I would never—

GIRL: And they'll say things. About me. 'Cause I live here. And I'm the girl. So they'll call me a slut. And a whore and a skank. And my friends will talk. And make up so much more. And then I'll start hearing things at school. And whispers at lunch. And I'll walk down the street and everyone will stare at me. On my own street. In my own town. And I'll wonder what my sister heard. And I'll wonder what my parents heard. And the lies won't even matter. Because I'll know there's enough truth. And I'll cry. Every night. And I'll hate you. And I'll hate myself. And I'll hate you for making me hate myself. And I'll hate myself for hating you. And you'll be there for me through it all, and that will make it all so much worse. 'Cause I'll know we were right. And I'll know we were in love. And in the end, when I have sacrificed everything, I'll know it was for you. And I won't even regret it. But I'll have lost so much. I'll have lost too much. And we'll never fall asleep together. And we'll never spend the night. And you'll never...kiss my forehead. And we'll never last. (*beat*) And then I'll start dating someone else. And I'll do all the things we never did with *him*. And it'll be so good. Until eventually I won't remember you at all. I won't remember anything about you. Except some nights when I'm all alone. And then I'll cry and cry. But only until the morning. And only because of this one kiss.

Beat.

BOY: You said you wouldn't even regret it.

She shakes her head no.

BOY: Okay.

He kisses her. Gently at first, but then more passionately. He breaks away. Beat.

They just look at each other.

He kisses her again. She kisses back and obviously wants to as well, but at the same time there's an almost stoic quality about her as if what she is doing has been predetermined and she is merely fulfilling her part in their destiny. They break away again.

BOY: I love you.

GIRL: I love you.

BOY: I'm sorry.

GIRL: (*simply*) That's life.

Lights down as they kiss. As the lights are almost out, a couple walks on stage and stops, seeing them. Blackout.

The End

Third Person

A One-Act Play for Two Actors

by Brandon Wicke

About the playwright

Brandon Wicke is currently finishing up his final year of a playwriting major at Concordia University in Montreal, Quebec. His introduction to theatre came when he performed with the Stratford Shakespeare Festival for two seasons in his hometown, Stratford, Ontario. Since that time he has written and acted in several of his short plays, which have been produced throughout high school and as part of small theatre festivals in Stratford and Montreal. *Third Person* premiered as a part of Concordia University's Fall SIPA/Short Works Festival (Student Initiated Production Assignments) in November 2011. The cast and crew of the debut production was as follows: director, Brandon Wicke; stage manager, Megan Holt; designer, Veronica Derby; Byron, Nicolas Turcotte; GEORGE, Kevin Ray.

Characters

GEORGE
BYRON

Setting

The stage is bare, with only a small two-person tent somewhere upstage.

Note: In this play, stage directions in ***bold typeface*** *are to be scrolled across the upstage wall or similar big, flat surface by use of a projector. These directions are not to be actually followed by the actors or any technical aspects, unless otherwise specified by normal, unbolded directions.*

The stage is dark.

Lights up.

The stage remains dark.

Pause.

The stage is dark.

Lights up. We are faced with BYRON *and* GEORGE. BYRON *opens his mouth very wide, making an "Ahhhh" noise, and* GEORGE *looks/pokes around in there.*

Two idiots sit, God knows where. They are discussing which one is to be cannibalized first, as they are dying of starvation.

BYRON: D'you see anything in there?

GEORGE: Mmm, I don't think so… Which one is it that hurts again?

BYRON: Uhh, back left.

GEORGE: Hmmm, is it this one?

BYRON: (*shaking his head*) Unh unh.

GEORGE: This one?

BYRON: (*pause. Again shakes his head*) Unh unh.

GEORGE: This one then.

BYRON: (*gagging, and ejecting the fingers from his mouth*) No, not that one either.

GEORGE: Well, you're sure it was on the left? Couldn't have been on the right?

BYRON: Of course I'm sure it was on the left. I guess it's just not hurting now. It comes and goes, y'know.

Upon examining his friend's teeth, the idiot decides that they are indeed capable of rending flesh, and volunteers himself to be devoured.

GEORGE: (*standing up*) Well, just let me know when it starts hurting again, I suppose, and we'll try to yank the bastard out.

BYRON: Okay.

GEORGE: Did you sleep all right last night?

Pause.

GEORGE: Byron.

BYRON: What?

GEORGE: Did you sleep well last night?

BYRON: Oh, yes, fine.

GEORGE: No bad dreams?

BYRON: Oh, one or two. None too scary.

GEORGE: What were they about?

BYRON: The usual: scary things. Ghosts, murderers, y'know…

Suddenly, a faint 'roar' is heard. Clearly some distant monster is on the loose.

GEORGE: No Minotaur, or…

GEORGE notices the writing for the first time. It is still lingering on the wall behind them. BYRON notices that GEORGE is distracted.

BYRON: What is it? George?

GEORGE: Oh, nothing, nothing. I was just thinking of a joke I heard earlier.

BYRON: A joke? You don't look like you were thinking of a joke.

Another 'roar,' this time a bit louder than before. It's getting closer.

GEORGE: (*absently, preoccupied with the text*) It wasn't a very funny joke…

BYRON sees the new words.

BYRON: What — What're those?

GEORGE: Words…

BYRON: I know they're words, what are they doing there?

The words vanish.

GEORGE: Shhh, I just…need to listen for a second.

BYRON: What 'roar'? What's getting closer?

GEORGE: Shhh!

The two wait, listening. They hear nothing. Eventually BYRON interrupts, and the text changes (conveniently) at the same time.

BYRON: What are we listening for? What did it say before?

Byron's interruption masks the sound of a third 'roar,' this one even louder than before. His interjection has prevented George from hearing it, but the beast is closer than ever, perhaps just yards away…

The two read the new text.

GEORGE: I don't know. I don't know what it is —

BYRON: It says it's closer.

GEORGE: If only you had let me listen —

BYRON: What d'we do?

GEORGE: Then maybe I'd know what it was!

George is lying to protect Byron. He, of course, knows the true nature of the mysterious beast. The clearing fills with an eerie silence, as the beast prepares to make its kill…

BYRON: What? It says you know! What is it, George?

GEORGE: (*urgently*) I don't know. Did you hear anything? Back then?

BYRON: Don't lie! What is it, tell me!

GEORGE: (*with anger*) I don't know! Okay? I don't know!

In his anger, George prepares to strike Byron.

The two read the new direction. Pause.

BYRON: You'd 'strike' me?

— But reconsiders…

GEORGE: No, of course not!

BYRON: It said you would!

GEORGE: I wouldn't! I'd never do that, ever!

BYRON: (*pointing to the text*) Oh, but you thought about it, huh?

GEORGE: No, it's lying! I swear!

BYRON: Why would it lie?

GEORGE: Byron, listen, we don't have time for this. We've gotta figure out if—

The beast pounces.

GEORGE: RUN!

GEORGE pulls Byron and runs with him into the tent. He zips up the doorway urgently.

Silence.

Heh heh heh.

A flashlight turns on inside the tent.

GEORGE: Can you see anything?

Silence.

GEORGE: Can you hear anything?

Silence.

GEORGE: Byron? ...Are you okay?

Silence.

GEORGE: I'm sorry, okay? I really wasn't ever going to hit you, I promise. I would never do that. Don't you believe me?

BYRON hesitates.

GEORGE: Pinkie swear?

A brief pause.

BYRON: Okay...

GEORGE: Okay... Do you see anything out there?

BYRON: No, I don't think so...

GEORGE: Me neither...what d'we do?

BYRON: I dunno...maybe open up that little window thing at the back, see if the writing's still up there?

GEORGE: Okay, good idea. Just hold on a second.

George opens the back window of the tent.

Sounds of shifting around inside the tent, as GEORGE moves to the back window. The window unzips.

BYRON: Well? Is it still there?

GEORGE: Yeah, it says, "George opens the back window of the tent."

BYRON: Well, it's got that right at least... Nothing about the monster?

GEORGE: No, it doesn't say…just unzip a teensy bit of the front door and take a look, would you?

BYRON: But what if it's waiting there?

GEORGE: I don't think it will be, just a teensy bit, real quiet.

BYRON: Okay, I guess.

BYRON very quietly unzips the front door an almost imperceptible amount, and peeks out. He zips it back up.

GEORGE: Anything?

BYRON: Nope.

GEORGE: Okay, I thought not.

Upon seeing nothing, Byron thinks to himself that the monster must in fact be invisible.

GEORGE: Oh! The words changed again!

BYRON: What do they say?

GEORGE: "Upon seeing nothing, Byron thinks to himself that the monster must in fact be invisible." Did you really think that?

BYRON: Well, now I certainly do!

GEORGE: Well, hold on, let me take a look out the front, and you keep an eye on the words, see if they change.

BYRON: Okay, switch positions.

Shuffling inside the tent as the characters switch places. The front unzips again, and GEORGE peeks through. Now that BYRON is the one watching the wall, new text is added. It now says:

Upon seeing nothing, Byron thinks to himself that the monster must in fact be invisible. A fact which George has known since the beginning.

BYRON: What did you say was written when you last looked?

GEORGE: Umm, "Upon seeing nothing, Byron thinks to himself that the monster must, in fact, be invisible." Why? Does it say something else now?

BYRON: It says that you knew that from the beginning.

GEORGE: What? Let me see that.

GEORGE's face disappears from the tent door. Urgent shifting in the tent.

GEORGE: It didn't say that before!

BYRON: Are you *sure* you didn't know the monster was invisible?

The text fades.

GEORGE: No, I didn't! I don't! I'm starting to doubt there's even a monster out there!

BYRON: You pinkie sweared me…

GEORGE: (*calming himself*) I know, and I was telling the truth, I promise. I don't know what's going on, but those words aren't always telling the truth here… I wouldn't lie to you.

BYRON: … So d'you think it's safe to go out there again?

GEORGE: I'm not sure. I'd like to figure out what that writing's up to before we go doing anything…

BYRON: Well…how can we figure it out? Keep watching it?

GEORGE thinks.

GEORGE: Has it said anything that we *absolutely* know was true?

BYRON: Umm…

GEORGE: Oh! Yes, it said, "George opens the back window of the tent" when I looked out to see if it was still there.

BYRON: Oh, right.

GEORGE: — But we had been talking about it beforehand. And I didn't *see* the words go up, they were already there when I looked out.

BYRON: So…could whatever it is have heard us talking and switched the words to what it *knew* we would do, just to trick us into believing it?

GEORGE: What d'you mean, 'whatever it is?'

BYRON: Well…y'know, the words…I mean they themselves aren't doing it, right? Something's gotta be putting them up there.

GEORGE: I suppose…

BYRON: So maybe this thing can hear us, right?

GEORGE: Right, and then it writes what *we* say we're gonna do, right before we do it, so that we think that *it's* predetermined it for us! Byron, you're a genius!

BYRON: Thank you, you're too kind.

GEORGE: So, I'm gonna open the tent up and go back outside. You keep an eye on it and see if it tries any funny business…

BYRON: Okay, got it.

Shuffling around as GEORGE unzips the door and makes his way cautiously out. BYRON remains inside, keeping an eye on the wall, which has remained curiously bereft of writings. BYRON shouts from inside the tent.

BYRON: No! It didn't say a thing while you were getting out!

GEORGE: Hmm, maybe we're on to something here… You can c'mon out now, I think. There doesn't seem to be anything amiss.

BYRON stumbles out from the tent.

GEORGE: If only we could test it somehow —

The text on the wall writes exactly what GEORGE is about to say, at exactly the same time as GEORGE himself.

GEORGE: For instance, if we keep watch on it, and wait for its next prediction and just do the opposite, no matter what it says, we'll be able to prove it wrong. It'll just be a matter of making sure that it can't write something new when our backs are turned…

"For instance, if we keep watch on it, and wait for its next prediction and just do the opposite, no matter what it says, we'll be able to prove it wrong. It'll just be a matter of making sure that it can't write something new when our backs are turned… "

GEORGE notices BYRON reacting to the writing behind him. He turns around while finishing his speech, watching as it copies his last words.

BYRON: Uh oh.

Good plan, jackass.

A pause.

GEORGE: (*sits down, defeated*) Well, so much for that idea.

BYRON: It's okay, it was worth a try…

The words vanish.

GEORGE: I just don't understand!

BYRON: I know, me neither —

GEORGE: I mean, every time we try to do something to figure it out, it finds some way to get us all turned around!

BYRON: … Well, maybe we *should* just turn around. I mean, go back the way we came. Or, go somewhere new at least…I don't like this writing, whatever it is. I think we should get as far away from it as possible.

GEORGE: But where would we go?

BYRON: I dunno, anywhere. Anywhere but here. I don't like it here.

GEORGE: I suppose we could…but wouldn't it bother you to just leave? I mean, without figuring it out?

BYRON: No, I don't think so. What is there to figure out? It obviously doesn't like us, and it wants to scare us away, so let's just go. I just wanna get out of here.

GEORGE: Okay okay, you're probably right… (*disappointed*) You just sit tight and I'll… go look for a path to leave.

BYRON: Okay.

GEORGE sets off, exiting. He has been gone only a few seconds when the writing appears.

George leaves. He makes his way back the way he and Byron came, trying to find the path. However, unbeknownst to him, he is being watched. Strange eyes follow his progress, lurking in the shadows.

BYRON, reading this, shouts to GEORGE.

BYRON: George, wait!

GEORGE: (*off*) What?

BYRON: Come back!

GEORGE comes back onstage.

GEORGE: What's wrong?

BYRON points out the writing.

BYRON: Look!

GEORGE reads.

GEORGE: Don't worry, it's probably just like the monster, all nonsense.

BYRON: But what if the monster really was invisible? It might be dangerous, it could be telling the truth!

GEORGE: It'll be all right, I swear. I'll keep my eyes peeled. I'll be really careful. I'd know if I was being watched. I'd feel it.

BYRON: Okay, but be quick.

GEORGE: All right. And whatever the words say, don't pay any attention. In fact, don't look at them. Look anywhere but at the words.

BYRON: Okay, deal.

GEORGE: All right. Wish me luck.

GEORGE heads off.

BYRON: Good luck.

Now left alone, BYRON dedicatedly avoids looking anywhere near the wall. As the words begin to appear (beginning slowly, but building gradually in speed) BYRON has still not seen them, but his anxiety and urge to look behind him builds. It is as if BYRON is caught in a cycle of thinking exactly what the writing suggests, even though he cannot see it.

Oh, tsk tsk, splitting up… Don't you know that's just a recipe for disaster? He won't be back. He'll wander around, looking for a way out, and he'll get lost. He won't be able to find his way back to you… He'll be calling out for you, but you won't be able to hear him, will you?

The writing vanishes, and continues.

And who knows what could be waiting out there for its next unsuspecting victim… What'll you do without him, I wonder? You're nothing with him gone. You're certainly no match for ME on your own… You're not clever enough. So predictable: Any second now you'll turn around and see—

The tension is palpable. Sometime during the above, BYRON has closed his eyes against the urge to look. Suddenly he cracks under the pressure and spins quickly around to face upstage. The words instantly vanish before BYRON can see them, and are replaced:

Now I've got you.

BYRON releases a squeak of terror and stands rigid, unable to turn back around. The text is replaced and begins again, scrolling quickly.

I know you. I know you inside out. I know where you'll go, and what you'll do when you get there. I know everywhere you've ever been, and everywhere you ever will be. I know which tooth of yours it is that hurts: right-side molar, second from the back, because part of a sesame seed is lodged in your gum behind it. Everything about you… Every decision you make, I've made for you, eons before you were even born…

BYRON: (*calls out, feebly*) George…

He can't hear you. Right now he's struggling to find the path you took to get here, but he won't. He'll give up. You're not going to leave here. You'll have my company for the rest of your days.

BYRON: (*feebly, perhaps a bit louder than before*) George!

The writing speeds up. GEORGE *can be heard calling faintly from offstage, "Byron? What's wrong?"*

You're stuck. You'll never be a free man again. I am the Minotaur in your nightmares, chasing you around the corners, through the corridors. And I'll always be there, right behind you until I've got you at a dead end and then —

BYRON: (*like a child screaming out for his parents upon waking up from a nightmare*) GEORGE!

The words fade. GEORGE *comes dashing in, just in time to see* BYRON *faint, falling to the floor like a puppet with its strings cut.*

GEORGE: What's wrong? — Oh, my God —

He rushes over.

GEORGE: (*frantically, tapping* BYRON*'s face to rouse him*) Byron, c'mon buddy, wake up. It's okay, just wake up. We'll be okay.

BYRON *regains consciousness, and moves his legs to a more comfortable position. He remains prone.*

BYRON: (*groggily*) Hi, George.

GEORGE: (*with an exasperated but relieved chuckle*) Hi, Byron.

BYRON: What happened?

GEORGE: You fainted…

BYRON: Oh… Why?

GEORGE: I'm not sure.

BYRON: He was saying something scary…

GEORGE: Who was saying something scary?

BYRON: The writing.

GEORGE: I see… Y'know, I told you you shouldn't look at it.

BYRON: I know, but I couldn't help it.

GEORGE: (*sympathetically*) No, of course.

A lengthy pause.

GEORGE: How're you feeling?

BYRON: (*still groggy*) Good, good.

GEORGE: Good. Y'wanna try getting up?

BYRON: Okay.

GEORGE *helps* BYRON *to sit up.*

GEORGE: Okay, how does that feel?

BYRON: Not bad…I feel sleepy.

GEORGE: All right, well, let's get you into the tent where you can lay down for a bit. Where it's nice and comfy.

BYRON: Okay.

The two stand up, GEORGE supporting BYRON. He leads him to the tent door.

BYRON: (*in unconscious and groggy reference to GEORGE's earlier warning*) And if the words say anything, don't pay any attention… In fact, don't even look at them. Look anywhere but at the words…

GEORGE: Okay, will do.

GEORGE helps BYRON into the tent, and leaves the door unzipped after him. GEORGE stays outside, and walks toward centre stage.

GEORGE: (*angrily advancing, pointing to the empty wall*) All right now, come out and play!

There is no response from the writing.

GEORGE: C'mon, don't you hide from me!

Still no response.

GEORGE: (*shouting*) Talk to me!

George rails futilely against the merciless actions of an unfeeling God.

GEORGE: Oh, no, don't you play that shit with me! You're not God. And where the fuck do you get off treating us like this?

Despite George's assertions to the contrary, he can't help but feel that perhaps he is dealing with a higher, all-knowing power.

GEORGE: Hey, no! Stop putting words in my mouth! You are NOT God!

His doubt is increasing, and he struggles to maintain his composure.

GEORGE: Stop it! You can't pull this stuff on me, I know what you're doing! Now cut it out with this third-person shit and talk to me!

Pause.

But I am the third person.

GEORGE: What?

I am the third person.

GEORGE: But what the fuck does that mean? You're the third person, like, a narrator? An observer?

Yes.

GEORGE: But anyone can call themselves an observer. Anyone can narrate! "Despite the mysterious writing's persistent assertions that it is omniscient, George remains profoundly fuckin' unimpressed." There, see?

George becomes belligerent and irrational when he discovers that he is incapable of comprehending the truth of the situation.

GEORGE: Excuse me, I'm perfectly capable of comprehending what you're suggesting, I just refuse to believe it! You don't control me. (*gestures to tent*) Or him, or anything else for that matter! You can't make us do anything we don't want to!

Correct.

GEORGE: (*taken aback*) Thank you!

But I know what you want to do. And I know what you will do.

GEORGE: … So? Then you're harmless! What power does that give you?

Absolutely none.

GEORGE: There you go! What were we even worried about? It's so absurd! We go where we want, we do what we want and you—

And what power does that give you?

GEORGE: What?

You're bugs in the sand. Go ahead, revel in your free will! What good does it do you when I already know the outcome of every decision you'll ever make?

GEORGE: (*troubled*) Yes, but…all that is, is knowledge… Even if you do know what you claim to—

And that's all I need. Your egotism is pathetic.

GEORGE: (*angry at the allegation*) I'm not an egotist! I am the be-all and end-all in matters of my own existence, and that's simply the fucking reality of it! You have no authority here!

Fine. Go on then, make your 'decisions.' Can you really say they have any significance now?

GEORGE: Oh, you're one to talk about egotism, you pompous…whatever the fuck you are! You're all talk, you've got nothing!

George has been left with only his newly unearthed doubts for company.

GEORGE: Don't start this again! (*furious, shouting*) Come back and talk to me!

GEORGE's shouts rouse BYRON from his sleep. His head emerges from the tent. A pause.

BYRON: George? What's wrong?

GEORGE: (*irritated*) Oh, no, nothing, it's okay.

BYRON: Y'know, I told you not to look at the words…

GEORGE: (*still irritated*) I know. But I couldn't help it.

BYRON: (*sympathetic*) No, of course not…

GEORGE: Are you feeling any better?

BYRON: Yeah, a bit. I was asleep. Your yelling woke me up though…

GEORGE: Sorry.

BYRON: What was it saying?

GEORGE: Oh, it was just trying to get under my skin.

BYRON: Well, I mean, with what? What did it say?

GEORGE: (*short*) I'd rather not discuss it, okay?

BYRON: Okay…

Pause.

BYRON: Y'know, you don't need to protect me.

GEORGE: What?

BYRON: By not telling me things. You don't have to protect me by not telling me things. I can handle it.

GEORGE: Look, this isn't about you, I just—

George realizes his folly in treating Byron like a child. He bursts into tears and rushes to Byron, hugging him.

The two read the directions.

BYRON: Aww, see? Sometimes I wish you were a bit more like that.

GEORGE: What? Are you kidding me? After what it's done to us, you're letting it get to you again? That's exactly what it wants!

BYRON: I'm not letting anything 'get to me!' I'm just saying I wish you'd stop treating me like I can't handle myself! You're the one who's freaking out…

GEORGE: No, but don't you see? It's trying to pit you against me!

BYRON: I'm not 'against you,' I'm just saying—

GEORGE: Okay, fine! You want to be treated like an adult? Whatever! We'll see how you feel when I'm not taking care of you every second of the day anymore!

BYRON: (*hurt*) We take care of *each other*! That's how it works! It's not all you, as much as you might think it is.

GEORGE, fuming, goes away and sits down.

The sun shines brightly, mirroring Byron and George's newfound hope and comfort with their place in the world.

GEORGE: (*in response to the writing*) Oh, shut the fuck up!

Pause.

Byron, realizing that he is an empowered, worthy, and independent human being, sets off on his own, knowing that George's negative attitude will only stand in his way.

Only BYRON sees this text. BYRON hesitates, and then makes his way over to GEORGE, sitting next to him.

BYRON: Y'know… Maybe what it's saying isn't *always* all that bad.

GEORGE: But, regardless of *what* it's saying, it's making us fight. It's causing *this.*

BYRON: It's not making us… Maybe it's just telling us a possible way things could go…and we could take it or leave it…

GEORGE is silent.

BYRON: My tooth is starting to hurt again.

Pause.

BYRON: You were right, it's actually on the right side… Second one from the back.

Pause.

BYRON: There's a piece of sesame seed stuck in there apparently…

Pause.

GEORGE: What d'you mean 'apparently?'

BYRON: Well, the writing told me.

GEORGE: Ahh.

BYRON picks a bit at his tooth.

GEORGE: What else did the 'almighty writing' tell you?

BYRON: It talked about my dreams… It was saying that it would be the Minotaur, always catching me in the end…

This rouses GEORGE's sympathy.

GEORGE: Oh…don't believe it, Byron, they're just dreams.

BYRON: Oh, I know… It was just scary is all.

GEORGE: No, of course.

A pause.

GEORGE: It was talking to me about how it knows everything we're gonna do before we do it.

BYRON: Oh, yeah, it mentioned that to me too.

GEORGE: Didn't that bother you?

BYRON: Umm, well it moved on pretty quick to the really scary stuff, so I didn't have much time to think about it.

GEORGE: See, for me, that *is* the really scary stuff… I mean, what good is making a decision if something already knows what you're gonna decide?

BYRON: I suppose… But it's still us deciding, right?

GEORGE: But is it, though? I mean, if he…if *it*, whatever it is… if it already knows, then doesn't that mean the decision's been made? I mean, before any of us have even had our say?

BYRON: Well, but if I'm…faced with some decision, right? Like, do I want a glass of milk or a glass of water, it's still me who chooses… Isn't it?

GEORGE: I guess, but… If what it's saying is true then…then all the effort we put into making the *right* decision is just, pointless… Isn't it? I mean if the result is predetermined.

BYRON: But… Isn't that kinda freeing? I mean, then we don't need to worry about it anymore. If we're just destined to decide what we're gonna decide.

GEORGE: But it means we don't have any control anymore! Over anything.

BYRON: Well, we have the same amount of control as we've ever had—

GEORGE: Which is apparently none!

BYRON: But…does it even matter? I mean, it doesn't need to have any bearing on anything! We can go on like it never even happened. Like we never found out.

GEORGE: But we haven't 'found out' anything! It's lying. It has to be!

BYRON: But it was right about my tooth…how it's really the right side…

GEORGE: Even I could've guessed that! That's all it's been, lucky guesses…

The two sit and mull.

GEORGE: It's not that things would be different, it's just…the principle of it…I don't want to be guided around by some predestiny… I don't like the idea of there being some *thing* out there that knows more about me than I do!

BYRON: I understand… But this always happens. You think yourself into a tizzy when maybe it's really all okay…

GEORGE: I'm not 'in a tizzy,' I just need to figure it out! It's okay for you, you can just leave it, and that's fine, and I wish I could too, but I can't!

A lengthy pause, as they ponder. BYRON *picks at his tooth.* GEORGE *looks up at the sky.*

BYRON: Maybe it really is the Minotaur…

GEORGE: What? Why?

Pause.

BYRON: Well, I never have any control in my *dreams* either…

GEORGE: Yes, but neither do I. I mean, nobody does. That doesn't mean that those words are some…personification of your nightmares!

BYRON: In last night's, he was chasing me in an old abandoned factory… Everything was kinda grey and cold, and it was really dark 'cause there weren't many windows—

GEORGE: Are you sure you wanna talk about this now?

BYRON: —And so, I went to the doors at the front, and pushed on them, y'know, on that big metal bar that goes across them, but it wouldn't open… And, I heard him behind me so I ran up the stairs and onto the second floor… And there were all these big machines, I dunno what they were for, but I found one of the biggest ones, and hid behind it. So then I heard him, his hooves clanging on the floor, y'know, that metal grate flooring, coming closer to me. And he pulled a switch and all the machines started moving and working away at whatever it is they do… And it startled me, so I jumped, and he saw me and started laughing, this horrible, big, *mean* belly-laugh… So I ran, and I came to a ladder so I started climbing, and I climbed for a really long time, and I could hear his breath echoing around below me and I knew if I looked back down behind me he'd be right there, about to grab onto my foot or something… So the ladder finally ends, on this new platform, but now I'm in the top of a bell tower, and there's nowhere to go anymore. And I look back at the ladder and his hand is just on the top rung… And suddenly he's up, and he's got me stuck… And I can see his red eyes, and whenever he exhales there're these puffs of grey smoke coming from his nostrils… And he laughs, and just walks towards me until my toes are right on the ledge… Then I wake up.

A lengthy pause.

BYRON: It's always the same… I'm always running to open doors that I know will just be locked, or climbing up ladders that will always lead to dead ends… Sometimes I wonder why I bother running in the first place… He always gets me in the end.

GEORGE: (*to himself*) Delaying the inevitable…

BYRON: Yeah, but for what? So I can spend more time terrified that he's gonna get me? More time running?

A lengthy pause.

GEORGE: Have you ever tried confronting the Minotaur? Like, fighting him?

BYRON: I couldn't. Whenever I'm in there it's just too scary… And I guess I just hope that 'this time it'll be different.'

GEORGE: (*again, to himself*) But it never is…

BYRON: Right. And even if I did confront him, what would I do? He's like, nine feet tall, he's got big horns and hooves… Arms like tree trunks—

GEORGE: But it's your dream, right? It's *yours*. No one else's.

BYRON: Yeah, I guess…

GEORGE ponders.

GEORGE: Does he ever try to trick you? I mean, like go somewhere that makes you think you're safe, and then suddenly cut you off? Or something like that?

BYRON: Umm, yeah, I'm sure he has. Like lulling me into a false sense of security.

GEORGE: Yeah! You see, it's just like the writing! Your Minotaur! The writing has tricked us plenty of times: told us there were monsters, said I was thinking of hitting you—

BYRON: Uh huh?

GEORGE: So it's toying with you, right? And, maybe, the only way to stop it from toying with you is to realize that you're being toyed with, and refuse to play into it. Refuse to be scared. And that's all we need to do to get the writing to stop toying with us as well!

BYRON: But…even if he's not toying with us, he'll still get me…

GEORGE: Okay, well, he can't chase if he's got no one to chase, right? So just remove yourself from the equation.

BYRON: Well…how do I do that? I mean, short of…

BYRON makes a gesture implying suicide. The two pause. It was certainly not GEORGE's intent to arrive at this conclusion.

Bravo, Bravo! You've finally arrived at it: The only option.

GEORGE: Oh, no. No, no. This is that 'toying with us' thing, so we just can't play into it.

All right, but as Byron so eloquently put it, 'I'll still get you' in the end.

GEORGE: (*grabs BYRON around the shoulders*) We refuse to be scared of you.

Fine, it makes no difference. You've got two options: Move on, deluding yourself by denying my existence so you can stomach going on about your lives; or you can take yourself out of the equation. Your call. I have provisions for either, let me assure you.

BYRON: (*defeated*) Well…don't you already know what we're gonna do?

Of course.

GEORGE: (*an epiphany*) Then tell us!

BYRON: No! (*to the writing*) No, we don't want to know, we don't want to know!

GEORGE: (*quietly, to* BYRON) No, Byron, just let me—

BYRON: No!

All right, George, you've convinced me. You want me to tell you what you'll decide in the end?

GEORGE: Yes!

BYRON: NO!

The text begins to scroll, and BYRON*, screaming, pounces on* GEORGE *and clasps his hands over his eyes, blindfolding him and preventing him from seeing whatever the words will reveal. He, too, closes his eyes tightly and looks away.* GEORGE *struggles and totters about, screaming for* BYRON *to let him go.* BYRON *holds on for dear life, shouting as well.*

If you insist: You, like every human being before you, will face despair, will confront your own ignorance, will search for meaning… And never find it. You will carry on, as you always have and always will, as mindless, meaningless automatons, content with your superficial confidence in your own tiny 'place' in the universe. You will carry on and avoid confronting me, because you will never be capable of even comprehending, much less enacting, any alternative.

GEORGE*, with a huge battle cry, finally succeeds in wrenching* BYRON*'s hands from around his face, and throws him off of him and onto the ground in a rage. The text vanishes before* GEORGE *can see it, however, and noticing this,* GEORGE*'s rage builds. He screams at the wall, charging at it, pummelling it with his fists.*

GEORGE: No! Come back! Tell me! FUCK YOU!

Too late, missed your chance.

GEORGE *cannot find words for his anger.* BYRON *looks terrified. He quietly gets up, trying not to attract* GEORGE*'s attention. He attracts* GEORGE*'s attention.*

GEORGE: I can't believe you just did that!

BYRON: I'm sorry…

GEORGE: I could've figured it out, I could've proven him wrong, but no! You had to… to… GAH!

BYRON: I'm sorry…

BYRON *begins edging upstage and around* GEORGE*, towards the tent.*

GEORGE: Oh, of course! You're sorry! You're always sorry! God, I can't believe it!

BYRON: I was just trying to protect us.

GEORGE *is silent, fuming.* BYRON*, aiming to console him, approaches, and lays his hand on* GEORGE*'s shoulder.* GEORGE *freaks out, shouting, pulls off one of his shoes and flings it angrily in* BYRON*'s direction.* BYRON *flees into the tent.* GEORGE *removes his other shoe and hurls it at the writing surface.*

GEORGE: DAMMIT!

GEORGE *sits down.*

A very lengthy pause.

BYRON realizes that the tent is not a very secure hiding place, and zips up the front door in haste.

Silence. GEORGE is calming himself.

BYRON: (*from inside the tent*) I'm sorry, George. I didn't know you had a plan.

GEORGE takes a deep breath.

GEORGE: I know. It's okay.

BYRON: Can I come out now?

GEORGE: ... No, it's probably best if you stay in there for just a little longer.

BYRON: Okay.

A lengthy pause.

GEORGE: Okay, you can come out. This is silly.

BYRON slowly unzips the door, peeks out, and seeing that GEORGE is no longer hostile, steps out of the tent, and goes hesitantly to sit next to him.

GEORGE: I'm sorry, I overreacted... I just...felt like I was so close to figuring it out...

BYRON: Well, we can still get it. It'll just take a bit more work... I won't mess things up anymore, I promise.

GEORGE: No, that's not fair. It's not reasonable of me to criticize you for stopping us seeing... It's a scary thing to know... I wouldn't look either if I thought it would actually tell us the answer... I should've known, when it offered to say, that it was just tricking us again...

BYRON: Well, but how was it tricking us? I mean, if it weren't for me...

GEORGE: Yeah, but I think it was *betting* on you stopping me...that's the only reason it got my hopes up in the first place.

BYRON: But you wouldn't have looked?

GEORGE: No... No I don't think so...

Pause.

GEORGE: And I mean, we could never—

BYRON: Oh, no.

GEORGE: No. Definitely not...

BYRON: But... If you wouldn't have looked, then... Why did you ask?

GEORGE: 'Cause I don't think it could. Tell us the answer, that is.

BYRON: Well...why not?

GEORGE: Well, I don't think it can tell us, because then we could know what it predicted, and just do the opposite...

BYRON: Huh?

GEORGE: I mean, if it tells us "You're going to kill yourselves," then we can just decide not to do it, right? I mean, no one can make us kill ourselves... People can kill us, sure, but only *we* can kill ourselves.

BYRON: Fair enough.

GEORGE: (*clarifying for himself as he goes along*) So if it predicted that we'd kill ourselves, and then we don't do it, then we've proven it wrong, right? So then we know it can't predict the future, so it doesn't know everything we're gonna do! It's the same thing we were onto when we tried to trick it, except *that* time it beat us to it.

BYRON: Okay…and so… (*working through it*) It wouldn't say its predictions, even if it knew them…because if it did, we could prove it wrong…

GEORGE: Exactly.

BYRON: So there's no way it could prove *itself*?

GEORGE: No, I don't think so.

BYRON: But, wait… If it said "You'll kill yourselves," then we could prove it wrong by not doing it, right? But, what if it said that we didn't… The only way to prove that wrong would be…

GEORGE: Right.

BYRON: But…like we said, we could never…

GEORGE: No…

A lengthy pause.

GEORGE: Well, it's not that we *could* never… Not really. Just that we…we *would* never… I mean, we have the capacity to do it, even if we wouldn't… And that's the important thing.

BYRON: (*scared*) How important is this to you?

GEORGE: … Oh, no, I wouldn't, I swear!

BYRON: Because that's probably just what it wants.

GEORGE: No, I know. But if we could get it to make *another* prediction, one that we *can* control with our own decisions, then we could disprove it.

BYRON: (*thinks*) Like…how many fingers will I hold up, or something…

GEORGE: Right, excellent! So if it says one, I put up two; if it says two, I put up one! Even if we can't determine our own actions, it's only us who can actually carry them out, who can actually *act*. So it can't *tell* us what we're going to decide, until we've actually made the decisions, otherwise it gives us the opportunity to disprove it by doing the opposite! And so it really doesn't have anything we don't!

BYRON: So…then, all it can really do is just narrate? Like, tell us what we're doing, as we're doing it? *I* could do that!

All right. If you're willing to leave it at that: A possible explanation with no way to prove it.

A pause.

You can never know when I've been lying, and when I've been telling the truth. If I say "One finger" and you put up two, I could either have been proven wrong, or could just have been lying to you. You can never know which. Even if you set off now with the 'knowledge' you've gained, you can still never be sure of yourselves, truly.

BYRON looks troubled by this. He beckons GEORGE downstage, whispering conspiratorially.

BYRON: George… It's right, we've got nothing, right? I mean, we don't *know*, we're just guessing… For all we know, it could be telling the truth.

GEORGE: Right, I know… But, I mean… We haven't seen any examples of it telling the truth, at least not for certain… And if I'm right, it could never show us any. But we've definitely seen examples of it lying to us, so what choice do we have?

BYRON: Mhmm…

GEORGE: And even if it said anything, it could never prove to us whether it genuinely knew anything beforehand, or if it was just bluffing…

I know what you're saying, you morons…you don't have to whisper.

The two go on, not having noticed the new text.

BYRON: All right, so what's the game plan now?

GEORGE: Well, I think we should provide him with an ultimatum: He tells us a prediction, or we walk. That way, if he gives us one, we can try to disprove it, and if he doesn't, at least we'll know we tried.

BYRON: Okay, deal.

The two break from their conspiratorial huddling session.

Why, what in the world were you two POSSIBLY discussing? I haven't the foggiest notion.

GEORGE: All right, we've got a choice for you: I'm going to put up either one finger, or two. You can either predict which one I'll choose, or we walk out of here right now, and never come back.

BYRON: (*confidently*) So what'll it be?

You know my answer.

GEORGE: All right, Byron, you heard it. Let's pack up the tent.

You mean, that's it? All that effort and you leave it at THAT? Your solution is completely irrational! You can't fool me. You can't bluff your way out of this, and even if you could, what would it gain you? What merit is there in that?

Pause.

What, you can't win, so you counter with some embarrassing attempt to trick me? And then when it inevitably fails, as it was always destined to do, you pack up and abandon, saying "at least we tried"?

GEORGE: But, we—

I mean, of course, you've eventually got to admit you're fighting a battle you can never win, but I expected more of a last stand from you two than this!

GEORGE: Now come on!

All right, go. You're no fun anymore anyway. What a waste of time.

GEORGE: Hey, if you really know all you claim to, you knew this would be how it turned out!

I know but it's somehow SO much more disappointing when it actually comes!

A pause. GEORGE *is downtrodden, and sits down.*

GEORGE: Every time we think we've gotten somewhere…

BYRON: But, don't you think it'll always be that way? I mean, as long as we keep trying?

GEORGE: Yeah, probably…

BYRON: I mean, it's better at this than us. It's too clever.

GEORGE: But, there's nothing that just *can't* be figured out… I mean, with enough time—

BYRON: But how much are you willing to give to this thing, to try and 'figure it out?' Are we gonna spend years here arguing with it?

GEORGE: Well, it couldn't take *years*…

BYRON: I mean, if it was worth *that* much, we might as *well* kill ourselves…

A lengthy pause.

GEORGE: It tried to get me to think it was God…

BYRON: Well…it couldn't be God, right? It lied to us. God doesn't lie.

GEORGE: But, God's all-powerful, right? I guess God *could* lie…

BYRON: The devil lies… Is it the devil?

Call me what you will: God, the Devil… I am the third person. I know all there is to know about you, about everything… And that knowledge is there for you, if you just reach out and take it.

GEORGE: (*angry*) But you'll never let that happen!

BYRON: George, it's trying to tempt you to try and figure it out again. That's a pretty good indication to me that we shouldn't listen.

That's right, I'll never let that happen. But you could try… If you can outwit me, maybe get a glimpse?

BYRON: What's the point, George? How long are we gonna spend here?

GEORGE: It's just so hard to admit…

BYRON: C'mon, what is this worth to you?

Pause.

GEORGE: I'm scared.

BYRON: Scared of what?

GEORGE: Scared of… Going away without knowing.

BYRON: It's… It's just like you said: We refuse to be scared! It can't toy with you if you refuse to be scared.

GEORGE: But it'll still get us in the end, just like your Minotaur…

A pause. Suddenly, BYRON *has a stroke of genius. It all comes clear.*

BYRON: But wait! The Minotaur doesn't get me in the end, ever! I mean, it seems like it, yes, but — But, I wake up! I mean, I'm still here, aren't I?

GEORGE: What d'you mean?

BYRON: (*very excited*) I mean, sure he corners me, so it seems like there's no escape, but I get out, right? I wake up! I never actually die: the Minotaur never lays a finger on me, he can't! Just like the writing! Because even when I can't escape, I wake up. I…transcend!

GEORGE: — Byron, you're a genius! You're a fucking genius! How could I not see it? We were just taking it as a given that in your dreams the monster wins, but it doesn't, YOU win, YOU escape! Here I've been getting myself into this, into this —

BYRON: Tizzy?

GEORGE: Tizzy, thank you! And all because I thought there was no way to get out! He said it himself, "I'm the Minotaur in your nightmares." But, your nightmares aren't about…aren't *about* you being trapped, about having no escape… It's about struggling against what seem to be insurmountable odds, until you've got no options left, until your toes are on the edge, about to give up, and then suddenly realizing that there's this escape route that you never would've thought of before, not in a million years… And then, lo and behold, in all your nightmares, you escape, you wake up… You win! So all we need to, to do is, wake up! To go where he can't get us!

In his joy GEORGE emphatically hugs BYRON.

How disgustingly poetic…

GEORGE: But how do we apply that to real life? I mean…we can't…wake up, when we're already awake…

BYRON ponders.

BYRON: I dunno, but…maybe we're closer than we think. I mean, maybe it's as *simple* as waking up? As simple as just…snapping your fingers, or shutting your eyes tight and *realizing* that there *is* a place out there that it can't get to us… After all, that's all that waking yourself up from a nightmare is, isn't it? Realizing that you're dreaming, and suddenly remembering that there's *real life*, and that you can go there to be safe from whatever it is that's after you.

GEORGE: So even if we can't…escape…we can transcend.

BYRON: At least we can try.

Transcend, Ha. How self-aggrandizing. "Oh, how noble an idea: To simply rise above the lowly, useless pursuit of knowledge." Victory by surrender, a very sensible course of action.

BYRON: Going to where *you* can't follow us!

Where I can't follow? Tell me, Byron. Do you still dream? Even after you wake up, won't the Minotaur be back the next night? The night after?

BYRON: But it doesn't matter now! 'Cause now I know, I win! Sure I'll be scared, but that doesn't matter! Like George said, "I refuse to be scared." And the same goes for you: You may have us fooled, but if we refuse to be scared, scared of…not-knowing, then we can wake up!

And, if I follow you?

BYRON: Then it's just a matter of waking up again. Of rising above the fear!

—And remaining in ignorance.

BYRON turns to GEORGE.

BYRON: C'mon, George, let's get out of here… What d'you say?

A pause.

However you choose to put it: Wake up, Transcend—it doesn't matter. You're evading. You're turning down the tremendous opportunity to explore the sort of knowledge that no human being has ever before been permitted. The search for meaning, purpose, destiny—You could have it all, through me, but you give up because you're not up for a little challenge? Just think: With a little effort, you could look up at the stars and truly KNOW.

GEORGE: Byron, I—

BYRON: No, George, c'mon. He's just tempting us again!

You're on the threshold of something great, George.

GEORGE: (*to* BYRON) But how can we know?

BYRON: We can't, we can't, but that's okay! It's okay not to know! …Listen, if it could really tell you all that, if it had so much to offer, it wouldn't *lie* to us, it wouldn't be scaring us down corridors like this! We've gotta *wake up*, remember? Just like we talked about. Trust me.

BYRON takes GEORGE's arm and gently pulls him towards the tent, which he begins to pack up.

Hmmm, giving up: How anti-climactic.

BYRON: C'mon. We take care of each other… That's how this works.

This seems to rally GEORGE's spirits. He assists in packing up the tent.

BYRON: I know, it's tough… I'm lucky, I've had plenty of experience admitting *I* can't figure things out…

The two chuckle. As they work, they don't look to the writing anymore. They pack up the tent rather quickly and messily, and set off, heading offstage.

GEORGE: … Maybe someday it'll all come clear… Whether it was telling the truth.

BYRON: Maybe.

GEORGE: Maybe, when we die…

A brief pause.

BYRON: Maybe… What's important is that we're gonna keep going… That's the best we can do.

And so, Byron and George set off again, to trudge on through their mindless, vegetable existence… They'll grow old, and die in ignorance. One day, they will lose each other.

They don't see the writing.

GEORGE: It's okay.

BYRON: It's okay.

They exit.

And they will never know.

The text remains for a moment, and fades away. A brief pause.

Lights out.

The lights go out.

The End

Kiss Me Outside the Box

by Carmen Cartterfield

About the playwright

Carmen Cartterfield is a first-time playwright from Cambridge, MA, who received her B.F.A. in theatre and development from Concordia University. Despite acting and directing in a variety of productions over the years, Carmen's passion lies in teaching, and she has spent the last three summers working with theatre and youth in Upstate New York. Carmen hopes to continue teaching and writing in the future.

Characters

RILEY — 18 years old. A first-year student.
NICO — 18 years old. A first-year student.

Setting

Montreal. Two rooms in a university dormitory. Although these rooms are in the same building, they are not actually situated side by side. They are dorm rooms and should have similar layouts and furniture, including a bed, mirror, and dresser. Personal touches should distinguish them.

Lights up on RILEY*'s bedroom.*

RILEY: (*rushes into her room and closes the door*) I just slept with a girl.

NICO: (*lights up on* NICO*'s room*) I just slept with a straight girl.

RILEY: Holy shit. First semester of college, first *month* of college and I've already slept with a girl.

NICO: Was she straight? She certainly didn't act like it.

RILEY: Am I gay? (*thinks about it*) Oh, my God. Am I gay? No. That doesn't sound right. No, definitely not.

NICO: Number one rule, Nico: Don't fuck around with straight girls. They are psychotic. They will use you as their science project, and then break your heart.

RILEY: A girl, it was a girl, I had sex with a girl. I mean, it's not like it was bad. It wasn't bad. It was good. It was really good. (*thinks about it*) What if it wasn't good? What if I was terrible? I mean I, like… (*mimes the act of fingering*) I've never done that before. Is that gross? Why would that be gross, Riley? I mean, that's normal, right? Normal for lesbians. And I was drunk. Was I drunk? Am I still drunk? Shit.

NICO: Maybe, maybe she just thinks she's straight and I've just blown her mind and she just didn't know she was a lesbian. She does have that I'm-not-entirely-straight vibe. No, rule number two: There are no exceptions to the straight girl rule. No matter how good you think you are, you did not just convert her.

RILEY: Ok, I'm ok. This is ok. I drunkenly hooked up with someone, who just happened to be a girl. That does not make me a lesbian. In fact, it's kinda cool. I'm that really crazy girl who sometimes sleeps with girls. That's hot. Wait, is that a terrible thing to say?

NICO: I wonder what she's thinking. She's probably freaking out, trying to figure out how she should oh-so-subtly break it to me that we should be friends. Stupid, I'm so stupid. (*beat*) I should text her. Is that clingy?

RILEY: What if she wants more? What if she wants a relationship? I can't have a relationship with a *girl.* You'd be like friends who have sex. That's weird. I should just tell her we should be friends who don't have sex. I mean, I need friends. And she's the only American I know in this godforsaken country of nice people, even if she is a New Yorker. And I like her. I mean, not like *that* but… I'm just gonna tell her we should be friends.

NICO: (*texting into her phone*) So, that was fun. You should come downstairs for round two. (*looks at the phone and quickly deletes it*) Round two? Really, Nico?

RILEY: I'm just gonna go down there and tell her, 'Hey, that was fun. But I don't really swing that way. So, let's be friends!' Ok, maybe not like that. (*She walks out the door, then turns around and comes back.*) Tomorrow. I'll just tell her tomorrow.

NICO: (*texting on her phone*) Hey. Can't sleep. You wanna hang out? (*stares at it and then types again*) We could just talk? (*no longer typing*) Or you could just crush my hopes of ever sleeping with you again.

RILEY: (*goes to open door again and then stops*) No, it's 2:00 am. Friends don't tell friends they're just gonna be friends at 2:00 am. Especially after they've just had sex.

NICO: Fuck it. (*sends the text message*)

RILEY's phone starts to ring loudly. She watches it until it stops. Then she cautiously goes to pick it up and reads the text message. She stands there for a moment staring at the phone. Exits. Lights go down on RILEY's room. RILEY appears at NICO's door. She stands staring at the door. Finally, she knocks. NICO opens the door.

NICO: (*surprised*) Hey.

RILEY: Hey. I got your text.

NICO opens the door further and RILEY enters.

NICO: So this is my room.

RILEY: Yeah, I know. We — I — we, ya know. I was just here.

NICO: Oh, yeah, right. How could I forget?

Beat.

RILEY: So…you couldn't sleep?

NICO: Yeah.

RILEY: Me neither.

NICO: I figured.

Pause.

RILEY: So…

NICO: Yeah.

RILEY: I wanted to…

NICO: (*overlapping*) I'm hungry.

RILEY: What?

NICO: Uh… I'm hungry?

RILEY: It's 2:00 am. I don't think anything's open that late in Montreal, which is weird, you'd think it would be.

NICO: I know. I hate this city. If we were in New York, we could walk around the corner and have disgustingly delicious diner food.

RILEY: It's weird how much I miss about the States. Stupid little things, ya know? Like dollar bills.

NICO: Yes! Nothing like the greenback.

RILEY: The way they feel…

NICO: The way they smell…

RILEY: The way they smell?

NICO: Ya know, fresh money.

RILEY: You smell your dollar bills? What are you, a drug dealer?

NICO: (*smiling impishly*) Maybe.

RILEY laughs.

NICO: And they have stupid names. Loonies? Toonies? I mean, they totally ripped off the Looney Toons.

RILEY: And I'm always losing them.

NICO: And then you're short six bucks like *that.* (*snaps her fingers*)

Pause.

RILEY: It's good to have a fellow American.

NICO: I know, right?

Pause.

RILEY: I'm not gay.

NICO: What?

RILEY: I just didn't want you to think I was gay.

NICO: Uh, I didn't.

RILEY: You didn't?

NICO: No, um, I sort of figured you were straight.

RILEY: Why? (*suddenly mortified*) Was I really that bad?

NICO: (*laughs*) No, I mean, I just sort of guessed.

RILEY: I'm sorry. I just made things really awkward, didn't I? I'm sorry.

NICO: Stop apologizing. (*beat*) So that was your first time with a girl…

RILEY: Yeah, I mean, I've drunkenly made out with my friends…

NICO: Yeah, that doesn't count. That's just straight girls trying to turn on straight guys.

RILEY: True. Maybe we should've talked before all of our clothes came off.

NICO: What's the fun in that?

Beat.

RILEY: Do you think we could just be friends? I know that sounds really cliché and terrible and bad, but I don't mean it like that. People always say, 'Let's be friends' and mean something else, which totally screws it up for all of us who do mean it. It's just, I like you. And I'm sure what I just did was a really typical straight girl thing to do. I just think you're really cool, and you're the only American I know, and you live downstairs and… I just keep digging myself a hole, don't I?

NICO: No, yeah, uh, friends would be great.

RILEY: Yeah?

NICO: Yeah. I'm really glad you said that.

RILEY: Yeah?

NICO: Yup.

RILEY: Great. (*beat*) Well, I'm glad that's out of the way, 'cause these Canadians are driving me crazy. They're too nice for their own good. I think I'm definitely going to need someone to fight with.

NICO: Well, you can always count on me.

RILEY: Thank God. (*pause*) So I guess I should call it a night.

NICO: Right. Yeah. You're welcome to stay if you want.

RILEY: I have class tomorrow morning…

NICO: Right, yeah, totally. Do you want me to walk you back to your room?

RILEY: It's just upstairs.

NICO: Right.

RILEY begins to leave. NICO hesitates, then speaks.

NICO: Hey, you wanna maybe go bowling tomorrow? I saw this place around the corner. We could, like, drink beer and steal shoes and have a friend playdate.

RILEY: Yes. I've always wanted bowling shoes.

NICO: Awesome. I'll give you a call.

RILEY: Right. Goodnight, friend.

NICO: Night.

RILEY exits.

NICO: Friend. Rule Number One, Nico.

Lights go down on NICO's room. Lights up on RILEY's room. She enters wearing different clothes and a pair of bowling shoes. She dials the phone.

RILEY: Hey, it's me. I'm just calling to say I had a great time last night. And again, I'm sorry for dropping the ball on your foot and spilling beer all over you. And, yeah, almost getting us caught trying to steal shoes. But I'm wearing them now and it makes it all worth it. And I was just wondering if you wanna grab some dinner tonight. Okay. Gimme me a call back. Bye.

Lights down on RILEY's room. Lights come up on NICO in her room, dialing the phone.

NICO: Hey, me here. That Chinese food definitely gave me food poisoning, never trust anything under five dollars. But I'm recovering smoothly and I'm thinking we need a playdate, so call me back.

Lights down on NICO's room. Lights up on RILEY's room. She's in bed. She picks up her phone, hesitates for a minute, and then dials.

RILEY: Hey, it's me. I know it's late, you're probably asleep. I just wanted a distraction and, yeah. Um, so you should call me back tomorrow so we can play. Ok, I'll talk to you tomorrow. Bye.

Lights up on both RILEY and NICO's room. They both enter, talking on the phone.

NICO: So we're gonna get shit-faced tonight. No chickening out.

RILEY: Yes, darling. I am prepared to dance, drink, and wreak havoc.

NICO: Good. Come down when you're ready.

Both girls start to change into something they would wear to a club. They're both picky in their own right and change multiple times. Lights dim on RILEY's room as NICO speaks.

NICO: I'm totally falling for her. It's not really my fault. She's just so fucking lovable. For instance, when we went bowling, she wore a dress and bowled granny style. Like, through the legs. (*mimes bowling*) I mean, seriously? That's just unfair. That's the thing about straight girls—they're completely oblivious to their sex appeal. They'll change in front of you. Hug you. Cuddle with you. Sleep in your bed. (*beat*) Yes, she's started sleeping in my bed. Ya know, as friends, of course. Fucking "friends." I hate that word. It's like a death sentence. And it's just worse because we had sex. Once. Now I can't stop thinking about it. Like, let's say you have the best hamburger in the whole world but then you're forced to be a vegetarian. And you have to see that hamburger wherever you go and know you can't have it because you have to be a vegetarian. In fact, because the hamburger told you that you had to be a vegetarian. It's kinda like that.

RILEY checks her reflection in the mirror and then grabs a coat and exits. Lights down on RILEY's room.

NICO: So we're just gonna go out, have a good time, and be friendly, because that's what friends do. Friends where one person isn't in love with the other. (*beat*) Ya know, you feel this way and you're, like, it can't be one-sided, that would make me crazy, right? But no, it is. It's completely one-sided. And I'm just that pathetic douche bag.

NICO grabs her coat and exits. Lights out on NICO's room. Lights change. NICO and RILEY come stumbling up to NICO's door. Both are drunk, but RILEY is visibly more drunk than NICO. NICO fumbles for her keys and opens the door, RILEY follows her in.

NICO: Whoa. Whaddya forget where you live?

RILEY: Lemme sleep in your bed.

NICO: What?

RILEY: It's just so big. Come on. Please. It's not like we haven't done it before.

NICO: Yeah, but that's when we were both slightly more sober. And your clothes weren't as revealing or falling off as they are now.

RILEY: I am not that drunk.

NICO: Whatever you say, my dear.

RILEY: You think we're gonna have sex, don't you?

NICO: Uh, that's not really what I said. But that is what happened last time we were drunk and in a bed together.

RILEY: But that was a one-time thing.

NICO: Yes, it was.

RILEY: Because I'm not gay.

NICO: No, you're not.

RILEY: Not that you're not attractive.

NICO: Thank you. I think.

RILEY: Because you are. I'm just not gay.

NICO: Right. I'm pretty sure that's been established.

RILEY: And we're friends.

NICO: Yes, good ol' friends.

RILEY: Really great friends. I think we make great friends.

NICO: Yup, we're pretty great.

RILEY: So I think you should take advantage of me.

NICO: What?

RILEY: Like the first night we met.

NICO: Whoa, whoa, whoa. I did not take advantage of you. You were totally all over me.

RILEY: I was not.

NICO: Yes, you were.

RILEY: I was being friendly.

NICO: Right, because that's what friends do, they fuck each other.

RILEY: Maybe.

NICO: Maybe? (*beat*) Are you trying to tell me we're those kinda friends?

RILEY: Maybe.

NICO: (*stares at her for a minute*) I'm not doing this. You're drunk. You have no idea what you're saying.

RILEY: (*whining*) Come on.

NICO: This really would be taking advantage of you.

RILEY: But you know you wanna.

NICO: Wow. Well, first of all, yes. And second of all, that's sorta beside the point.

RILEY: That's totally the point.

NICO: So you wanna have sex with me because I wanna have sex with you?

RILEY: Don't you?

NICO: I don't even know what we're talking about anymore. What are we talking about?

RILEY: Having sex.

NICO: I thought we were friends. I thought you were straight.

RILEY: Whatever.

RILEY starts taking off her clothes slowly. She's attempting to be alluring but her drunken demeanor causes it to be a tad awkward.

NICO: Riley, what are you doing? (NICO *starts picking up each piece of clothing* RILEY *takes off, trying not to look at her. In the end,* NICO *is holding all of* RILEY'*s clothes.*) Please put this back on. Riley. Please. God, why are you crazy?

At this point RILEY is completely naked. NICO, holding all of her clothes, finally looks up at her.

NICO: And why are you so incredibly hot?

NICO drops the clothes and takes RILEY to the bed. Lights go down.

Lights come up on RILEY *and* NICO *in bed.* RILEY *is sitting up in bed.* NICO *is asleep next to her.*

RILEY: What am I doing? What the fuck am I doing? It's like I can't think straight. That's really a terrible joke, you know, but I guess it's true. I have all these feelings I don't know what to do with. (*looks at* NICO) Like, I know she makes me laugh. I know I really like hanging out with her. I know that sometimes when she looks at me, I actually start to blush. I know I miss her when I'm not with her. I know sometimes when she's talking I stop listening 'cause I'm too busy just staring at her. And I want her to want me. I do. And I enjoy it, the sex, but I don't think I could do it when I'm sober. It's like my head turns on and I freeze up. Like my body's betraying my mind, or maybe it's the other way around. I'm not gay. I can't be gay. It just doesn't sound right. Is it possible that it's just her? That it's just you who makes me feel this way?

NICO *wakes up.*

NICO: Mornin.'

RILEY: Hey.

NICO: You okay?

RILEY: Yeah. I just couldn't sleep.

NICO: How's your head?

RILEY: It feels like there's a little man in there jumping up and down and pounding on the walls.

NICO: Sounds about right.

Pause.

RILEY: Look, I—

NICO: Don't. Don't say anything.

RILEY: Why?

NICO: 'Cause let's just be hungover right now.

RILEY: Nico—

NICO: We're friends, right?

RILEY: Right. I really like being your friend.

NICO: As do I.

RILEY: I know what I did last night was confusing. I'm sorry. This whole thing's just a little crazy.

NICO: What whole thing?

RILEY: This. (*pointing to herself and* NICO)

NICO: What?

RILEY: You know what I'm talking about.

NICO: Why is this so crazy?

RILEY: Because it is. Because this is not who I am.

NICO: What do you mean it's not who you are?

RILEY: I'm not gay.

NICO: Says who? What does that word even mean?

RILEY: Well, you're gay, aren't you?

NICO: Yeah, I guess. Yeah.

RILEY: How long have you known?

NICO: Girls are just hotter. But it's not like I haven't thought about being attracted to guys. I dated one, once, in eighth grade. It was weird.

RILEY: But I *have* been with guys. I've dated guys. I've slept with guys. They're all I've ever known. I've always thought I was straight.

NICO: Does it have to be one or the other?

RILEY: Doesn't it?

NICO: Does it? I don't think so. Why can't you just be whatever you are?

RILEY: Because that's not really how it works. We have to define ourselves. To a certain extent, we have to create these boxes for ourselves that fit us. And right now I feel like my box just exploded, and now I'm left here all boxless. Like, what if I am gay? That would mean I haven't known something about myself for eighteen years. That's crazy.

NICO: Why can't you just make a new box? It could even be a trapezoid. Or a circle. Or you could have two different boxes with spikes. (*beat*) Look, I don't wanna make anything hard for you. But I'm not gonna lie to you — I like you, a little more than in a friend way, as you can probably tell. That being said, I'm really cool with doing whatever you wanna do.

RILEY: But I don't know what I want to do.

NICO: Do you wanna be friends? Because we can do that. We were doing that. Pretty well, I think.

RILEY: I know.

NICO: But we could also... I mean... What happened last night for you?

RILEY: I don't know. I just sometimes have an urge to kiss you. Hence really-confused-box syndrome.

NICO: (*laughing*) You gotta stop saying it like that.

RILEY: (*realizing*) Seriously...

NICO: Ok, fine, really-confused-box girl. So sometimes you have the urge to kiss me...

RILEY: Yes.

NICO: Well, that's sort of good news.

RILEY laughs.

NICO: What if, when you have the urge to kiss me, you just kiss me, and we'll take it from there. We'll just be friends who fuck up sometimes.

RILEY: That's a terrible idea. Friends with benefits never work. Don't you watch television?

NICO: Well, it's a good thing this is *reality*.

RILEY: No, seriously. Things get messy and emotional and end terribly.

NICO: Things are messy right now. We just, as friends, slept together...again. So let's just take our boxes, throw 'em out the window, and see what happens. Seriously, what's to say we can't make this work?

RILEY: Because other people can't.

NICO: You hate other people. You're the one always complaining about how other people ruin phrases like 'Let's be friends' because they really mean something else. So let's not be other people. Let's be friends with benefits and *really* mean it. We'll be the exception who lives outside the box — Taco Bell style.

RILEY: I hate you, you know that?

NICO: So is this one of those times where you're having an urge to kiss me?

RILEY: No. (*RILEY throws a pillow at NICO.*)

NICO: Oh, good. Does that mean we can go back to sleep?

RILEY: Yes.

They lie down and NICO wraps her arm around RILEY. Lights go down on NICO's room.

Lights up on RILEY's room. It's a different morning. RILEY enters wearing heels and a dress. She looks tired and a little disheveled. She quickly changes into normal clothes and gathers things she needs for school. She looks around desperately for something she can't find. She realizes something, stops, grabs her bag and exits. Lights down on RILEY's room.

Lights up on NICO's room. She's in bed. The room looks messier than it did in the previous scene, with clothes strewn all over the floor. RILEY appears at NICO's door, quietly opens it and sneaks inside. RILEY begins to look for something quietly in the mess. NICO wakes up.

NICO: Don't you knock?

RILEY: Oh, shit. I didn't mean to wake you. I left my notebook here.

NICO: Good luck finding it. (*NICO sits up in bed, waking up slowly.*)

RILEY: Do you ever clean?

NICO: Nope. Half this shit is yours anyway, since you've been living here for the past month. Maybe you should start cleaning, my little housewife.

RILEY: (*without looking up*) In your dreams, sweetheart.

NICO: Where'd you end up last night? We were all looking for you.

RILEY: Yeah, right. You were too busy talking up a storm with what's-her-face. Be careful, you know she's in love with you.

NICO: Oh, please, I saw you grinding up on that guy in that hot little number you were wearing. Saw you give him your number, too.

RILEY: You saw nothing. I'm never gonna find this notebook.

NICO: Did you go home with him?

RILEY: Oh, yeah, I went home with him and let him fuck me stupid.

NICO: Good, I hate smart girls.

RILEY: I just thought I'd spend the night in my own bed...for once.

NICO: Yeah, so you could think of an excuse to come wake me up in the morning?

RILEY: I really did leave my notebook here.

NICO: Uh-huh. Get over here.

RILEY: I can't. I have class —

NICO: Get over here.

RILEY scampers over to the bed and hops on. NICO tickles her and drags her over to her until they're both lying down again. NICO tries to kiss her, but RILEY dodges the kiss. NICO, oblivious, keeps kissing her neck and tries to take off her shirt. RILEY stops her.

NICO: What's wrong?

RILEY: I just — nothing. I'm just not really in the mood, that's all.

NICO: All right.

RILEY: I just have to go to class.

RILEY gets up and keeps looking for her notebook.

NICO: You haven't been havin' many urges lately.

RILEY: What?

NICO: Ya know, your urges…

RILEY: I have no idea what you're talking about.

NICO: We haven't had sex. I mean, you've been crashing here almost every night for the past month, but we haven't…

RILEY: I've been tired and stressed, you know that. You aren't mad, are you?

NICO: No, why would I be mad?

RILEY: I dunno.

NICO: Is it because you're not attracted to me anymore?

RILEY: (*stops searching and looks up at NICO*) What? No. I just really have to go to class right now. Attraction intact. Okay?

NICO: Okay.

RILEY: Good. (*kisses her quickly.*) I really gotta go. (*grabs her bag and heads for the door*)

NICO: Call me tonight?

RILEY: Maybe. Yeah. (*exits*)

Lights change. NICO is asleep again. RILEY sneaks into the room quietly. She gets into bed with her. NICO rolls over, looks at RILEY, then looks out at the audience.

Lights change. It is morning. RILEY lies in bed, awake. She gets up and starts getting dressed in NICO's clothes. NICO wakes up.

NICO: Where are you going?

RILEY: (*startled*) Um, I'm just gonna go back to my room. Get some work done.

NICO: It's, like, 6:00 am. (*beat*) Where were you last night?

RILEY: What?

NICO: Last night. Where were you? I wanna know where you've been every night for the past month.

RILEY: I was just out.

NICO: With who?

RILEY: Jesus, when did you become my mother?

NICO: You know what? Forget it.

RILEY: I don't know if you woke up on the wrong side of the bed, but I'm gonna go.

NICO: That's great. Go. Do whatever you want. Because the world revolves around what Riley wants. When Riley wants to come sleep in my bed, she does. When she doesn't, she doesn't. When you wanna have sex, we do, but then halfway through it we stop because all of a sudden it's too much for you—

RILEY: So that's what this is about? Sex? I'm sorry I'm confused and don't want to have sex all the time, but it's not really my fault you decided to fuck a straight girl.

NICO: So now you're straight. What does that even mean?

RILEY: I don't know, Nico. Cut me some slack.

NICO: Of course, you don't know. How could I forget? You never know. Well, let me enlighten you.

RILEY: Go right ahead.

NICO: Maybe you're not fucking me because you're too busy fucking that guy you met at the club.

RILEY: Excuse me?

NICO: You think I'm stupid, right? I was there when you met him. I saw you give him your number.

RILEY: I don't know what you're talking about.

NICO: Right. Where were you before you climbed into my bed last night?

RILEY: I was out.

NICO: With him?

Pause.

RILEY: Yes.

NICO: Yes?

RILEY: Yes. What does it matter if I was with him? We're just friends with benefits, right?

NICO: Wow.

RILEY: What? I thought we were on the same page.

NICO: And what page is that, Riley?

RILEY: The one where I'm straight, Nico. The one where my whole entire world is getting flipped on its head. And that, yes, I'm sleeping with this guy because, I don't know, it's easier. Because I don't have any feelings for him, and it's familiar and I feel like I'm in control. Fuck, Nico. Do you know how hard this is for me?

NICO: Do you know how hard this is for me? I'm fucking in love with you.

RILEY: What?

NICO: I love you.

Pause.

RILEY: I have to go.

NICO: Seriously?

RILEY looks at NICO and exits. She reappears in her room. Each girl takes a moment to process what just happened.

NICO: Fuck.

RILEY: Fuck.

NICO picks up her phone and stares at it. RILEY goes to open the door, hand on the doorknob, and stands there. NICO puts the phone down. RILEY slides down the door to the floor, then picks up her phone and stares at it. NICO gets off the bed and goes to the door. She kicks it and then gets back into bed.

RILEY: She loves me. Why does she have to love me?

NICO: Why am I doing this to myself? This is just gonna get worse.

RILEY: Oh, fuck.

NICO: You knew she was straight. You knew this was gonna happen.

RILEY: Fuck.

NICO: Maybe we can just go back to being friends. She'll be with this guy and we'll figure it out.

RILEY: Fuck me.

NICO: We'll just take some time apart.

RILEY: I'm in love with her.

RILEY goes to get her phone and begins to text. NICO begins to get dressed.

RILEY: I'm not texting that. Fuck. I have to tell her.

NICO leaves her room. Lights down in NICO's room.

RILEY goes to her door. NICO appears at the door and stands there. RILEY opens the door as NICO goes to knock. RILEY opens the door and jumps back.

RILEY: Hi!

NICO: Hey.

RILEY: What are you doing here?

NICO: I came to talk.

RILEY: Yeah, I was coming to, uh, never mind. Come in.

They both enter the room. Long pause.

NICO: I'm sorry.

RILEY: No, I'm sorry.

NICO: I didn't mean half of what I said. I guess we should just be friends.

RILEY: (*overlapping*) I love you.

BOTH: What?

NICO: What did you say?

RILEY: No, what did you say?

NICO: Forget what I said. Did you just say what I think you said? (*pause*) Did you just say you were in love with me?

Pause.

RILEY: Yeah.

NICO: Yeah?

RILEY: Yeah. (*beat*) I'm sorry I'm such a fuck-up.

NICO: Shut up.

She kisses RILEY. They keep kissing and move to the bed and begin to fool around. RILEY pulls away.

NICO: What's wrong? Did I hurt you?

RILEY: No. No, it's not that.

Pause.

NICO: You don't wanna do this.

RILEY: I just—

NICO: It's okay. We don't have to do this.

They lie together in silence.

NICO: Do you know what it is? About the sex, I mean.

RILEY: Not really. It's just overwhelming for some reason.

NICO: But only sometimes?

RILEY: I really don't understand it. Sometimes I'm totally in it with you, and other times I just can't get out of my head. It has nothing to do with how I feel about you.

NICO: I know. I mean, I'm glad I know that now.

Pause.

RILEY: What are we gonna do if this keeps being hard for me?

NICO: We'll make it work. We're already living outside the box, right? We'll just keep making up our own rules.

RILEY: Are you saying you can live without sex?

NICO: Wait. Are you saying you wanna stop having sex altogether?

RILEY: No. I just can't promise I'm gonna stop being confused.

NICO: Do you need time?

RILEY: No, I mean, yes, but I want to be with you now.

NICO: Would it help if you could keep sleeping with him?

RILEY: What?

NICO: If you need to keep sleeping with him because it makes you feel in control or sane or whatever, then maybe that's what you should do. I just wanna be in love with you.

RILEY: You'd be okay with that?

NICO: As long as you love me, that's all that matters.

RILEY: But what about you?

NICO: What about me?

RILEY: Who are you gonna sleep with?

NICO: I'm gonna sleep with you.

RILEY: But—

NICO: Only when you want to.

RILEY: I don't like it. We need to find you someone. What about what's-her-face?

NICO: I am not doing that.

RILEY: Why not? She's totally crazy about you.

NICO: You think you'd be okay with it, but you wouldn't.

RILEY: If you can do it, I can do it. You love me, right?

NICO: Fuck yes.

RILEY: Then it doesn't matter. You'll always be mine, no matter what you do with what's-her-face. Only one rule—don't fall in love with her.

NICO: You don't need to worry about that. (*kisses her*) See? Who needs boxes when you can just make 'em up as you go along?

RILEY: Only other people need boxes.

NICO: Those poor other people.

RILEY: I love you.

NICO: I love you.

They kiss. Lights out.

Lights up on NICO*'s room.* RILEY *comes to the door, she's been crying, she's very upset. She knocks.*

RILEY: C'mon, Nico. (*She knocks again, frantically.*) C'mon, where the fuck are you? (*She opens the door. There's no one there. She picks up her phone and dials.*) C'mon, c'mon. Pick up. Please. (*gets answering machine*) Hey. I know you're with what's-her-face but I really need you to come home. I had a really shitty night. He's just an asshole. Come home, please. I'm waiting in your room.

She hangs up the phone. She crawls into NICO*'s bed and finds a large black bra in the bed, obviously not* RILEY*'s. She stares at it a moment and then puts it back.*

Lights change. Morning. RILEY *wakes up and* NICO*'s still not there. She sits staring out the window. The door opens,* NICO *enters.*

NICO: Hey! What are you doing here?

RILEY: Did you get my message?

NICO: Nah. My phone died last night. Weren't you supposed to be with dickwad?

RILEY: You didn't get my message?

NICO: No, my phone was off.

RILEY: It died or it was off?

NICO: It died. What's going on?

RILEY: I really needed you last night.

NICO: I'm sorry. I'm here now. (*tries to kiss her. RILEY pulls away.*)

RILEY: Did you shower?

NICO: Um, no.

RILEY: You smell like her.

NICO: Riley… (*pause. NICO pulls back*) You gonna tell me what happened last night?

RILEY: I don't really wanna talk about it. He was just being an asshole.

NICO: What did he do?

RILEY: Nothing.

NICO: You know I'll kick his ass.

RILEY: (*smiles weakly*) I just don't really wanna see him anymore.

NICO: You don't have to. (*NICO goes to her.*)

Pause.

RILEY: I've missed you lately.

NICO: I've missed you.

RILEY: You've been gone a lot.

NICO: Well, so have you.

RILEY: How's slut monkey?

NICO: Just a slut.

RILEY: Really?

NICO: Really. (*beat*) Is everything ok?

Pause.

RILEY: Would you stop seeing her if I asked you to?

Pause. NICO pulls away.

NICO: Why? Because you stopped seeing him?

RILEY: Well, yeah.

NICO: Jesus, Riley…

RILEY: What? She's just some slut, right? Why wouldn't you stop seeing her?

NICO: Do you hear yourself right now? You want me to stop seeing her because he broke up with you? Do you know how selfish that is?

RILEY: I thought this is what you wanted.

NICO: None of this is what I wanted! I wanted to be with you from the beginning and only you.

RILEY: So stop seeing her.

NICO: That's not the point, Riley. I'm always just supposed to do what you want. Nothing's changed. I'm still bending over backwards. Still wondering every single day if you're just gonna wake up and figure out you're not in love with me anymore. Do you know how terrifying that is?

RILEY: Nico, I love you. I know it took me a while to say that. But I'm here now. And I wanna be with you.

NICO: Only because you're not with him anymore.

RILEY: That was your idea for me to keep sleeping with him.

NICO: And you said yes. I did whatever it took so I didn't lose you. But you make it so fucking hard to hold on sometimes I wonder why I do it.

RILEY: What are you saying?

NICO: Falling in love's always scary. Being in love's always scary. It has nothing to do with whether you're straight or gay or confused or whatever, it's just scary. *(beat)* Look, I don't want to fight with you.

RILEY: I don't wanna fight either. I'm sorry.

NICO: Ok.

RILEY: Can you come here?

NICO gets in bed with her.

RILEY: I love you. I really do.

NICO: I love you, too.

RILEY: (*cautiously*) So will you end it?

Pause.

NICO: Yeah.

RILEY: Tonight?

NICO: Yeah.

RILEY starts kissing NICO's neck. NICO doesn't kiss back.

RILEY: What's wrong?

NICO: I haven't showered, remember?

RILEY pulls back and rolls away. Silence. Lights out.

Lights up on RILEY's room. She sits at first, then tries to distract herself but can't focus on any one thing. She picks up her phone and fidgets with it. Finally, she dials. Lights up on NICO's room. There is no one there. NICO's phone is on the desk. It rings and goes to voicemail.

RILEY: Hey, I know you're probably still with her. Um, will you just call me when you get back. I don't care how late it is. I'm gonna go to bed, but please call. And Nico, I'm sorry for being so crazy. I love you. (*She hangs up the phone and gets into bed.*)

Lights change. RILEY is asleep in her room.

NICO enters her own room, checks her phone and listens to the message. She puts the phone down and goes to bed. Lights change.

Morning. RILEY wakes up, looks at her phone. No new messages. She gets dressed and leaves the room. She reappears at NICO's door. She thinks about opening the door, but knocks instead. No answer. NICO wakes up to the knock. RILEY knocks again. NICO slowly gets up and opens the door.

NICO: Hey.

RILEY: Can I come in?

NICO: It's early.

RILEY: You didn't call me last night.

NICO opens the door to let RILEY in. RILEY walks by her and notices hickeys on her neck.

RILEY: What happened?

NICO: You know what happened.

RILEY: No, I don't think I do.

NICO: I ended it.

RILEY: Yeah, before or after you fucked her?

NICO: What?

RILEY: You're gonna stand there and lie to me? Who sucked on your neck, Nico?

NICO: Riley—

RILEY: Who sucked on your neck, Nico?

NICO: Riley—

RILEY: You fucked her, didn't you?

NICO: Riley, lemme explain.

RILEY: What? Explain what? You went over there to tell her it was over. You went over there to tell slut monkey that you were done using her as your cunt.

NICO: (*overlapping*) She has a name.

RILEY: Excuse me.

Pause.

NICO: She has a name. Her name is—

RILEY: I know her name.

Pause.

RILEY: You didn't do it, did you?

NICO: Of course I did it.

RILEY: All that shit you said yesterday, the whole reason you were so pissed off is because you wanted to keep seeing her, didn't you?

NICO: Riley…

RILEY: Because you wanted to keep fucking her?

NICO: Riley, calm down.

RILEY: Why did you sleep with her?

NICO: It's complicated.

RILEY: Enlighten me.

NICO: You can't just sleep with someone and not have feelings for them.

RILEY: Yes, yes you can.

NICO: Maybe *you* can. But I'm not that person.

RILEY: If you knew that, you shouldn't have fucked her in the first place. That was one of the rules, remember? Don't fall in love with her. I never, *never* had feelings for him.

NICO: You asked me to fuck her. You *asked* me to.

RILEY: You promised me we wouldn't be other people. You said we'd make this work.

NICO: I ended it, didn't I? What does it matter if I fucked her one more time? I've been fucking her for months. And it's over. Isn't that what you wanted?

RILEY: Isn't that what you wanted?

Pause.

RILEY: Nico?

Pause.

RILEY: Nico?

Lights fade.

Lights up on RILEY's room. Different day. She gathers things that belong to NICO, looks around the room and exits. Lights up on NICO's room. RILEY appears with NICO's things and knocks. NICO opens the door.

NICO: Hey.

RILEY: Hey. I brought you these.

NICO: I really wanna talk.

RILEY: I know what you're gonna say.

NICO: You can't know what I'm going to—

RILEY: I'm not stupid.

NICO: I know.

RILEY: I know you learned a lot from me. I know this isn't my fault. I know you love me. At least, I know you did.

NICO: I always will.

RILEY: I know. I know you didn't want this to happen.

NICO: I wanted to make it work.

RILEY: I know. It was just easier to love her.

NICO: Riley…

RILEY: No. I want you to know I'm not mad. Not that I'm not broken or devastated, but it happens, right?

NICO: I don't know how it happened.

RILEY: I do. I made it really hard for you to love me, forced you to sleep with someone else who, because you're amazing, fell in love with you and made it easy for you to love her. It makes perfect sense to me. All I know is that in the end it doesn't matter if I'm gay or straight or whatever. I'm just a person finally in love with a person, getting my heart broken. And you're just a person, falling in love with another person who was actually ready to love you. That person just wasn't me. *(beat)* I want you to know you sort of changed my life.

NICO: You sort of changed mine. I mean it.

RILEY: So, let's not do this talk. Other people do this talk and that's not us.

NICO: Well, we certainly tried not to be other people.

RILEY: We gave it our best shot.

NICO: Yeah, we did.

Pause.

NICO: So what happens now?

RILEY: We'll be friends.

NICO: Friends?

RILEY: Yeah, friends. You think you can handle that?

NICO: I think I could try.

RILEY: Good.

RILEY goes to exit.

NICO: Riley—

RILEY turns around.

NICO: I, um…

RILEY: I know, me too. Bye.

NICO: Bye.

RILEY exits. NICO stands in her room. Lights up on RILEY's room. She enters and stands there. She begins to sob uncontrollably. Lights out.

The End

Red

by Jordan Hall

About the playwright

Jordan Hall is an emerging artist whose work has been dubbed "stellar, insightful" by *Plank Magazine*, "thoughtful" by CBC Radio, and "vivid, memorable" by *NOW*. Her writing for the stage includes her short works *Annie & Izzy*, *The Second Last Man on Earth*, *Asleep at the Wheel*, and *The Possible Lives of Dolores Garcia Rodriguez*, as well as her full-length play, *Kayak*, which won Samuel French's 2010 Canadian Playwright's competition. Jordan's plays have been produced across the country, most recently at the 2011 Vancouver Fringe and 2010 SummerWorks Festival. She is developing her newest work, *Travelling Light*, as an Associate with the Playwrights' Theatre Centre. Her first short film, *Love Sucks*, is currently in post-production in Toronto, and her second, *Run Dry*, is one of the winners of the 2011 Crazy8s short film competition. As a dramaturg, Jordan recently worked on the Dora-nominated *Belle of Winnipeg* with Keystone Theatre, sits on the Board of Foundry Theatre, and is a mentor for UBC's Booming Ground program. Visit her at www.jordanhall.ca.

Characters

ROSE (F) — maybe 16 or 17
WOLF (M) — about 20, tall, dark and twitchy
THE WOLF — something monstrous, not human. (This character should be designed as an "idea" of a wolf. A monstrous and frightening figure. Above all, it is critical that this character remain metaphoric and not fall into a clichéd "Cats" version of a human costumed as an animal.)

Red, warm darkness, like the inside of an eyelid. A muffled thumping, like the beating of an enormous heart.

Onstage, a spill of red cloth running upstage to downstage. At the upstage edge of the cloth sits ROSE*, curled into a ball. Her hair is red, and she wears a simple red shift, so it might look as though she and her dress and the path are of a piece.*

ROSE *rocks back and forth. She hums "To Grandmother's house we go."**

In the shadows at the back of the stage, there is a flicker of movement. A flash of blue electrical light. Something big. Not human. ROSE *sees it.*

ROSE: Here's the problem with wolves: they're hungry. You think it's that other stuff: the big eyes, big ears, big teeth—but it isn't. A wolf is born with a great big hole inside. An emptiness that howls and howls to be filled—and the wolf'll do just about anything to fill it. Including swallow you whole.

The movement/flicker again. ROSE *gets to her feet. She starts to walk away from the creature, down the trail of red cloth, never touching the floor beyond the cloth.*

ROSE: This is a story that begins with a girl. She's on her way to her grandmother's house.

Let's call her "Red." She likes that better than "Freckles" or "Ginger." Those are names for regular girls. But call a girl "Red"? Red has blood-coloured curls that make men stare and she doesn't stay on paths and she isn't ever afraid. Even when there's a monster breathing hot at the back of her neck. Something my grandmother told my mother once: Some girls, you always knew they'd end up in the belly of a wolf.

A light hits the stage, creating a streetlamp glow off the path. In the light sits a basket covered with a red-checked cloth.

ROSE *steps off the path and becomes* RED*, maybe sixteen or seventeen. She heads to the basket, pulls off the cloth, and starts scarfing down Black Forest cake.*

The movement/flicker happens again. As it ends, WOLF *enters. He's a tall guy, maybe twenty, with a scarred face and a beaten leather jacket. He smiles at* RED.

WOLF: Hello, little girl. What's a sweet bite like you doing in a place like this?

RED: (*mouth full*) Down, Fido. I'm supposed to be taking this crap to Gram's. We gotta talk.

WOLF: Before or after you share your basket of goodies with me?

RED: Don't start that shit. We got a serious problem here. (*beat*) I'm late.

Awkwardness.

WOLF: Fuck.

RED: Two weeks.

WOLF: Are you sure?

---

* From "Over the River and Through the Woods" by Lydia Maria Child

RED: Don't be stupid.

Beat.

WOLF: So. Uh — what are you going to do?

RED: Well…end it.

WOLF: Oh.

RED: Mom can't find out. She thinks I go straight to Gram's without passing Go. If she knew I was here? With you? She's been warning me about guys like you since I was six.

WOLF: So tell Grandma. You been ferrying that old bag cake and sherry since time began.

RED: Grams flips if you spill shit on the fucking doilies. Her precious granddaughter ruining her life? She'll disinherit me.

WOLF: I could tell her how it is.

RED: Grams'll pay the fucking gardener to kill you with a shovel and bury you in the backyard.

WOLF: Jesus. Let's not get carried away here.

RED: I end it and neither of them ever has to know.

WOLF: Yeah. Yeah. (*beat*) But, okay — what if you didn't?

RED: Are you high?

WOLF: No. Well — yeah. But what if you didn't?

RED: And what?

WOLF: Us. We could keep it. Like — a family.

RED: Because you and me are such great Mommy-Daddy material?

WOLF: That's your tightass family talking. We can do this. I'll clean up. Get a job.

RED: No one's hiring you. You've got a record.

WOLF: (*scoffs*) Drunk and Disorderly. Howling at the moon.

RED: Aggravated assault. And you *bit* a guy in a bar fight. You were bragging about it when we met. (*beat*) It won't work.

WOLF: No. No. Listen. So — Okay, yeah — maybe no one'll hire me as a fucking stock boy. Maybe your family is a bunch of controlling bitches. But we can do this. That rat in the bar — I tore his throat out with my teeth. Because he looked at some girl I didn't give a damn about. Because he thought he could take what was *mine*. If I could do that when I didn't care — then for you, Red? For my kid — ? I will do anything. You're *mine*. You're both mine.

A beat.

RED: I — uh — should go. Grams is gonna bitch for days if I'm any later.

He grabs her arm.

RED: I'll think about it.

The streetlight dies and WOLF *disappears into the movement/flicker. There's some kind of high electric whine and the thumping of the heart returns.* RED *becomes* ROSE, *standing at the downstage edge of the cloth.*

THE WOLF, the apparition that frightened her earlier, appears at the upstage edge of the cloth.

ROSE: There's a monster here. On the inside. Something growing in the dark. All eyes and teeth and hunger.

THE WOLF begins to stalk her. ROSE crawls underneath the fabric of the trail like a little child under the covers. Once she's underneath, she draws up the end to make herself a hood of red cloth.

ROSE: It doesn't scare Red. This is the first story she heard as a child, the first her child will hear. In Red's story, you're as safe in a little red cloak as a child under blankets, as a baby in the womb. The wolf will be carved open and everyone trapped inside will come blinking out into the light. Red almost feels sorry for the wolf. For the way it has to take because nothing is given. For the story that kills it again and again.

She stands up, still holding onto the hood, as though the trail is the train of some enormous cloak. As she speaks, THE WOLF sneaks under the upstage edge of the train and begins to crawl towards her under the fabric.

ROSE: But there's something she's forgotten: Feeling sorry for a monster doesn't mean it's not a monster. The wolf has a story too. Here's how it ends: The cloak tears and you get dragged out into the dark, screaming. The wolf pulls open your belly and rips your insides into pretty red ribbons. Red isn't afraid, but she should be. The only one getting out of this alive is the wolf.

From under the cloth THE WOLF grabs ROSE with a snarl, drags her under. There's a shriek and a scuffle. The electric whine. The flicker.

Soft, early evening light. The scuffle becomes tumbling and laughter. As they emerge from the cloth ROSE becomes RED, THE WOLF becomes WOLF. WOLF looks cleaner, but exhausted.

WOLF: (*laughing*) My — What big eyes you've got!

RED: (*giggling*) The better to roll them at you!

WOLF: My — What big lips you've got! (*he leans in to kiss her*)

RED: (*pouting, but willing to be kissed*) The better to —

He interrupts her with a kiss that blossoms into more serious making out. He grabs her ass.

WOLF: My — What a big —

RED: Don't you even *think* it, loser! (*beat*) Damn, I'm hungry. We got anything in the fridge?

WOLF: Yeah. Sure — you want some of that chicken we had yesterday?

RED: Mmm. No. Not the chicken.

WOLF: I think we got Cheerios.

RED: The milk's gone bad. (*looks at her stomach*) But that's okay. You know what the monster wants? Steak. Garlic Mashed Potatoes. Asparagus in butter.

WOLF: Monster and me both.

Beat.

RED: You know. If it's a girl—

WOLF: He's a boy.

RED: But if it's a girl—

WOLF: Never happen.

RED: I—I wanna name her Rose. After Grams.

WOLF: What? Why?

RED: It's a family name.

WOLF: Of a family that doesn't return your phone calls.

RED: Actually, she did—

WOLF: She? Called you?

RED: Yeah. Yeah. Mom still won't speak to me. But Grams—we talked—and—I miss her is all.

WOLF: You can barely stand her.

RED: I know she's all snotty, but I miss—like—how she gives you a dirty look if you try to make tea in a mug instead of the teapot, or sprays you with rosewater because "perfume is for prostitutes." (*beat*) I even miss those stupid baskets. I'd always snitch something and she'd pretend she didn't notice. Oooh—Black Forest cake! Just dripping with cherries and cream—

WOLF: Is that how you paid the hydro bill?

RED: What?

WOLF: Did you ask her for money? You what—? Thought I wouldn't notice?

RED: Leave it alone.

WOLF: She just calls you up out of the blue. You weren't missing the finer things, Princess?

RED: Stop it—you'll upset the baby.

WOLF: She going to pay you to name it after her? Huh? Put you back in the will, Red?

RED: That's not fair—

WOLF: You think it's easy? What I do? You think I just grab a neck and squeeze and they hand the money over? People do crazy shit when they think they're gonna die. Accountants whack you with briefcases. Girls wearing fucking "fur is murder" shirts go clawing at your eyes. And all you get is forty dollars and a bunch of credit cards you can't use. I do it for you. Every day. I am dogfucking tired. You think you can just go running back at the first sign of trouble?

RED: Seriously? The first sign of trouble? I'm pregnant, you asshole. They were going to shut off the hydro. The OB needed to do a second sonogram to check—I don't know—my goddamn placenta. The fucking milk has gone bad. So I did what I had to do. Because day-old chicken and no name Cheerios are not gonna cut it. (*beat*) If it doesn't get better I'm going to live with Grams.

WOLF: You are not taking my kid.

RED: Yours?

WOLF: You think you can just walk away from this?

RED: We had a deal. And you are not holding up your end.

WOLF: Fine, baby doll. Run home to Grandma. Maybe I'll visit. Maybe I'll see you real soon. (*starts lalala-ing the tune of* "To Grandmother's house we go" *in an obnoxious voice*)

RED: You're a fucking psycho.

The giant heart is thundering and faltering. The electrical whine. The blue flicker. WOLF leaves. RED collapses, becomes ROSE. She's struggling to breathe.

ROSE: What if you could choose? Would you be the wolf? Or the girl?

Opposite ROSE is the apparition of THE WOLF. They circle each other warily.

ROSE: Behind the teapots and make-up and tampons, under the monthly reek of blood, the rules and regulations, the girl is beloved. She'll never go hungry. She belongs.

As she speaks, she gathers up the path. Wrapping it and rolling it into the shape of a swaddled child in her arms. THE WOLF advances, growling, threatening.

ROSE: The wolf learns loneliness early. Kills its mother crawling out of her belly. Takes what it needs. Leaves her bleeding and never looks back.

She darts left and right, trying to keep the baby away from THE WOLF. It cuts her off at every attempt.

ROSE: Sooner or later you have to decide. There are a thousand versions. Stories inside stories inside stories — but the choice is always the same. Red? Or the Wolf? Maybe it's impossible to love a monster, but — something else my grandmother told my mother — if you're a woman, you're gonna bleed.

ROSE turns, becomes RED. Underneath her dress the bundle of fabric is now a pregnant belly. THE WOLF fades back into the shadows.

RED: "At the first cut, he saw the little red cloak, and after a few more slashes the little girl sprang out and cried — " (*She puts down the book as the baby kicks.*) What? You don't like that? You've heard it a thousand times —

A scuffle offstage. A sidelight flows across RED like a door being opened into a dark room. In the door is WOLF, mid-burglary, with an old lady's nightgown on one arm.

RED: You are fucking kidding me.

WOLF: Shit.

RED: Are you fucking burglarizing my grandmother's house?

WOLF: Kind of.

RED: Kind of?

WOLF: Sort of.

RED: Sort of?

WOLF: You're supposed to be asleep!

RED: Oh. Well, no need to call the cops then.

WOLF: I'm doing this for you. For us!

RED: Get out. I'll give you five minutes before I dial 911.

WOLF: Nobody's calling the cops.

RED: You're lucky it's me. Grams would've had a heart attack if she'd come down first.

WOLF: Yeah. Well.

RED flags that he's got her grandmother's nightgown. The pieces fall into place.

RED: You son of a bitch!

WOLF: It was an accident!

RED: Murderer!

She turns to run out of the room. He rushes her. A struggle.

WOLF: Stop it, \ Red! Red!

RED: (*overlapping*) Stop calling me that! \ Stop—

WOLF: (*overlapping*) I don't want to hurt you—

She scratches him. He backhands her. She drops. Screams. She's in serious pain. He backs off, hyperventilating.

WOLF: No. No. I didn't mean to.

RED: Something's wrong. Something's—

WOLF: I didn't mean to do that!

A contraction hits her.

RED: Oh, God. Call an ambulance.

Silence. She flags that he isn't going to do it. For the first time, she's terrified.

RED: No. No. You don't do this. Not to *me*. Not to the baby! (*beat*) We'll die—don't you understand? We'll both die. (*contraction*) Oh, God. Oh, God. It's too fast—there's too much—Oh, God. (*contraction. She whispers in horror.*) There's a wolf inside me. You put a wolf inside me.

As she speaks, WOLF has the fabric in his hands like they're covered in blood. He backs away in horror, pulling the fabric out from under RED's dress, like a flood of blood. He runs.

RED: (*whispering*) She warned me. You're gonna bleed. If you're a woman. You're gonna bleed. (*She passes out.*)

The heartbeat thunders, thunders, falters. The whine-jolt-flicker. THE WOLF apparition returns, pulling the fabric away from ROSE. ROSE retreats, trying to hold on.

THE WOLF: This is a story. That begins with a girl. Let's call her \ Rose.

ROSE: (*overlapping*) Rose. She was named for her mother's grandmother.

THE WOLF: Rose's mother tells her a story.

ROSE: Before she's even been born.

THE WOLF: And when Rose listens, her mother is—

ROSE: Little Red Riding Hood.

THE WOLF: And her father—

ROSE: Is a wolf.

THE WOLF: But something goes wrong. The story is the same.

BOTH: Girl. Wolf. Path.

ROSE: But it means something different.

THE WOLF: The path is a river of blood. The girl is dying—

ROSE: If you're the girl, you're dying—

THE WOLF: —but if you're the wolf—

ROSE: —if you're the wolf—

THE WOLF: —they cut Little Red Riding Hood open and her daughter—

ROSE: —the only one who gets out alive—

BOTH: —is the Wolf.

The great heart flatlines. ROSE *turns her face up.*

ROSE: I'm so sorry, Red.

THE WOLF *removes some part of its costume and places it on* ROSE. *Uncostumed,* THE WOLF *fades away. During the following the shocks of the defibrillator happen once, twice, three times.*

ROSE (as THE WOLF):

Here's the problem with wolves: they're survivors. Catch one in a trap, it'll chew off its own leg. You can learn to live without a leg. Without a lot of things.

There are words for what happened: Trauma. Abruption. Hemorrhage. What they mean is: she was bleeding. Red. And I let her. That was the choice, and I let her bleed. The police will come for my father. Put him down like a dog when he runs. They'll give me to my grandmother. Her mother. But it's already too late. She'll know it the moment they show her the crib behind the plexiglass wall. My little face, howling, still red with blood and afterbirth. She'll be afraid. She should be. I'm a wolf.

As the lights fall, the flatline becomes the sound of a baby crying.

The End

Almost, Again

by Briana Brown

About the playwright

Originally from rural Ontario, Briana Brown spent several years in Toronto after graduating from York University (B.A. Theatre Studies), and is currently completing her M.F.A. in creative writing at the University of British Columbia. Her plays have been workshopped through Factory Theatre's LabCab Festival, Tarragon Theatre's Spring Arts Fair, Nightwood Theatre's Write from the Hip program, and the TheatreKairos writers' circle, where she took on the role of Program Director. In the 2010–2011 season, she was the Program Director for the Paprika Festival's Playwrights in Residence Program. Her one-act play *Cassandra* toured Fringe Festivals in London, Ottawa, Victoria, and Vancouver in the summer of 2006, with a second production at the London Fringe in 2010. The play was also included as part of Winnipeg's FemFest in 2007. In 2009, Briana was commissioned by SeriousFUN! Theatre Company to develop a script based on the experiences of the ten young women in their company's Going Pro program, entitled *The Line*. As a director, she had the opportunity to assist Brad Fraser on the Canadian premiere of *True Love Lies* (Factory Theatre), and has directed productions at the Theatre Passe Muraille's Buzz Festival, the Toronto Fringe, HotScrawls festival, the New Ideas Festival, the Paprika Festival (Tenth Anniversary Celebration, 2010), and V-Day Toronto (*The Vagina Monologues*, 2009). *Almost, Again* debuted at the Toronto Fringe Festival in 2010 and went on to be included in the Best of Fringe under Briana's direction. The production starred Roger Bainbridge and Haley McGee, with set and costume design by Katie Horrill, original composition by Rob D'Ambrumenil, and stage management by Alex Kentris. It was produced by Liz Sheffield and go go go productions.

Characters

JACK — mid-20s. A mathematician.
GINGER — mid-20s. A poet.
They are co-workers at a large chain bookstore.

Setting

GINGER's chaotic apartment, and JACK's spotless apartment.

Scene 1

JACK and GINGER burst into GINGER's apartment in a fit of laughter and alcohol. GINGER snorts. There are books, pillows and clothing scattered everywhere.

JACK: Oh, my God, we made it.

GINGER: That was epic.

JACK: But we persevered.

GINGER: We did!

JACK: Not even the tragic death of a mouse could ruin our evening!

GINGER: (*laughs. Then:*) That was sad.

JACK: Should we have — we couldn't really do anything.

GINGER: We could have buried him.

JACK: Do you want to go back?

GINGER: No. Is that bad?

JACK: No.

GINGER: Can I get you a drink? You can put your coat anywhere.

JACK: I can see that.

GINGER: I'm not the tidiest.

JACK: I didn't mean —

GINGER: I know, I just —

Pause.

JACK: I would love a drink.

GINGER: Great.

She goes to retrieve it. JACK checks out her place.

GINGER: So… I only have vodka.

JACK: You mean business.

GINGER: I'm going to be a mess tomorrow.

She brings two glasses over — straight vodka.

JACK: Cheers.

GINGER: To an absolutely ridiculous evening —

They drink.

GINGER: Thank you. I needed it.

JACK: I know you did.

GINGER: Yeah?

JACK: I've got mad perception skills.

GINGER: (*beat*) Noted.

JACK: Ben also mentioned that you told Margo you were going to quit.

GINGER: *If things don't change* I'm going to quit. That's what I said. (*beat*) Is that why you were so nice to me tonight?

JACK: No. What needs to change?

GINGER: As of next week, we're only allowed to have three Staff Picks at a time. You know this?

JACK: I'd heard whispers of it, yes.

GINGER: It's ludicrous! It's like they don't want *anyone* to read—not even the employees!

JACK: Are we allowed to recommend stationery and s'more-making kits?

GINGER: Yes! YES, WE ARE.

JACK: That was a joke.

GINGER: I know it was—you did that thing with your eyebrow—and I would have laughed if it weren't TOTALLY TRUE!

JACK: That is crazy. (*beat*) I do something with my eyebrow?

GINGER: —Yes.

JACK: What?

GINGER: Just you raise it kind of—expectantly when you make a joke.

JACK: Huh. Jack recommends: the campfire-scented candle. You're right, I do.

GINGER: I also have mad perception skills. Anyway, I'm not going to quit. Yet.

JACK: Good.

Pause.

JACK: All right. Enough pretense. Let's get to it.

GINGER: What?

JACK: The big moment.

A look of panic crosses GINGER*'s face at* JACK*'s sudden forwardness.*

JACK: (*laughing*) I'm sorry—shit—your face! I meant your poem. You said you were going to share tonight's bout of inspiration.

GINGER: Right. Oh, my God. My face is really red, isn't it?

JACK: Little bit.

GINGER: Okay. (*fumbling with her bag*) Oh, shit! I used it to cover up the mouse. I only have the last bit—napkin number two. This is why I will never finish the book!

JACK: Because you're always using your poems as shrouds?

GINGER: No, because I can never get it together enough to buy a notebook.

JACK: (*customer service*) Has anyone mentioned our summer stationery sale? Fifteen percent off all stationery products—this week only.

GINGER: Thanks, I'll consider it. That was funny, by the way—the shroud.

JACK: Thanks. Wait, I know that trick. Poem. Go. Now.

GINGER: Yes. Poem. Oh, God, this is pointless but anyway—it was about a rabbit... Okay!

Our Petrie, young rabbit that he so comfortably was
did happily, hoppily, unstoppably go
Despite the knowledge that this decision would
disappointingly, aggressively, and unapologetically
fill his poor sister to the brim with woe.

And so. And so.
Our tale of Petrie, young reader
must unhappily flow
out and across and above and below
gently, majestically and indisputably so
into the abyss that we all — regrettably — know:

'the end.'

JACK: Wow. (*beat*) That —

GINGER: Are you thinking full-blown verse is the antithesis of children's literature?

JACK: No, I think that's cool. I was just — that was a lot of adverbs.

GINGER: It makes me really happy that you noticed that.

JACK: Oh — so —

GINGER: It was intentional, yes! Wow, that's really great that you noticed that. I read an article that said in fifty years, adverbs will have vanished from the English language.

JACK: Wow, th —

GINGER: Laziness. I'm doing my small part to fight the extinction of the adverb.

JACK: Cheers. Never would have dreamt that the girl shelving books next to me every day at work is actually *singlehandedly* fighting the fight of the dying adverb.

GINGER: That gets a high five.

They do.

GINGER: I feel the same. I had no idea you were a moonlighting mathematician. I thought you were a struggling comedian. I guess you're always scribbling calculations, not jokes.

JACK: Is that the —

BOTH: — mad perception skills —

GINGER: — yes. You're always scribbling stuff down in your book. Joke. Book. Joke. Book. Oh, my God — are you inventing the formula for laughter?

JACK: (*laughs*) No, unfortunately. Doesn't have much to do with math or comedy. It's more about "how do I get myself through another day working at a chain bookstore without completely losing my mind?"

GINGER: And how do you get yourself through another day working at a chain bookstore without completely losing your mind?

JACK: Well…

He goes to tell her, but starts laughing before he can get out the first word.

GINGER: C'mon.

JACK: I'm sorry—this is—(*vocalization of frustration*) The thing is, it's not even that big a deal. Ah! Okay.

GINGER: Go!

JACK: I have a system.

GINGER: A system.

JACK: A points system. I get one point if I make someone smile, two points for a laugh. A snort—gets me five big ones. Which is why I hang around you so much.

GINGER: Hey! Okay, so then what happens to these points?

JACK: 150 points: geeky magazine. I can usually rack that up in a week, and it makes my day bright. BUT. If I wait to collect 500 points, then I get to purchase something for the kitchen—lemon zester, garlic peeler or new, very specific, knife. And if I can hold off to 1000 points—(*shaking his head*) I take myself to see the newest blockbuster hit with my self-created 100 percent guilt free pass.

GINGER: Is it an actual physical pass?

JACK: No! It's just—a metaphorical pass.

GINGER: And the guilt—

JACK: You know. Supporting the man. Financially contributing to the problem. All that. I'm trying to balance the effect I have on society.

GINGER: Right. (*beat*) Well, I'd say that's hardly embarrassing at all.

JACK: Hardly?

GINGER: Yeah. Oh.

They high five.

GINGER: Wait—is hardly an adverb or does it just happen to end in L-Y?

JACK shrugs. Long pause.

JACK: I wish I was creating the formula for laughter.

Struggling to find something to say, GINGER awkwardly begins sliding forward off the couch. As she tries to stop herself, JACK begins to mirror the action to prevent embarrassment. A silent agreement. They both slide off the couch and onto the floor. GINGER notices something on her bookshelf.

GINGER: Can I just say something? I don't know if I need to or not, but I really just want to address it in case I do.

JACK: Okay.

GINGER: When I had my back turned earlier to get the drinks, you probably noticed that I own the hardcover illustrated edition of *The Da Vinci Code*—

JACK: I hadn't, no—

GINGER: I just want you know that it was a gift from my aunt, who barely knows me because of my whole Paris thing. I need you know that.

JACK: I now know that.

GINGER: Okay.

JACK: To estranged aunts.

GINGER: … And to expressive eyebrows.

Cheers. Long pause. Almost simultaneously:

JACK: So—

GINGER: So—

Beat.

JACK: Yeah, I should—

GINGER: Yeah? Okay, sure—

JACK: I mean—

GINGER: No, that's—

JACK: Yeah?

GINGER: Okay.

JACK: Okay.

GINGER goes to get a drink, which he misinterprets as getting up to say goodbye.

GINGER: Well—

JACK: So I'll—

GINGER: Go? Yeah, I'll see you—

JACK: Tomorrow. Yeah.

GINGER: Tomorrow.

A long moment.

GINGER: (*whispering*) I really want to kiss you.

JACK: (*whispering back*) Okay.

GINGER: (*still whispering*) But I don't think I should kiss you.

JACK: (*whispering back*) Okay. Why?

GINGER: I just—I don't want this to end up like that.

JACK: Like…

GINGER: I mean—I guess it doesn't matter. I've kissed a lot of people when I'm drunk.

JACK: Yeah.

GINGER: No, like—a *lot.*

JACK: (*laughing*) Not where I thought that was going.

GINGER: But—yeah. Let's—

JACK: If you don't—then I don't want to—

GINGER: No, it's fine. Let's—

JACK: I don't want you to—

GINGER: No, I won't. I know it's something I want to do even when I'm sober.

JACK: Yeah?

GINGER: I've thought about it.

JACK: Me too.

GINGER: Really?

JACK: Yeah.

GINGER: Great. I feel better.

JACK: Glad to be of service.

GINGER: You're a smooth talker.

JACK: Ha.

GINGER: You're a good — convincer.

JACK: And you're drunk.

GINGER: Yes — wait — so are you! Hey — do you not want to —

JACK: I do, I just — *(beat)* I'm kind of a 'moment' guy.

GINGER: Oh?

JACK: And I think maybe we missed our moment. Tonight.

GINGER: Okay. So let's just sneak up on the moment when it isn't looking.

JACK: That's not what I meant.

GINGER: But I think it's a really good idea.

JACK: Okay. *(pause)* So…now?

GINGER: Yeah… Now. I could do now. Let's do it now. I'm going to kiss you now.

They move in closer.

JACK: So…

GINGER: I'm going to.

JACK: So… ?

GINGER: Oh, I'm about to.

JACK: Okay…

GINGER: All right.

JACK: All right.

GINGER: Okay.

He moves in to kiss her.

GINGER: *(breaking away)* Nope. Don't want to. I think we over-talked it. We're setting ourselves up for just about the worst kiss in history. And — I think we'd be really good at this. At some point.

JACK: I agree.

GINGER: Yeah?

JACK: We'll do this again. We'll drink a little less.

GINGER: Yeah. I like you. I mean, it's nice that it's not going to be another drunken hook-up. I like that. Is this going to be weird?

JACK: *Absolutely* not.

They high five.

JACK: Same team.

GINGER: I like that. Hey, can we just totally start over?

JACK: Isn't that what we just—

GINGER: No. Like really. Start over. Just wipe this away completely. And commit to doing a good job next time. A fantastic job.

JACK: ... Sure.

GINGER: But we can't talk about what we're doing or even hint at what it is we're doing. It's like a secret, but from *ourselves.*

JACK: Okay.

GINGER: And you need to be just as nervous with your 'Oh, hey—if you wanted to, I was totally planning to attend your favourite poet's first reading in ten years—randomly—but if you want to join me that'd be cool.'

JACK: Hey, if we're backing everything up it only seems fair that I get to do that part better, too.

GINGER: (*she thinks*) Yes, that's okay.

JACK: Okay.

GINGER: Really?

JACK: Sure.

GINGER: So tonight you didn't say that. We finished the display and then you turned to me and said—

They pretend they're back at the bookstore, re-enacting an alternative ending to the night.

JACK: 'Finished.'

GINGER: Yes.

JACK: What are you up to tonight?

GINGER: Revisions. You?

JACK: Just going to a thing. I don't even know where it is or what it's called, but it's not interesting at all.

GINGER: (*shooting him a look.*) Great. Well—you on tomorrow?

JACK: You bet. Think I'd miss the arrival of the Messiah herself?

GINGER: You know how I feel about people referring to Heather as the Messiah. Even in jest, it's problematic.

JACK: I'll see you tomorrow then.

GINGER: Goodnight!

JACK: Goodnight.

He winks and whispers:

JACK: Goodnight.

GINGER: (*returning the whisper*) Goodnight.

JACK exits.

Scene 2

In a semi-blackout, JACK and GINGER collect the books from the floor, straighten them on the shelves, as though they are working at the bookstore. Flirtation. Eventually it becomes: JACK's spotless apartment. JACK is onstage, making final adjustments in preparation for GINGER's arrival. GINGER enters with gusto.

GINGER: Sorry I'm late!

JACK: It's fine. Make yourself at home—there's a fine-looking dessert on the way—be ready in twenty.

GINGER: Dessert?

JACK: Yes.

GINGER: Am I that late?

JACK: Wha—?

GINGER: You ate without me?

JACK: No, we said you were coming for dessert because you had a thing to—

She starts laughing.

GINGER: Oh, Jack, I'm teasing you. Thought we could both use a bit of a laugh about all this.

JACK: You are a horrible human being.

GINGER: I couldn't resist. It smells amazing.

JACK: Get out of this apartment immediately and come back in.

GINGER: Yessir.

She spins around and re-enters.

GINGER: Sorry I'm late.

JACK: Dessert will be ready in twenty.

GINGER: Smells delicious!

JACK: Thank you. I'm making cheesecake.

GINGER: Wow. From scratch?

JACK: Yes. May I offer you a glass of wine? Or would you prefer straight vodka?

GINGER: I have no idea what that is in reference to. Wine would be lovely. Wow. You are really organized.

She wanders to his bookshelf and eventually begins smelling some of the books.

JACK: Here you are.

GINGER: Thanks. I just like the way they smell.

JACK: I didn't say anything.

GINGER: Thank you.

JACK: I have seen you around books once or twice.

GINGER: Okay, Jack. Explain the system.

JACK: What system?

GINGER: I know there's a system, but I'm clearly not brainy enough to figure it out. I've ruled out alphabetical and by subject.

JACK: Then you're wrong.

GINGER: What?

JACK: It's very, very complicated.

GINGER: I love it. Go.

JACK: It's also a secret.

GINGER: C'mon.

JACK: It is alphabetical. Second letter of each title. I don't want to be that person, but I am that person. So I try to disguise it.

GINGER: Simplistic, and stealthy.

He goes to put on some music.

GINGER: I like this.

JACK: Thanks.

GINGER: I don't know it.

JACK: (*shrugs*) No associations.

GINGER: Yeah.

JACK: (*clearing his throat in preparation*) For this, our very first date, I thought it would be nice to pay homage to our history—

GINGER: Whoa, I did not prepare anything—

He holds up a finger to silence her, continues.

JACK: —to give thanks that we're finally here, and behind us forever are all the painful conversations that brought us to this moment.

He takes a stance which indicates their typical 'bookstore pose.' A game. GINGER catches on. As they pretend they're in the bookstore, they are also commenting upon their past behaviour.

JACK: Morning, Ginger.

GINGER: Morning, Jack. What did you get up to last night?

JACK: I sat at home—alone. Bored. You?

GINGER: I also sat at home, alone and bored. What are you going to do tonight?

JACK: The same. You?

GINGER: The same.

Moment of awkward tension. They break, laugh, shake it off and dive back in.

GINGER: Okay. Morning, Jack.

JACK: Morning, Ginger. What did you get up to last night?

GINGER: Oh, not much. Finally had someone in to fix my heater. I've been freezing for days.

JACK: I thought there was a rule that they have to come within twenty-four hours—

GINGER: I didn't call 'til yesterday. I'm bad like that. I always sort of wait and hope it works itself out.

JACK: I'm pretty good with that stuff—

GINGER: You call right away?

JACK: No, I mean, fixing things. If it happens again I could—

GINGER: Oh, you don't have to do that—it's my own fault. I don't like calling people.

JACK: It might be easier to call a friend.

Beat.

GINGER: I wouldn't want to trouble you.

JACK: It wouldn't be any trouble.

GINGER: I'm gonna—

JACK: Yeah—

They break away from the tension and return.

GINGER: Morning, Jack.

JACK: Morning, Ginger. What'd you get up to last night?

GINGER: Nothing—you?

JACK: Nothing.

GINGER: What are you doing tonight?

JACK: I was thinking of maybe going to see a movie or something.

GINGER: There are so many movies I want to see right now.

JACK: Me too.

GINGER: Which one are you going to?

JACK: *Relinquishment.* It's, uh—

GINGER: From Denmark?

JACK: Yeah!

GINGER: I really want to see that.

JACK: Cool. Me too. Obviously.

Beat.

JACK: You could—

GINGER: Well—

BOTH: Oh.

Beat.

GINGER: Have fun!

JACK: For sure!

GINGER: Later!

JACK: See ya!

BOTH: Goddamnit.

They break apart a final time, laughing.

GINGER: Oh, my God, we're losers.

JACK: We're — careful.

GINGER: And insecure. Tell me, Jack, are we meant to learn something from that little trip?

JACK: (*stepping in closer*) Mmm...patience is a virtue?

GINGER: Actions speak louder than words?

A moment of tension, mirroring the moments just experienced above. She breaks it.

GINGER: Glad we're past that.

JACK: Absolutely.

They high five. Pause.

GINGER: We use far too many words when we're together, Jack.

JACK: You started talking.

GINGER: I did. I panicked. But now we need to stop. And when we do start talking again — which will be after I finish this sentence and after the mind-blowing sex —

JACK: — no pressure —

GINGER: We need to use words with *significantly* fewer syllables.

They high five.

JACK: ...yes.

GINGER: Okay.

JACK: Just — one second. I'm going t —

GINGER: No. Shhhh.

JACK: But I just —

She cups his face in her hands.

JACK: Yes?

She launches into a kiss. Current music shifts into something over the top and epic-sounding. They both clock it, but try to get over it. Finally GINGER *falls into a fit of laughter.*

GINGER: Talk about pressure!

JACK: Fuck.

GINGER: I feel like you're going off to war or something!

JACK: (*as he tries to turn it off*) I'm sorry, okay?

GINGER: Whoa — it's okay. It's hilarious.

JACK: Dessert?

GINGER: Hey, I can deal with your terrible taste in music. Just...sit down.

JACK: I tried to go turn it off.

GINGER: It's fine.

JACK: No — I. I just wish you —

GINGER: Hadn't kissed you?

JACK: No. Had given me a second.

Long pause.

GINGER: Jack… ?

JACK: I really did think this through.

GINGER: And it's been wonderful. Still is.

JACK: But—it's just… Look. If we're into second chances, we might as well have a third, right? Just a few tweaks and adjustments, and we'll get this thing polished to a shine. Am I right? I'd like to exercise my right to start again.

GINGER: (*starts laughing*) Oh, this could get dangerous.

JACK: Whaddaya say?

There's a 'ding' from the kitchen.

JACK: Cheesecake?

GINGER: Ahh! Yes Jack, I'd love to stay and eat a piece of cheesecake with you and then pretend it never happened.

JACK: I'm honoured. I probably over-thought tonight.

GINGER: You should read *The Power of Now.* It's really—(*stops herself*) Okay, now we're both embarrassed. Resetting to zero…commencing.

JACK: Not until after dessert.

They exit towards the kitchen, leaving their glasses.

Scene 3

The following scene is a theatrical montage. Between the vignettes, the actors maintain a fluid motion in half-light. All the glasses used remain on stage.

JACK is seated on the bench, while GINGER stands, mid-way through her poem.

GINGER: *He seemed a bit too princely—that prince.*
And relatively difficult to convince
That his princely crown
Was but a frown

One he wore with pride.

You see.
He.
Was incredibly
Surly.

JACK: You know surly—

GINGER: —I know surly isn't an adverb, yes.

JACK: Just checking.

GINGER: If it was an adverb, I wouldn't have been able to use an adverb to describe it.

JACK: (*beat*) That's not true…

GINGER: What?

JACK: An adverb *can* describe another adverb, but—

Pause. GINGER is horrified.

GINGER: (*handing him her glass*) Um, call me?

GINGER exits.

***Transition** where JACK and GINGER meet in half-light to cheers and drink. Moving into: GINGER seated downstage on a cushion in a meditative state as JACK pokes his head into the apartment.*

JACK: (*whispering*) Heeey… Hey!

GINGER: Jack?

JACK: I just—before we start, I have a couple of questions about your email.

GINGER: Jack! You can't talk to me about it! That's the whole point.

JACK: Well, I have no idea what you mean by "gaze longingly but confidently into my eyes, as though searching for something in me that you've already found."

GINGER: I don't think I could have been much more explicit.

***Transition** into GINGER's apartment. JACK is seated.*

GINGER: I'm just going to throw on some music to set the tone of our evening…

She does. Music begins. GINGER seats herself next to JACK, expectant.

JACK: They played this at my grandmother's funeral.

She slowly gets up, walks across the room and turns off the music.

GINGER: Are you free on Saturday?

***Transition** into JACK's apartment. JACK stares at GINGER, helpless.*

GINGER: GOD HELP ME! Calm down, Ginger. Calm the hell down. He likes you! (*to JACK*) I'm sorry—I keep telling myself to be cool, and I'm all ready to be cool, but then I see you and I'm a mess. I actually can't control it and I just—it's really frustrating. (*starts crying*)

Email me, I have to go. It's way too soon for this. I'm sorry if it makes you afraid of getting to know me. It's just that this feels like a lot of pressure and it's not like I'm not good under pressure because I can be so—like, on it—but… Okay, I'm leaving.

(*dramatic hand motion*) Clean slate clean slate clean slate.

Goodnight.

*She exits. **Transition.** They meet again in half light for a cheers. This time it is a desperate kind of gulping. They move into: Arms around one another entering GINGER's apartment, post-date.*

GINGER: (*whispering*) That went well.

JACK: It did.

Pause. She takes an enthusiastic step forward to kiss him, on to his foot.

JACK: Shit!

GINGER: Oh, my God, I'm sorry!

JACK: (*hopping around in pain*) Fuck! Fuck! FUCK!

GINGER: Okay, Jack — override the pain. We can still get it back.

JACK: Really? This is the one you want to go with?

Scene 4

With the same fluid motion transition, they move into JACK*'s apartment.* GINGER *enters, with a significantly sexier wardrobe than usual.*

GINGER: Hey.

JACK: Hey! Just let me grab my jacket and I'm ready to go.

GINGER: Can I have a glass of wine, Jack?

JACK: Oh — sure. I — guess we've got time.

GINGER: We have all the time, Jack.

JACK: I'll just give the restaurant a call and push back the reservations —

GINGER: Um, Jack. I was thinking that maybe we could — stay in.

JACK: Oh…kay. I'm still going to need to call the restaurant.

GINGER *gives an over-exaggerated laugh and touches his arm lightly.*

GINGER: That was hilarious!

JACK: No, it wasn't.

She looks at him intently and starts batting her eyelashes.

JACK: Oh! — are you — high?

GINGER: What? No. (*hurt*) Jeez, Jack.

JACK: Sorry — I just — I'm not with you here.

She makes an exaggerated hand gesture.

GINGER: Jack.

JACK: Yes. (*mimicking her*) What is this?

GINGER: It's a time out.

JACK: We're allowed to call time outs?

GINGER: Of course.

JACK: Do you know how many times I was dying for a time out?

GINGER: Sorry. I thought you knew. Listen. I think we're flirting dangerously close to becoming best friends instead of lovers.

JACK: So instead of dinner —

GINGER: There is a small window of time left for us to become lovers — and we need to squeeze through that window tonight.

She repeats the gesture and retakes her position on the couch, indicating they are now in their 'present.'

GINGER: Wine?

JACK: Wait—

GINGER: We're back.

JACK: No—I wanted to say something. (*using the gesture, but doing it incorrectly*) This is a time out.

GINGER: Okay.

JACK: I understand your point. But you've created a situation with even more pressure than we were under before. Can we please just—work our way up to this a little?

GINGER: It's too late, Jack—one more delightful conversation over a piece of cheesecake and it's gone for good.

JACK: You really think so.

GINGER: Absolutely.

He attempts to give her a high five.

GINGER: See—no! That used to be flirtatious and now it's like a couple of married people who don't have anything new to say to each other. Look, we can do this, okay?

JACK: Okay.

They repeat the gesture in unison. Time out over.

JACK: Wine.

JACK goes to retrieve the wine. They drink. Eye flirting. A sip. A sip. She verges on guzzling. He follows her lead. The glasses are empty. He sets his down. She sets hers down. She puts her hand on his leg and begins counting under her breath.

JACK: What are you—

GINGER: Nothing.

JACK: Are you counting?

GINGER: Maybe!

JACK: What are you counting?

GINGER: Nothing.

JACK: Ginger, what are you counting?

GINGER: (*beat*) I read in *Cosmopolitan*—

JACK: *Cosmopolitan*—

GINGER: Yes, *Cosmopolitan*.

JACK: The magazine?

GINGER: Shut up! I read the first one in my life today, okay?

JACK: You kind of seem like a subscriber—

GINGER: IT SAID that to be truly seductive you have to leave your hand on someone's leg for over three seconds. Just longer than usual so they know. For sure. It's game time.

JACK: Three seconds, huh?

GINGER: Yes. That's my cue to you that I am ready to have sex with you. (*beat*) I wonder about that, though. About the poor women who just leave their hands resting a little longer than average. Women who don't know the code.

JACK: They must just be beating men off with sticks.

GINGER: Yeah, I guess. God, I did it again! I was doing really well, too.

JACK: Maybe you need to rest your hand on my leg again.

GINGER: No, that's obviously been ruined.

Long pause.

GINGER: Okay. I didn't think it would come to this but it has. Plan B.

JACK: Oh, my.

GINGER: We're doing this.

She sifts through her purse, finds her iPod, hooks it up. Dramatic, synthesized, sexy music. GINGER *begins to do a poorly choreographed dance. She sings along. After a while, she gestures for* JACK *to take the lead.*

JACK: I—don't know the words.

GINGER: Yes, you do.

JACK: No, I don't.

GINGER: Yes, you do!

In an effort to save the moment, GINGER *gets* JACK *on his feet and leads him through a dance. This goes well, so once again she indicates it is his turn to take on the lead vocals, in a grand gesture. He passionately sings the wrong lyrics.*

GINGER: I can't believe you don't know any of the words.

JACK: Sorry—I haven't seen it in a while.

Still dancing. She is leading him through various steps trying to keep the mood intact.

GINGER: Haven't seen what?

JACK: *Dirty Dancing.*

GINGER: Oh, I've never seen that.

JACK: —Oh.

GINGER: I just love the song. Singing it with someone as a means of seduction is my ultimate fantasy.

JACK: Singing "Hungry Eyes"?

GINGER: Yes.

JACK: And you've never seen *Dirty Dancing*?

GINGER: No!

JACK: 'Cause that's kind of what happens in *Dirty Dancing*. Well, they don't sing, but they—dance.

GINGER: Okay! Well, (*stops dancing*) it doesn't matter because I just sacrificed that fantasy, didn't I? I will never be able to have that moment now.

JACK: I can look at the words…

GINGER: Oh, my God, it doesn't work like that. Now I'll know that you're just thinking about some movie—

JACK: Anyone you did that with would be thinking about the movie! (*beat*) I'm—sorry. If I'd known I would have prepared.

GINGER: The joy comes from the spontaneity, Jack.

Long pause.

GINGER: I am feeling incredibly discouraged, Jack. Do not high five me. I have my eyes closed so I can't tell whether or not you were going to high five me.

JACK: I wasn't going to.

GINGER: Okay. But. I just—I'm getting really afraid that this is never going to happen. Why aren't you worried that this is never going to happen?

He puts his arm around her and kisses her forehead.

GINGER: See—friends.

He goes to take his arm away.

GINGER: (*putting it back around her*) No, that feels amazing and I'm really embarrassed right now, so it's totally working for me. I just thought I would point that out. Please tell me you're still attracted to me, Jack. That all this hasn't wiped that away.

JACK: (*makes sure she's looking at him*) Yep.

Scene 5

JACK and GINGER throw books and pillows around the stage, carrying the frustration from the last scene until they create: GINGER's apartment. They enter, a bit tipsy. Very tongue-in-cheek.

JACK: Now *that* was a great first date.

GINGER: You know, it really was.

JACK: I enjoyed it immensely.

A second-nature high five—it's actually more like a secret handshake now—a bit elaborate.

GINGER: Me too. It was great getting to know you outside of work.

JACK: Wasn't it? I had no idea you were a poet.

GINGER: I had no idea you were a mathematician.

JACK: And that poem about the prince—

GINGER: Epic?

JACK: But interesting. I could just listen to it again and again.

GINGER: If you're lucky, you will. (*throwing something on the ground*) I'm not the tidiest.

JACK: Hadn't noticed.

GINGER: Straight vodka?

JACK: How did you know?

Cheers. They drink.

GINGER: You're clever, Jack.

JACK: You're clever, Ginger.

GINGER: I like your vocabulary.

JACK: I like your — spirit.

GINGER: My spirit?

JACK: Your spirit is filled with whimsy.

GINGER: I like your vocabulary.

JACK: You said that.

GINGER: Tonight?

JACK: Just now.

GINGER: You remind me of Mick Jagger.

JACK: (*laughing*) And you remind *me* of Mick Jagger.

GINGER: (*laughing*) Making you laugh makes me feel like I'm high on something way more hardcore than pot.

Beat.

JACK: I make it a personal mission to find ways to restock in your section.

GINGER: I've read all the 'Jack recommends' selections. And not by accident, even though I tried to pretend sometimes it was by accident.

JACK: I've calculated that 21.37 percent of the books you touch end up flying out of your hands and onto the floor.

GINGER: I like your specificity.

JACK: I like your clumsiness.

GINGER: Whenever I'm around you, all of the hairs on my body stand up on edge, extending to their longest possibility in the hopes of coming into contact with your skin. (*beat*) Blah.

GINGER goes to pour another drink.

JACK: Wha —

GINGER: It's just — it's like I'm standing outside my body watching myself behave this way and I'm like, "ew — who is that girl and what is she saying?"

JACK: It's honesty. Honesty's sexy.

GINGER: That's gross.

JACK: Okay.

GINGER: I'm sorry, that was rude. But don't lie.

JACK: I wasn't.

GINGER: Honesty's only sexy until you hear something you don't want to. Then it's too much honesty. It's all bullshit.

Pause.

JACK: Hey… I've been having fun.

GINGER: That's it?

JACK: It's enough. I like you. I wanted to see what happened next. And I liked the idea of having a really kick-ass 'how we got together' story.

GINGER: So you're…

JACK: I haven't been waiting for it to start. Look — I like what you said.

GINGER: Thank you.

JACK: I meant what I said.

GINGER: Me too.

JACK: I don't think we can achieve perfection, but I think we can get close.

GINGER: I find that problematic.

JACK: I thought you might.

GINGER: Why aim low? Why would you ever do that?

JACK: Because people screw up.

GINGER: See — that's what people say. You spend your childhood being told to dream big, that anything is possible and then bam — you grow up and you're a fool for believing the same thing. And if you believe in *other* people? That's just totally crazy.

JACK: Ginger, I… (*beat*) You know when you're trying to create a moment? You try to choose the perfect piece of music to underscore that moment. And you find it. Words are *perfect.* The mood it's creating — *perfect.* But then you remember that it was used in that pivotal episode of *Dawson's Creek*, and later it was used in a Pepsi commercial — so instead of someone hearing the perfect sound and lyrics — instead they're thinking about James van der Beek, Pepsi or Scientology. Right?

GINGER: Like *Dirty Dancing*.

JACK: Right. Well — I love you. You've had experiences with that phrase that I have no control over. All I can do is tell you how I feel. And those words are the right ones to describe it. I love you. Not I love you *and* or I love you *but*. Just that. I can't speak to anything beyond that right now and I'm not going to try.

GINGER: That was…

JACK: Just kiss me.

GINGER: Perfect.

JACK goes to kiss GINGER.

GINGER: Can we just sit in this for a minute?

JACK: Hey. We got it right this time.

GINGER: My head's spinning.

JACK: I know.

GINGER: I just want to keep this. I don't want to hate you.

JACK: You think I'll be that terrible?

GINGER: People screw up, right? No matter what happens — we cross this line, and at some point I'll hate you.

JACK: That's a little —

GINGER: Even if we're married thirty years — At some point, you'll hurt me. Eventually, you'll disappoint me. And I don't want to be disappointed. I want — this. Just this. Here. Again and again and again. Is that crazy?

JACK: Well — it just. It isn't possible. But.

He kisses her. She allows it.

GINGER: We *are* really good at this.

They kiss again.

GINGER: Jack?

JACK: Yes?

GINGER: I can't do this. Please don't hate me.

JACK: I really don't understand.

GINGER: I'm sorry.

JACK: Wow.

GINGER: I know. I'm sorry. I didn't know this going in, I promise.

JACK waits.

GINGER: I'm sorry.

JACK waits.

GINGER: It's just — I'm always choosing the experience over the regret of not having one, but I can't keep doing that to myself. Rationalizing the greater purpose of all the bullshit I put myself through. Justifying my terrible decisions by taking pride in all I've *learned* from them. I'm not saying this is a terrible decision but — Jack — it can only end one way. And I can't... I think, sometimes, living with the regret of not having done something might actually be better than ruining the thing that you already have.

JACK: That — you must know that doesn't actually make sense.

GINGER: It does.

JACK: But that's not who you are.

GINGER: That's how important you are. I know it'll be hard. But maybe — we can pass through this and be — friends. (*knowing this is pointless*) Then we get to be in each other's lives forever.

JACK: Or maybe in a few months you'll actually move to Paris like you're always talking about and I'll never see you again. Who knows. Ginger, this is a mistake. You think you're preserving something but you just made it disappear. I'm not going to force it, but — I'm strongly voicing my opinion.

GINGER: Strongly.

Silence.

JACK: I'm going to stop using so many words — and I'm going to say 'goodnight.'

GINGER: Jack — This is all coming from a really good place, so I don't think you can be angry at me.

JACK: But I can be disappointed. And I can be hurt.

GINGER: Okay. We can't just…use the reset button one last time to pretend the last couple months never happened?

JACK: I'm not going to do that, Ginger.

GINGER: Okay. I'll see you tomorrow?

JACK: You will.

GINGER: Absolutely.

JACK puts his hand up. A slow high five.

JACK: 'Night, Ginger.

GINGER: 'Night, Jack.

JACK exits. GINGER looks around the apartment and begins clearing the mountains of glasses which have accumulated throughout the production. GINGER exits, glasses in her arms.

The End

Crazy Love

A Dark Comedy

by David Sklar

About the playwright

David Sklar is an actor/playwright who currently resides in Montreal. He is a graduate from Dawson College Professional Theatre Program and the Bristol Old Vic Theatre School in England. He is also a graduate from Concordia University in the playwriting program. David has toured with The Montreal Shakespeare Theatre Company in *A Midsummer Night's Dream* and *Hamlet* as well as their mainstage production of *Titus Andronicus*. Under the tutelage of Kit Brennan, David devised *Crazy Love,* which had its debut at the twenty-first Annual Montreal Fringe Festival: director, David Sklar; dramaturge/set designer, Nico Racicot, stage manager Alycia O'Keefe; Leo, Braulio Elicer, Rebecca, Amy Kitz. Other written plays include *Dance with Desire*, on the life and times of Canadian poet Irving Layton. It had its first staged reading at the Dapopo Theatre in Halifax in October, 2011.

Characters

LEO — young, urban
REBECCA — young, urban

Setting

LEO's apartment. In the centre of the stage there is a worn-out couch. Next to the couch is a mini-fridge filled with water and beer bottles. There is a chair and a door to signify a bathroom. Off-stage is a kitchen and another door for the apartment hallway. Behind the couch there is a guitar.

Note: The songs performed in the play should reflect LEO*'s current mood in the scene.*

As the lights come up, we hear LEO *talking to his girlfriend on his cellphone.*

LEO: (*laughing from off-stage*) No, you stop it. Well, I don't know? Whatever you want, baby. No, no, I've got a better idea. Why don't *you* come over and I'll cook you an amazing Linguini Montanara followed by a mouthwatering… store-bought apple pie. Hahahaha. Okay, good, but you bring the wine. I don't care, it all tastes the same to me. So get your butt over here, pronto. I'm just going to run out now and pick up some supplies. Can't wait to see you. Mucho love, bye, bye bye.

He grabs his jacket and just as he opens the door to his apartment, REBECCA *is standing there. She is wearing XL grey sweats and hoodie. She looks slightly dazed. At first, she appears quiet and timid.*

LEO: Whoa! Shit, you scared me.

REBECCA: Hi.

LEO: Rebecca, what are you doing here?

REBECCA: I thought I'd stop by. Say "Hi."

LEO: Okay. Hi. But, why?

REBECCA: Can I come in?

LEO: I'm sorry, but I was just running out. To pick up some food for Katherine and myself.

REBECCA: Oh, come on, it'll be just a few minutes. Please, it's important.

LEO: (*pause*) All right. Make yourself at home.

REBECCA: That's easy. This used to be my home.

LEO: Want a beer?

REBECCA: No thanks.

LEO: Juice, water?

REBECCA: Water, please. I could really use some. Hot outside, if you're going out, you don't need a jacket.

LEO: Here you go.

REBECCA: Thanks. Ahhhh. So, how have you been?

LEO: Fine. Just fine.

REBECCA: And… Katherine?

LEO: She's good. Yup. All good.

REBECCA: Well, I think we should all get together for dinner sometime soon.

LEO: Really?

REBECCA: I think we can all be mature about this situation.

LEO: As opposed to last time, where you dumped your soup all over her?

REBECCA: I already told you, that was an accident. Besides, she looked like she needed some food in her.

LEO: So what did you need to tell me?

REBECCA: Right. Well, you know how we used to, date…for two years and how it seemed…so wonderful. And then you ended it. Suddenly. But for some stupid reason, we still loved getting drunk and having sex. With each other. And I personally think that you will never find anyone who gives better head than me! I guess that's why you kept on seeing me even after Katherine appeared.

LEO: That only happened once and it was a mistake. You said you were never going to bring it up again.

REBECCA: And I won't. But you're going to have to, sooner or later.

LEO: What do you mean?

REBECCA: As I was saying after "nobody gives better head than me," the night we got smashed and did what we can't talk about or won't talk about or whatever fucked-up bullshit rule you implemented...well, I guess...wow, I practiced this speech like twenty times yesterday. I told myself "no crying"; I can't believe I'm doing this.

LEO: Rebecca, what's up? Hey. It's okay. Whatever it is, I'll help. You need more money? You sick?

REBECCA: Yeah.

LEO: Okay, what's wrong? Did you go to a doctor?

REBECCA: I've been feeling nauseous for a while. Throwing up.

LEO: What did the doctor say?

REBECCA: Oh, so now that I'm sick, you're here for me, but you don't return my calls beforehand.

LEO: I've been busy. I'm sorry. Look, you came over to see me. I'm here now for you. So what's the problem?

REBECCA: Well, he told me... I'm a gravida.

LEO: Huh?

REBECCA: Well, he didn't actually say that, I looked that up on Wikipedia, they have everything you could possibly want. Yay, Wikipedia.

LEO: Becca, what's going on?

REBECCA: I'm...pregnant.

LEO: What?

REBECCA: With child. Fertile. Expecting. Prolific. Heavy, teeming and my favourite, preggers.

LEO: So you've been hanging onto this for a long time.

REBECCA: I know we both didn't mean for this to happen, but it did. Like all those crappy movies, where they both get really drunk on cheap wine, rip off each other's clothes — you actually broke my bra strap, by the way — and just dive right in.

LEO: Whoa, whoa, whoa. We're talking about the last time we did it, right? That's impossible, I remember I wore a condom.

REBECCA: We were so drunk, it probably fell off.

LEO: But...it was still on me when we woke up.

REBECCA: I guess we were that one percent.

LEO: You're fucking with me, right?

REBECCA: Sorry. No.

LEO: Serious?

REBECCA: Yup. Serious.

LEO: Okay, really, really honest to God not screwing with me?

REBECCA: It's real. Get over it. Pro-Care doesn't lie.

LEO: They can make a mistake.

REBECCA: I took two tests.

LEO: Can I see them?

REBECCA: You want to see two urine-soaked pregnancy kits? I'm sorry, but I didn't bring them with me. I didn't know I was going to get harangued by you for knocking me up. Why is it that everyone always blames the girl for getting pregnant?

LEO: Okay. Okay. I…we, we can figure this out. It's not so bad, there's a solution to everything.

REBECCA: You mean an abortion!

LEO: I didn't say that. That was nowhere near my mind. But now that you brought it up…are you… ?

REBECCA: I don't know.

LEO: Would you… ?

REBECCA: I just don't want to talk about that.

LEO: You came here because you did want to talk.

REBECCA: Well, I don't want to talk about that!

LEO: Jesus, I can't believe this is happening to me.

REBECCA: Uh, hello, you're not the one with a fetus floating around in his womb.

LEO: Point taken.

REBECCA: Listen, I don't expect you to be a part of it. Whatever choice I make will be my choice and I won't hold it against you if you don't want to be a part of it.

LEO: I can't do that. You remember what happened with my dad. So whatever, I'll support you. I'll be there for you.

REBECCA: I was hoping you'd say that.

She moves closer to grab his thigh. His cellphone buzzes.

LEO: Ahhhh! Hello, hi, hi, baby. What's up? Uh… I don't care. Okay, red's fine. Yup, I'm there right now. Well, I see chocolate cake, vanilla cake, uhhhh, brownnnnorange cake. What do you like? Okay, sure. See you soon. Bye, baby. Look, Rebecca, you sprang this on me at a really shitty time. Kat will be over any minute now. I don't think you guys should re-run into each other.

REBECCA: I don't mind.

LEO: Huh?

REBECCA: Well, she's going to find out about this sooner or later, right? It might as well be today, like any minute now.

LEO: Hahahahaha. Rebecca, look, I promise you we'll talk about this tomorrow. We can go over all of this and I promise I will now be there for you. But right now is a really bad time. (*He goes to open the door.*) You can't be seen here, I'm sure you understand, so if you don't mind. Hey, you okay?

REBECCA: NO! (*She runs to the bathroom.*)

LEO: Fuck. Rebecca, are you okay? Rebecca?

REBECCA: (*off-stage*) Fine. Just blew chunks all over your toilet.

LEO: Great. Do you need water?

REBECCA: (*exits the bathroom*) Sorry.

LEO: For?

REBECCA: For putting you through all this. You're right, I shouldn't have showed up today. I'm so stupid. God, I don't know what I'm going to do. I can't afford a baby. I can't even take care of myself. Last night for dinner all I had in my house was cat food.

LEO: You ate cat food?

REBECCA: I may be poor but I'm not crazy. I fed the cat and went to bed on an empty stomach.

LEO: You can't do that, not only for the baby but for yourself.

REBECCA: I know. I know.

LEO: I can lend you money. Here.

REBECCA: No, I don't want your money. I already owe you like 1,200 dollars.

LEO: Actually 1,400.

REBECCA: I gave you 200.

LEO: I know and now that makes it 1,400. But it doesn't matter. Take some.

REBECCA: No. I'll ask my mom for a loan.

LEO: Your mom. I didn't even see that coming. Have you told her?

REBECCA: Not yet.

LEO: Well, your mom was your age when she had you.

REBECCA: I know and look at me. (*beat*) Okay, look, I need to go. I'll speak to you tomorrow.

LEO: No, wait, you're right. I have to tell Kat. And you should be here.

REBECCA: Leo, if I was still dating you and found out that you knocked up another girl while still dating me, I don't think she would be safe in the same building as me.

LEO: No, I need to fess up and you two are the two most important girls in my life right now.

REBECCA: Hey, you might have to make room for a third. Too soon?

LEO: I thought you would have lost your bad baby sense of humour.

REBECCA: Are you kidding me? Dead baby jokes are the first thing I'll teach my kid, thanks to you.

LEO: Ha ha. Remember the first one I told you?

REBECCA: And how I acted all shocked?

LEO: I knew you were pretending.

REBECCA leans in for a kiss.

LEO: Whoa, whoa, whoa!

REBECCA: I'm sorry. I thought I picked up on a vibe there.

LEO: Rebecca, it's over between us. I have someone new.

REBECCA: I know, I just thought we shared a moment. That's all. You always say go with your instincts.

LEO: When did I say that?

REBECCA: Well, someone said it somewhere.

LEO: Look, just because this might be my baby it doesn't mean…

REBECCA: Might? Might be your baby? What do you mean by that?

LEO: Nothing, look, I'm just saying…

REBECCA: It's yours.

LEO: How? How do you know for sure? You weren't with anyone else after we broke up?

REBECCA: No.

LEO: No.

REBECCA: NO!

LEO: That's not what I've been hearing.

REBECCA: From who?

LEO: Uhhhh…Nick.

REBECCA: What the fuck does Nick know?

LEO: Look, I don't want to get him in trouble, so don't be pissed at him, but he said he was at your place two weeks ago and that you had some guy over for dinner.

REBECCA: So, dinner doesn't mean sex.

LEO: Sure.

REBECCA: Fuck you! I didn't come here to be attacked because I also found someone else.

LEO: So you *were* with him.

REBECCA: Whether I was or not is none of your business. I just know it's yours.

LEO: How, how can you be a hundred percent sure that I'm the guy without taking one of those DNA test things.

REBECCA: You want a test. Fine, here's your test. I didn't sleep with him! I just sucked his cock.

LEO: What is that? Number thirty-one?

REBECCA: Thirty-two, fuck you. At least I don't cheat on my girlfriend, then lie to her about shopping for a fucking dessert cake.

LEO: At least I can spend one day without shoving something in my mouth.

REBECCA: At least I don't break up with someone who I've been together with for one year, five months, and two weeks for no reason.

LEO: No reason?

REBECCA: We are not bringing that up again.

LEO: Fine, but you're the one who keeps bringing it up. God, you know you haven't changed one bit. You are still the insecure, obnoxious…

REBECCA: You turn your back on the people who need you the most!

LEO: What the hell are you talking about? I was there for you and I fell for it.

REBECCA: Well…at least I'm not an asshole! Fine, have it your way. Tomorrow I'll go to my doctor and make sure everything is hunky-dory with my baby.

LEO: You can't just get an appointment in one day.

REBECCA: I made it as soon as I took the pregnancy test.

LEO: So what the hell were we fighting for?

REBECCA: I just wanted to know where we stood. And you answered it. Thank you.

She goes to leave.

LEO: Hey…wait, I'm sorry…for not trusting you.

REBECCA: I guess "we" were easy to forget.

LEO: No, it's not that, it's just from the last time…

A knock on the door.

REBECCA: That's her, I guess. Don't worry, your secret is safe with me. But if I were you, I'd tell her. Women have a way of getting back at people who hurt them. Enjoy your quality time.

LEO: Thanks. (*LEO walks over to his guitar.*)

REBECCA: If you want, I can swing by tomorrow, with the results.

LEO: Fine.

REBECCA: Good luck. Hope she doesn't bust your balls. Or maybe you like that now.

She opens the door and sees Katherine.

REBECCA: Hi, Katherine. Long time no see. Leo's all ready for you now. And I think he has so much to tell you. Toodles. Bye, Leo.

LEO bangs a note directly after "Bye, Leo."

Lights immediately go bright to show time has frozen. After a couple of beats, the lights go back to the original setting. LEO strums a few more notes on his guitar and quietly sings. He continues until there is a knock on the door. LEO jumps up and starts to clean up his room in a panic. He rushes over to open the door and REBECCA, now wearing a dress, is standing in the hallway.

REBECCA: …Leo?

LEO: I take it you're Rebecca?

REBECCA: Thank God. You're not ugly. I can't begin to tell you how many guys Nick set me up with that turned out to be butt ass ugly.

LEO: Uh, thanks, I guess.

REBECCA: So, aren't you going to invite me in?

LEO: Oh, yeah, please come on in.

REBECCA: Uh-huh. Nice-ish place you got here.

LEO: Thanks.

REBECCA: No, I don't mean it like that. It's good. It's got a real "realness" to it.

LEO: Uh-huh.

REBECCA: Oh. I'm killing it here, aren't I? You know sometimes I just shoot off my mouth and it keeps going. I talk when I get nervous. Yeah, so now you know a secret about me, I should know a secret about you.

LEO: Uh, I can cook, I guess.

REBECCA: Mmmmmm, what's cooking? Ha-ha-ha. Get it?

LEO: Yeah. Linguini Montanara.

REBECCA: MON-T-NERA?

LEO: Montanara. It's a traditional Italian meat sauce but you add just a little bit of Alfredo cream.

REBECCA: Hmmm. You can cook.

LEO: Kinda. My dad taught me. He used to consider himself quite the chef.

REBECCA: Used to? Is he retired?

LEO: No idea. Haven't seen him in over ten years.

REBECCA: Oh. Sorry.

LEO: I'm not. He just picked up one day and left my mom and me.

REBECCA: Now that's a secret. So, your dad ran away? Well, mine's dead.

LEO: Oh, well, it looks like we have something sort of in common.

REBECCA: Maybe Nick didn't screw up this time.

LEO: Yeah, I was surprised I even said "yes." I guess I was getting a little desperate.

REBECCA: Desperate?

LEO: I don't mean desperate…just…

REBECCA: Cat got your tongue?

LEO: Ha-ha-ha. I mean, I usually don't listen to Nick's advice. But I couldn't believe he was friends with someone I'd never met before.

REBECCA: I know. I thought I knew all his buddies. Where's your washroom?

LEO: Over there.

REBECCA: I think your light is out.

LEO: Yeah, it occasionally does that. Cheap rent equals bad lighting, I guess. (*beat*) So what do you do?

REBECCA: I'm studying to be a doctor.

LEO: Really? That's awesome. What field?

REBECCA: Oh, you know, with patients and gauze. What about you?

LEO: Well, I used to go to university but I work at a café now. I need to save up some money to help my mom out.

REBECCA: Why, she's too lazy to work?

LEO: Well, she would work if she didn't have progressive relapsing multiple sclerosis.

REBECCA: Uh. Sorry. Again. It's like I have diarrhea coming out of my mouth. Oh, shit, you must be having a horrible image racing through your brain right now. I didn't mean to insult your mother, I'm sure she is the very opposite of lazy. Total workforce, a real go-getter. And believe me I crammed like five Trident into my mouth before I came over here so my breath can't smell anything like diarrhea…

LEO goes in for a slow kiss.

LEO: You're right. It smells more like a dead baby.

REBECCA: That's disgusting.

LEO: Not a fan of dead baby jokes?

REBECCA: Absolutely not.

LEO: How do you know a baby is dead?

REBECCA: (*putting her hands to her ears*) La-la-la-la-la-la-la-la-la-la-la-la-la-la-la-la.

LEO: It doesn't cry if you nail its feet to the ceiling.

REBECCA: That's awful.

LEO: I didn't think you were listening, I thought you were la-la-laing.

REBECCA: I can do two things at the same time. I never want to hear another dead baby joke again. You, you're losing points with me.

LEO: I'll check on dinner then. (*exits*)

REBECCA: You play?

LEO: Just started learning.

REBECCA: You cook, you play, you're good-looking. You're sure you're not gay?

LEO: I just kissed you.

REBECCA: Many a gay man has done that before. What's for dessert?

LEO: Dessert?

REBECCA: For after the meal?

LEO: Oh, I didn't think of that. If you just me give some time, I'm sure I can whip up something.

REBECCA: Not a big deal, but next time you should know my favourite is sweet apple pie.

LEO enters with two wine glasses.

LEO: So there will be a next time? I've regained all my points?

REBECCA: (*downing the entire glass of wine*) Seeing as how there is no pie, what will we do after the meal?

LEO: Monopoly?

REBECCA: We could play a board game or we could play hide 'n' seek.

LEO: What about the pasta?

REBECCA: It can wait. Now, close your eyes and count to ten. (*She makes her way to LEO's bedroom.*)

LEO: One, two, three, four—

REBECCA: No peeking. Oh, and could you wear your guitar? Just your guitar.

LEO: Ha-ha. (*he picks it up*) *five, six, seven, eight, nine, ten!*

As he is counting, he follows her into his room and shuts the door. Once the door shuts, the lights go immediately bright as they did previously and return to normal. LEO*'s cellphone starts ringing from the bedroom.* LEO *opens the door and is already on the phone. He is wearing a T-shirt now.*

LEO: ... Uh-huh. Uh-huh. No, *I'm* sorry. My mind was somewhere else last night. My mom. I didn't tell you 'cause I didn't want you to worry. She called before you came over...yes, and before Rebecca showed up. Look, I told you, she just showed up like that. She just came by to give me some of my old stuff. I'm sorry, I can't. I'm supposed to take my mom to the doctor's. I just didn't want to worry you, that's all, but I guess it showed, huh? Okay, I promise, no more secrets.

There is a knock on the door.

LEO: That? That's my mom. I'll tell her you said "feel better." Bye. Yeah, love you too.

LEO *goes to the door and opens it slowly.*

REBECCA: Hello.

LEO: So?

REBECCA: Can I come in first?

LEO: Sorry.

She enters.

LEO: So?

REBECCA: What?

LEO: The doctor?

REBECCA: I went.

LEO: And?

REBECCA: You'll never believe it. I get there and I take a seat in the waiting room. I'm there for a good forty-five minutes reading the same *Gourmet* magazine article over and over again, when all of a sudden the secretary informs all of us waiting that the doctor isn't coming in today, 'cause she's, like, in some sort of car accident or something. Can you believe that? If I got into a car accident and I wasn't dying, my work would still expect me to be on time.

LEO: You couldn't see another doctor.

REBECCA: She's my OBGYN. I don't want some random stranger looking down there.

LEO: OBGEEEE?

REBECCA: Vagina doctor.

LEO: Right. So what are you going to do?

REBECCA: I had to reschedule for next week. If she's taking the bus, it had better not break down.

LEO: I'm going with you next week.

REBECCA: You don't have to do that.

LEO: I want to. I'll switch around my work schedule.

REBECCA: I'm a big girl.

LEO: Yes. But I want to be there for you.

REBECCA: Suit yourself. Anything else?

LEO: Other than that, how are you feeling…overall?

REBECCA: Overall? Beyond no drinking, smoking or sleeping, I'd say the puking is the best part.

LEO: Sorry I was so cold last night. You just completely took me by surprise.

REBECCA: I've been trying to call you, but you never returned my calls.

LEO: Look, I've been thinking a lot and even though you're the one carrying the baby, I think we have to…

REBECCA: I'm keeping it.

LEO: I see.

REBECCA: I'm all for abortion for others, I just can't kill a living thing inside of me. (*pause*) So…now that we put that to bed, you wanna catch a movie? Or we could just stay here and order a double pizza. My treat.

LEO: No. Not really in the mood.

REBECCA: Well, I didn't come all the way over just to stay for a minute. I thought we were doing something tonight.

LEO: Listen, I don't feel like doing anything right now.

REBECCA: Oh, so yesterday you say you're here for me, but now not so much.

LEO: What do you want me to say, Rebecca? I just found out my life is completely fucked and you want me to act like everything is the way it used to be.

REBECCA: I'm trying to make the best of this situation. You wanna just forget about it? What, kill it, so when you're bumping around with Katherine, you won't feel so bad? How can you be so blasé about killing your own kid?

LEO: There's no way you or I can raise a kid, so that's exactly why I want to do it. He'd be fucked up for life.

REBECCA: You said you would support my decision.

LEO: Because I thought you would be smart and make the right decision, or at least give it up for adoption.

REBECCA: I couldn't live with myself, knowing someone else was raising my child. I'm going to be its mom.

LEO: Look at you, look at us. We're young, we have our whole lives ahead of us. Why throw it all away? We can't afford a baby. We can barely pay for the lives we have now.

REBECCA: I work. I can take the year for maternity leave and I make enough to survive for the both of us.

LEO: Listen to yourself. You're acting like you're so grown-up but you still haven't even managed to tell your mom, right? You need to get her advice. You shouldn't…we shouldn't be the only ones in this.

REBECCA: This is my body and my choice.

LEO: It's not your choice, only. It's your baby's life, too. Do you really think it will have a good life if you raise it?

REBECCA: You'd think I'd be a bad mom?

LEO: No, you will be a kind, supportive, nurturing mother who gives her child all the attention she deserves. Come on, look at your mother and how she raised you.

REBECCA: That's exactly why I would be different. I don't want to fuck up its life the way she screwed up mine. You know what? I can take a hint. You don't want to be a part of us, fine.

LEO: You know I wouldn't do that. You know all about my dad. How hard it was for my mom and me. I'm not broken-hearted about it, I don't sit down and weep over him, but I couldn't look at myself with respect if I did the same thing. Fuck! Why the fuck did I sleep with you? I finally meet someone I really like and she's not going to stay once she finds out about this.

REBECCA: You haven't told her yet?

LEO: I couldn't. I was still hoping I was in some bad dream.

REBECCA: (*During this, she moves towards* LEO *and begins giving him a massage.*) Leo, the last thing I want is for you to hate me. We are connected now more than ever. It might be hard, but think on the bright side. A kid. Ours. We created it. That's a beautiful thing. It can bring so much to our lives. We can spend the day in the park, having a picnic, you can teach him or her soccer and then come back home for dinner. You don't have to live with us, but I heard it's better for a child's development to sense its parents in the same surroundings.

LEO: You know, there should be a rule, when people break up, they can't see each other for at least a year.

REBECCA: A year? You don't want to see the birth of our child?

LEO: That's not what I mean and you know it.

REBECCA: All I know is that for all your talk about being here and committing to your child, you're beginning to look like your father.

LEO: I'm nothing like him.

REBECCA: Running out on your responsibilities. Leaving a family in need. Who knows, maybe your dad accidentally knocked up your mom and resented her until he couldn't take it any longer and escaped. I'd rather you do that now before your kid asks on its fifth birthday, "Where's Daddy"?

LEO: (*lifts up his hand as if to slap her, but stops*) Get this through your thick, fucking head. Whatever happens down there, *this* is finished. This does not exist. I've been patient with you, but I give up. I will not, not even for the sake of our kid, get back together with you. Is that why you wanna keep the baby? For us? Pull me back in, huh? You think in your fucked-up head that if you kept the kid, I'd run into your arms. If that's your plan, you are already an unfit mother.

REBECCA slaps him across the face. She goes to attack him. He stops her and tries to hold her back but accidentally hits her stomach.

REBECCA: Awwwwwwwww!

REBECCA sinks to the floor.

REBECCA: Awwwwwww! I think something's wrong. Awwwwww!

LEO looks at her.

REBECCA: Something's wrong…with the baby!

LEO stands frozen.

REBECCA: LEO!

LEO: Fuck. Come on! (*He picks her up slowly.*) I'm taking you to the hospital.

Once they close the door, the lights go bright. They flicker for a beat but return to normal. The couple re-enters but have switched sides. REBECCA has a scarf around her neck.

LEO: Come on. I got ya. Slowly, take it easy.

REBECCA: I'm okay. Seriously, I'm fine. He just took me by surprise.

LEO: I tried to chase after him but I guess he got away.

REBECCA: Ouch! Oh, I think I'm going to have a black eye. Great.

LEO: Hold on. (*gets a beer from the fridge to put over her eye*)

REBECCA: Fuck my life.

LEO: Here, let me. How's that?

REBECCA: Freezing.

LEO: Doesn't look like permanent damage. (*He kisses her.*) There. So, what the hell happened?

REBECCA: Jealous old boyfriend just doesn't know how to take a hint.

LEO: But how did he know where I live?

REBECCA: He must have followed me here. I called you outside your place 'cause you were late and all of a sudden he comes out of nowhere and starts begging to take me back. He said he wants me, he can't live without me. I told him to leave me alone, that I found someone better. I tried to walk away, but he got in my face, freaked out, smacked a good shiner here and pushed me down on the pavement. And then ran away like a pussy. Fucking asshole!

LEO: I'm going to fucking kill him, where does he live?

REBECCA: No, forget it.

LEO: I'm not going to let him forget it. I'm going to kill him. Where is he now?

REBECCA: Leo, Leo, please don't, don't go. I don't want to think about it ever again.

LEO: Then let's call the cops.

REBECCA: No. If we do, it will just go on forever. I don't want to have to think about him ever again. Please, I just want to forget about it. And I just want to hold onto you now. I just want to go to sleep.

LEO: All right. It's okay, baby. I'm here for you. Don't worry, I'm not going anywhere.

REBECCA: Promise?

LEO: Well, yeah, of course.

REBECCA: Good, 'cause I don't know what I'd do without you.

LEO: You'd find someone better-looking, with lots of money.

REBECCA: That's not funny. I don't ever want to find anyone else. I love you.

LEO: Thanks. I love you, too.

REBECCA: And I know that you will never find anyone better than me.

LEO: Unless she's better-looking and has lots of money.

REBECCA: Can you sing me something?

LEO: Yeah, sure, baby. You name it.

REBECCA: Our song.

LEO begins to sing the same song. REBECCA curls into a fetal position. LEO strikes the guitar and the lights go bright for a beat but then begin to flicker like a power drain. They do this for a couple of beats.

LEO: Fuck!

He puts down the guitar and it looks like he wants to say something but can't get it out. He goes to get a water bottle.

REBECCA: Can I have some?

He crosses over and leaves the half-empty bottle on the table. REBECCA weakly picks it up. It falls to the floor.

LEO: Fuck.

He goes to pick it up.

REBECCA: Sorry.

LEO: Don't worry about it.

REBECCA: I'm sorry.

LEO: I said don't worry.

REBECCA: I'm so sorry.

LEO: Jesus, Rebecca. Stop acting like this.

REBECCA: I can't help it.

LEO: YES YOU CAN.

REBECCA: I want to die. I want to fucking die.

She starts going into a nervous fit.

LEO: Just cool it, okay?

REBECCA: You don't know what it's like.

LEO: Yeah.

REBECCA: To have something…inside of you. And then just like that…gone.

LEO: You ready to go home?

REBECCA: Home? Where's home? I don't know where that is. Can I stay here with you tonight?

LEO: That's not a good idea.

REBECCA: Please. I can't be alone. Not now. Not tonight, please.

LEO: I'll call Nick. I'll ask him to stay with you.

REBECCA: NO! I don't want him or anyone to know about the baby.

LEO: Well, you're eventually going to have to tell people the truth.

REBECCA: I don't know what I'm going to do to myself if I'm alone.

LEO: Fine. Stay. What do I care?

REBECCA gets up and slowly makes her way to LEO's bedroom.

LEO: Where are you going?

REBECCA: To the bedroom.

LEO: I'll be out here.

REBECCA: Come with me.

LEO: What?

REBECCA: I can't go to sleep on my own. I just need someone to make sure I fall asleep.

LEO goes to the bathroom and grabs a pill bottle. He throws it to her.

LEO: Here. Take this, it'll calm you down.

REBECCA: Please, I really need you. I really need you. I don't have anyone left in my life. You leave me, then the baby leaves me. I can't be alone, I don't know what to do, please, please, please, please, plea… (*She's sobbing.*)

LEO: I'll make you a deal. I'll wait with you until you fall asleep, if you admit to me what really happened.

REBECCA: …about?

LEO: Rebecca. Rebecca!

REBECCA: What? What?

LEO: You want to tell me?

REBECCA: I don't know what you're talking about.

LEO: You got nothing?

REBECCA: No. What's going on?

LEO: Fine. Get out!

REBECCA: What?

LEO: Get out of my place, and get out of my life.

LEO lifts her up forcefully and grabs her by the arm.

REBECCA: Awwwwwwww. You're hurting me.

LEO: You promise?

REBECCA: You're scaring me. What? What do you want? I don't know what you're talking about. I don't know what you want. Just tell me. Tell me. I love you.

LEO: Shut up. Shut up! (*pause*) I was there, in the waiting room with you, remember? After rushing you to the hospital, you were complaining about those stomach cramps and they took you for some blood tests? About an hour later you burst through the doors crying, saying you lost the baby. I tried to comfort you but you just wanted to get out of the building. I thought you were just freaked out and needed to calm down. So once we left and I told you I forgot my jacket, I went to talk to your nurse.

REBECCA: No…no…no…

LEO: I said, "I'm sorry, my friend is really upset that she lost the baby. I just wanted to know what happened. How she lost it." The nurse looked at me, almost like this isn't the first time she has had to do this and told me, "We examined her, we couldn't find any fetus." I said, "Of course not, she lost it before she got here." "Even if that was the case," she told me, "there would still be evidence of a fetus in her body." I was, like, "wait, no, no, she took a pregnancy test and got the result that she was pregnant." And then, it was funny, 'cause she seemed to give a look of pity, she felt so bad for me and said, "She must have read the results wrong." I was dumbfounded, how is that possible? How can someone make a mistake between a plus and a minus sign? All she could say was, "She must have read the results wrong." It was like she was apologizing to me, for having to go through all of this.

REBECCA: No, I don't care what any nurse says. I know I was pregnant.

LEO: You lied then, you're still lying now. Just admit it!

REBECCA: I know what the test said. I read it. It told me I was pregnant.

LEO: Just like last time, when you said your first boyfriend gave you a black eye and then it turned out to be make-up. Do you have any idea what you put me through?

REBECCA: No, I'm telling, I swear I…thought I was pregnant. I thought I was…

LEO: You have a problem, Rebecca. You need help.

REBECCA: I thought I was. I really thought I was. I felt it, inside. After we had sex, I wasn't getting my period anymore, I felt sick. Oh, God. What did I do? I couldn't help myself.

She is sobbing on the floor.

LEO: I'm not falling for any of this shit anymore.

He pulls her up and shoves her out the door and slams it shut. The lights go bright but flicker on and off for a couple of seconds. LEO *turns around and is noticeably different. We can hear* REBECCA *laughing outside.*

REBECCA: (*drunkenly*) Hellooooooooooo! I think you forgot about me.

LEO: (*also drunkenly*) No thanks, I didn't order a pizza!

REBECCA: I got something better than a pizza.

LEO: Ah ha! What could that be?

REBECCA: Open the door and find out.

LEO: (*as they begin to make out*) Ahahahah! Maybe this isn't such a good idea. We broke up and I'm kinda…seeing someone.

REBECCA: Fine.

LEO: Hey, I didn't say go.

They continue making out.

REBECCA: What's her name?

LEO: Who? Oh…Katherine.

REBECCA: Well, is this Katherine as good at giving head as me?

LEO: Come on.

REBECCA: Just tell me. I won't be angry.

LEO: No.

REBECCA: So then?

LEO: Yeah. But I want to do it somewhere we haven't done it yet. The hallway?

REBECCA: Ha-ha. What about the neighbours?

LEO: I won't tell them if you won't.

REBECCA: You dirty little boy.

LEO: Not so little anymore.

REBECCA: Race you.

LEO: Give me one sec.

As he runs to his room to grab a condom, REBECCA *exits to the hallway.*

LEO: Ha-ha-ha. Look what I got.

The lights go out and LEO *trips and falls. As the lights struggle to come up again, time has already changed.*

LEO: Fuck this place.

We now hear REBECCA *on the outside, whimpering. She begins to bang her head on the wall. He ignores the sound, but then it stops and he grows concerned.*

LEO: Fuck me.

He opens the door and sees she is in stable condition.

LEO: Listen, I don't know what you might do to yourself if you're alone but I will not be blamed for it. One night. Just tonight. Tomorrow, you'll call your mom and tell her what you've been up to. Deal.

REBECCA: Thank you.

LEO: (*pause*) Water?

REBECCA: Please.

LEO: Or how about beer?

REBECCA: I guess. I'm really sorry.

LEO: Heard that before.

REBECCA: I can't imagine what I put you through.

LEO: I really don't want to bring this up because I can't guarantee what I'll do to you.

They both drink their beer in silence.

REBECCA: I can't stand this silence. Say something. Anything. Say you hate me. Say you want to punch me in the face until I get a real black eye.

LEO: I want to punch me in the face until you get a real black eye.

REBECCA: (*picks up a pillow*) Use this instead. It's softer.

LEO: It's always a joke with you. You never think about the consequences. What you're doing to other people? It's Rebecca, Rebecca, Rebecca, twenty-four hours a day, seven days a week. You're like a virus. You just drain the other person until there is nothing left. You think we would have been happy if we were back together? All sunshine? I was so tired of your lying, I couldn't wait to get out.

REBECCA: I did it for you. For love.

LEO: People who love each other don't fuck with each other.

REBECCA: You're doing that now with Katherine. You cheated on her and you never fessed up.

LEO: You set up that whole evening. So, what, ever since I found out that you not only never had a black eye or even a boyfriend, and I told you it was over, you've been what, plotting? Hatching a plan over a cauldron with snakes, toads and dead babies?

REBECCA: Dead…babies?

LEO: I said no fucking jokes! Ahhhhhhhhh. I want to hit you, but I can't. I want to throw you out of my life, but I can't. I want to see you suffering the way I did through this incredible mind game you put me through. You need to be locked up in one of those padded rooms, with a straitjacket, totally separated from the rest of society.

REBECCA: I screwed up. I lied to you the first time about my…supposed ex and lost you. I needed to find some way to have you back.

LEO: What do you think was going to happen when it became obvious you weren't pregnant?

REBECCA: I wasn't thinking like that.

LEO: You should have been. It's not safe to be around you.

REBECCA: Do you regret it?

LEO: What?

REBECCA: All of it. Our one year, five months, and two weeks.

LEO: What the hell does this have to do with our relationship?

REBECCA: I don't want you to look back on our time together and regret you ever went out with me.

LEO: I don't regret it but, well, I can't understand all the lying. Not even about big stuff. I always caught you in a lie that wasn't even about anything important.

REBECCA: I couldn't stop myself. Deep down, I knew what I was doing was wrong, but it was like I was possessed. One lie led to another and another and before I knew it, I was out of control. I think I need help.

LEO: You definitely need help. Despite the fact that I still hate you, that was pretty impressive.

REBECCA: What was?

LEO: This whole fiasco. You should go into acting.

Leo goes to the bathroom.

REBECCA: I think psychoanalysis would be my first pick.

LEO: Well, at least Katherine never found out.

REBECCA picks up the pill bottle LEO gave her and pops a handful into his beer.

REBECCA: Yeah, I was so jealous when I found out about you two. I just wanted to strangle her.

LEO: (*from the bathroom*) What?

REBECCA: Not literally.

LEO: Right. From now on, I'm going to tell her everything that goes on in my life.

He exits the bathroom and goes to take a drink from his beer.

REBECCA: I understand if you never want to see me again. But I hope you can forgive me and maybe we could still be friends? Or if not friends, at least not enemies.

LEO: I don't know. I feel a hundred different ways right now. I can't even believe I'm still talking to you.

REBECCA: You're the most decent man I know. That's why.

LEO: Yeah, I think it's because you have some strange voodoo hold over me.

REBECCA: You found out about my Leo doll? Kidding.

LEO: I wouldn't put it past you. Listen, don't get insulted, but I just want to practice, okay?

REBECCA: Wait. Can you…in front of me? I liked it when you used to.

LEO: All right. You're not going to go crazy on me, are you? Try to slip me some tongue?

REBECCA: I promise. Just to calm me down.

REBECCA gets ready for bed on the couch. As he sings, he begins to get sleepy. He hits one more note and falls asleep. Silence. The figure of REBECCA starts to move.

REBECCA: Leo? L-e-o?

She approaches LEO and removes his guitar. She then goes to get her purse. Once back in front of LEO, she removes his shirt. She digs in her purse and pulls out a camera. The lights begin to flicker and dim. As she gets on top of him, she positions the camera to include both of them in a photo.

REBECCA: (*slowly*) Smile for Katherine!

As the lights go to blackout, one flash goes off.

The End

Waterfront: The Blessing

by Leah Jane Esau

About the playwright

Leah Jane Esau was born in Winnipeg and currently lives in Montreal, where she attends the National Theatre School of Canada. Her plays include *Calvin* (Festival of Innovative and New Drama, 2006), *Shed* (SummerWorks 2010), and *The Death of Ashley Smith* (National Theatre School, 2011). She holds a B.A. honours in theatre history from the University of Victoria, an M.A. in drama from the University of Toronto, and a M.F.A. in creative writing from the University of Guelph. *Waterfront: The Blessing* was performed at SummerWorks 2011 with the following: Amanda Lockitch (director), Brian Drader (dramaturge), Nancy Perrin (set and costume design), Mary Keenan (stage manager), and performed by William MacDonald as Ed and Robert Fulton as Jeremy.

Characters

ED — 35
JEREMY — his younger brother, 32
GWENDOLYN — Ed's girlfriend, young 30s

Setting

A small town, a few hours north of Toronto. ED and JEREMY's father has passed away, and the play takes place in Dad's house, after the funeral. There are two adjoining rooms: a den, and Dad's bedroom.

Scene 1

ED sits on the couch in the den, surrounded by empty beer bottles. Three cases of beer are stacked against the wall. JEREMY is packing, in Dad's bedroom. Both are wearing suits, as Dad's funeral was a few hours earlier.

Silence.

ED: You'll let me know if you find Dad's jacket?

JEREMY: For the last time, yes.

Silence.

ED: I'm going out.

JEREMY: Okay. Where are you going?

ED: For a walk. Too quiet in here. Pick up some beer.

JEREMY: We have beer. I thought we had three cases of beer.

ED glances at the cases of beer.

ED: Do you need anything from the store?

JEREMY: No. (*beat*) You're *walking* to the store?

ED: Sure.

JEREMY: Aren't you going to take the truck?

ED: I want to walk.

JEREMY: All the way to town? That'll take hours.

ED: No. Maybe. Have you seen my wallet?

JEREMY: Just take the truck. Or the rental.

ED: Can I smoke in the rental?

JEREMY: After I puked in the back, sure. Why not. Maybe you'll get the smell out.

ED: Why'd ya puke anyway? You got food poisoning?

JEREMY: Probably something I ate on the plane.

ED: You always had a woman's stomach.

ED slaps JEREMY on the shoulder. JEREMY glares.

ED: Did you see the leaves, in the lake? Fall already. Feels like just yesterday I was riding my bike up to Lively.

JEREMY: Lively's far.

ED: About two hours. Got a girl up there.

JEREMY: You didn't tell me that.

ED: Got a gorgeous pair of legs on her. Works at the restaurant off the highway. Been dating since May.

JEREMY: That's a long time for you.

ED: What's that supposed to mean?

JEREMY: I've just never seen you with a girl longer than thirty seconds. She must be something else.

ED: Something else all right. My waitress. Wrote her number on my bill.

JEREMY: Really.

ED: Name and number. Bet you never had a girl do that.

JEREMY: I didn't see her at the funeral today.

ED: She's working.

JEREMY puts his beer on the coffee table.

ED: Careful with that.

JEREMY: What? The table?

ED: You're gonna stain it.

JEREMY: We got this table at the Salvation Army. It was ten dollars.

ED: You put beer down on your furniture at home? Huh? I'm sorry this isn't your expensive coffee table.

Beat.

JEREMY: You were never tidy. Dad was tidy.

ED: He wasn't. Not really.

JEREMY: He had a *coaster* obsession.

ED: Wasn't an obsession.

JEREMY: Every trip you took, he bought coasters.

ED: He liked the fucking furniture, okay! (*beat*) He was confined to the house for weeks: had to move a bed in here, so he could see the lake. So when you're in this house, you're gonna respect him, you're gonna use a coaster.

Uncomfortable beat.

ED: Got these ones in Mexico. Took Dad down there. He tell you?

JEREMY: Told me all about it when he came to visit me and Amanda.

ED: Wanted to see the place where I lost my tooth.

JEREMY: Right. The Tooth.

ED: When I was nineteen. Lost my tooth in a bar fight in Mexico. Had been hitchhiking for weeks trying to get south, down to South America, but it was raining—just pouring. Never seen anything like it—raining so hard it was flash flooding, the roads covered in mud, making it impossible to hitchhike.

JEREMY: Ed, you've told me—

ED: So I've been walking—wading really, wading through flooded countryside until I find the highway, and I get picked up by this trucker, this old man with grey hair. I get in, guy's name is Hal. We get to talking; he's a sweet old guy, wouldn't do nothing bad to nobody, has two grown sons and some grandkids. So we drive a couple hours, and we pull into this place off the highway, this local bar. Place is a junkyard, like an indoor junkyard, with strange shit lying around: a mattress without any fabric, a shopping cart, a scuba mask—real old, those tin ones they used to use with the round glass face and the oxygen tube. All this junk. A TV from the fifties without a screen.

JEREMY: Junk. Really.

ED: You know, for atmosphere. For the…décor. And a wall of antlers, this place, bone faces of moose and deer. Skulls. Mounted on the walls.

So we have a couple beers, and then it happens: end of the night, bar's closing, everyone's drunk, we get up to leave, and this guy grabs Hal's shoulder — outta nowhere — and says, "Gimme my jacket."

Hal was wearing a dark jacket when we came in, and he realizes he's wearing a similar jacket but too big.

So Hal's about to take the jacket off, about to apologize — you can see it on his face, an honest mistake, but the guy takes a swing and knocks Hal to the floor, right there, in the bar. Hal's blinking, all confused, and that made me so fucking mad, to knock down a nice old guy like that. So I get in a fight. Leave a gash on the guy's forehead — right above his eyebrow.

JEREMY: Thought you broke his arm.

ED: Things happened fast. Can't remember exactly what I did.

JEREMY: You remember the décor, but you can't remember if you broke a guy's arm.

ED: What would you know about it, huh? You've never been in a bar fight.

JEREMY: That's just fine with me.

ED: You've never even been outta Toronto.

JEREMY: I've lived in Boston.

ED: You think you're real smart, don't'cha?

JEREMY: No.

ED: You gotta contradict everything I say. You think that ivy-league school of yours was real life experience? You've never been punched in the face. Gotta get punched at some point in your life. Guy punched my tooth out when I was nineteen years old.

Beat.

ED: Just don't throw anything out — any of his stuff, all right? You gonna be here when I get back?

JEREMY: Probably.

ED: You could'da stayed here, you know. You didn't need to get some fancy hotel.

JEREMY: It's not fancy.

ED: There's a hot tub. That's as fancy as it gets around here. I got the futon all set up in the basement. Sheets and everything.

JEREMY: That's okay.

ED: What's wrong with this house, huh?

JEREMY: Nothing.

ED: Is this about your room?

JEREMY: No. I don't mind what you've done to my room. I think it's a nice improvement to the basement.

ED: You should see the new machine, she's a beauty. The thing adjusts to work everything: your quadriceps, your peroneus longus, your groin muscles. Pump up those chicken legs, eh? Go home to Amanda all pumped up, a new man, she won't even recognize you.

JEREMY: Aren't you going to the store?

ED: I'm gonna walk.

JEREMY: Jesus, Ed. We really need to get this done. Just take the rental.

ED: It smells like puke.

JEREMY: So take the truck.

ED: Do you have twenty bucks? I can't find my wallet.

JEREMY opens his wallet.

ED: Can I borrow your credit card?

JEREMY: No way.

ED: I just want chips and smokes. Maybe a skin rag, and another case of beer.

JEREMY: You're not borrowing my credit card, Ed.

ED: This *is* about your room, I can tell. First time you come home in ten years and you won't even stay here.

JEREMY: The hotel was free. Work pays for it.

ED: How'd you manage that?

JEREMY: I'm picking up a parcel so we don't have to ship it.

ED: Do you do that a lot?

JEREMY: Do what?

ED: Go on business trips.

JEREMY: It's not a business trip.

ED: You haven't changed a bit. You still keep your food separated?

JEREMY: What?

ED: Like, you still keep your mashed potatoes on one side of your plate, away from the corn, away from the turkey, away from the salad? You never liked mixing up your food. Wouldn't eat it if it touched something else on the plate.

JEREMY: I don't see what my eating habits have to do with anything.

ED: You're afraid to get out there, get your feet wet, go on an adventure.

JEREMY: An adventure.

ED: Don't you ever get bored of the same thing all the time?

JEREMY: No. Toronto's a big city.

ED: You *know* Toronto: North, South, East, West — you can't get lost. Don't you ever want to get lost sometimes? You gotta work the system — take advantage of what you got. See, if I had your job, I'd be traveling all the time. That's the life: start my own business, use company money to travel, take a couple of "business trips." Maybe go down south again.

Beat.

JEREMY: Thought you were never going back.

ED: Been back there lots.

JEREMY: To L.A?

ED: Further south. I'm talking Arizona, Nevada — the desert. It wouldn't be like last time. It wouldn't be just taking off, just leaving without warning, you know, abandoning you, or nothing.

JEREMY: You didn't abandon me.

ED: I'd be testing camping gear.

JEREMY: Testing camping gear?

ED: Well, sure. If I own a camping store, I gotta know how stuff works, how good it is. That's the problem with places around here: not enough experts.

I took my bike in the other day, only place in town. I wanted to change the shocks, there's these new European ones that are lighter. Wanted more information about them. And the guy hadn't heard of them — hadn't even *heard* of them. Why would I trust him to fix my bike?

You gotta start a business about something you love, see, something you're actually interested in. You gotta be an expert. Customers like that. And then you can hook 'em. When you recommend something, you gotta have a reason why they should use that particular product — a good story.

JEREMY: A good story.

ED: Like, nobody uses food canisters, you know, bear-resistant food canisters. Guys just tie up their food in a tree.

So I'm in Peru, up there on the Inca Trail, but off the beaten track, deep in the jungle without any tour guides or nothing, and I tie my food up in this tree, real high, like Dad taught me. I was nineteen or twenty at the time — I forget, but real young, right? — too young to know that hyenas climb trees.

JEREMY: Didn't know there were hyenas in Peru.

ED: Sure.

JEREMY: Thought it was a rainforest.

ED: It's more of a jungle, but it's got all kinds of animals you wouldn't think of: goats, and bears, lizards the size of kids — real big. So I'm in the jungle, sleeping out there under the stars, completely unprotected. And in the middle of the night, I hear them coming. I hear this noise, like laughing. I'm thinking: it sounds like an orangutan, like a monkey laugh but deeper — less of a screech.

JEREMY: Hyenas only laugh when they're in trouble.

ED: Maybe they were, I don't know. So I wake up and I'm surrounded, I'm surrounded by glowing eyes, and snarling, like low growling, like a big animal growls. They're not big, hyenas, but they sound big. I can hear 'em circling the tree where I hung my food. So I light a fire, and I see those guys, about five of 'em, five hyenas up in the tree: ripped the bag to shreds.

JEREMY: Hyenas.

ED: Next day, hiked up to a tourist town there in the mountains and bought a bear-resistant food canister. (*beat*) You see those guys who go camping — Dad's friends — and they don't get a canister. Well, I got a story for them: canister worked. Blocks the smell, keeps away the animals. I could sell a million of those, 'cause I've been there, I've had experience with the product, I know it works: I'm the expert.

JEREMY: Ed —

ED: So what do ya think?

JEREMY: Ed, it's…

ED: Great, right? We're in canoe country up here: whole town's surrounded by lakes. People like to go camping, fishing, hunting, and there isn't a single store in town that sells that stuff. You gotta drive an hour — sometimes in the wrong direction — to get to the nearest tackle shop. Doesn't make sense. (*beat*) All I need is a little bit of money to get it going.

Pause.

ED: You know, you've supported me all these years now —

JEREMY: Yeah.

ED: And I never really thanked you for it. Especially for keeping it to yourself, you know, for not telling anyone what really happened out there. In L.A. (*beat*) I'm sure it was hard to listen to all my problems, and to keep it to yourself — even away from Dad. Dad wouldn't have understood. (*beat*) Do you think Dad would've understood?

JEREMY: I don't know.

ED: My guy talks about that — support. You gotta surround yourself with supportive people, otherwise you might start doing stupid stuff. You might start using again. (*beat*) So what do you think?

JEREMY: A camping store is a good idea. It's always been a good idea.

ED is very pleased.

ED: Well, would ya look at that? He admits that his older brother's got a good idea.

JEREMY: Look, Ed, I have to talk to you about something.

ED: Looks like you're not the only businessman in the family, after all. I got the location picked out and everything. I'll take you down there tomorrow.

JEREMY: I'm leaving tomorrow.

ED: You are?

JEREMY: I have to work.

ED: I thought you were staying a couple of days.

JEREMY: Where'd you get that idea?

ED: Isn't that what people do? I mean, two days? Two days is not enough time to grieve and all that.

JEREMY: I'll be fine.

ED: Dad died, I mean he's… You gotta take some time to…

JEREMY: Do you need me to stay longer?

ED: I'm fine. It's fine with me.

JEREMY: I really can't get the time off.

ED: You can't *get* the time off, or you won't *take* the time off?

JEREMY: Running your own business is a lot of work, Ed. You can't just take off whenever you want.

ED: This is why Dad called you a "workaholic."

JEREMY: Really. When did he say that?

ED: All the time.

JEREMY: Recently?

ED: Sure.

JEREMY: I don't think he said it recently.

ED: For as long as I can remember, "The boy's too serious, the boy doesn't know how to have fun."

JEREMY: Yeah, yeah, "the boy."

ED: "The boy's gonna be a nerd if this continues. A square." Guess he was right, eh? I never understood you and Amanda. Talk about adventure: she wants adventure, that girl. Someone who jumps out of a plane at fifteen thousand feet: a real thrill seeker, that one.

Beat.

ED: Have you picked your guys yet?

JEREMY: Our guys?

ED: Yeah, you know, planned for the wedding?

JEREMY: Not yet.

ED: 'Cause, I was thinkin,' well, I'm gonna come up to Toronto, to see it.

JEREMY: I don't know if it'll be in Toronto.

ED: Isn't Amanda's family there?

JEREMY: We might elope.

ED: Oh. Yeah, she'd do that. (*beat*) Well, let me know what you decide to do.

JEREMY: Sure.

ED: It's just, if I was getting married, I'd ask you to be my best guy. The best man, you know?

JEREMY: Oh. Yeah—

ED: Unless you've got someone else in mind—

JEREMY: I'll think about it, Ed.

ED: You'd consider me?

JEREMY: Sure.

ED: Why don't you stay here tomorrow night—at least one more day? I thought we'd go fishing.

JEREMY: Fishing.

ED: Sure. Season closes soon. Good place to talk about stuff. Take the boat out for a spin one last time.

Beat.

JEREMY: Are you going to sell it?

ED: Is that okay?

JEREMY: You're the one who went fishing with him.

ED: Yeah, but where would I put it? It's a pretty big boat. Probably won't have a garage or even a driveway. (*beat*) At my new place.

Beat.

ED: Didn't I tell you? I'm moving into town. Shit, Jer, I thought I told you.

JEREMY: Why don't we just leave the boat here? In the driveway.

ED: I guess. Stays with the property. (*beat*) The Johnsons sold their place.

JEREMY: I saw the sign out front.

ED: Never thought they'd go. Been meaning to go over there and say goodbye, but Dave's gonna want to talk about Dad. You gonna go over there and say goodbye?

JEREMY: I'm thinking about it. (*beat*) It's too bad I'm not staying a couple more days, actually. I'd like to meet your girlfriend. What's her name?

ED: Who?

JEREMY: The waitress.

ED: What waitress?

JEREMY: The one with the gorgeous pair of legs. You've been dating since May. In Lively.

ED: Artist. She's an artist. It's just you said waitress, so I got thrown off about who you meant.

JEREMY: Your girl.

ED: Yeah. My girl up in Lively.

JEREMY: As opposed to your girl down here, or what?

ED: Whadd'ya mean?

JEREMY: Just sounds like you have other girls. "My girl in Lively" sounds like you've got other girls. "My girl in Sudbury. My girl in Muskoka. My girl in Toronto." (*beat*) So what kind of art does she do?

ED: Who?

JEREMY: Your girl in Lively. You just said she was an artist.

ED: Yeah.

JEREMY: So what kind of art does she do?

ED: I don't know. Art.

JEREMY: Is she a painter? Or a writer?

ED: We didn't talk about it.

JEREMY: You didn't talk about it. She's an artist but you didn't talk about what kind of art she does?

ED: I don't talk about that stuff.

JEREMY: Didn't you ask her?

ED: Why would I ask her?

JEREMY: It just seems like an obvious question to ask. "I'm an artist." "Oh, what kind of art do you do?"

ED: It doesn't make a difference to me.

JEREMY: So you don't *care* what kind of art she does.

ED: I didn't say that.

JEREMY: You didn't ask her.

ED: I'm not really interested in art. I'm interested in her. But I'm not really interested in art.

JEREMY: Me neither.

ED: Amen.

JEREMY: So you don't really know what she does.

ED: Sure I do. She's a waitress.

JEREMY: So what's her name?

ED: Gwendolyn.

JEREMY: Gwendolyn. Like the medieval princess.

ED: Gwen. I call her Gwen all the time.

JEREMY: So why didn't you just say "Gwen" in the first place?

ED: 'Cause her name is Gwendolyn.

JEREMY: Is that what you told Dad? Came home and said, "This gorgeous waitress wrote her name and number on my bill. Her name's Gwendolyn."

ED: Sure I told him, sure did — told him all about it, 'cause after she gave me her number, she said she had a break in five minutes. So I met her outside, and we drove into the backwoods, and had a quickie on her smoke break.

Beat.

JEREMY: In a car.

ED: Of course in a car.

JEREMY: Whose car? I mean, you had your bike.

ED: Her car. Bet you've never done it in a car. It'd be too weird for you, right?, too different. And the risk someone might catch you with your pants down.

JEREMY: Well, I guess Dad liked that story, huh, about you and Gwendolyn in the car? Probably bragged about you to the doctors.

ED: He sure did.

JEREMY: Gave him something to brag about.

ED: Like old times. Like when I'd win the MVP in football every year.

JEREMY: Or your adventure. You know, those couple of years down in Mexico. He sure liked to brag about that.

Beat.

ED: You got something to say to me, huh? You should just say it.

JEREMY: Have you told *Gwendolyn* you're moving into town?

ED: Yeah. (*beat*) My guy says it'd be good for me. He's been telling me I should move for a while, get out of the house, start something new, especially now that there's nothing to do here.

Beat.

ED: Everything's changing. Dad's gone, and the Johnsons sold their place, and the town is booming, like, putting up all these new buildings. I hardly recognize the place anymore. It's too quiet up here now, without Dad. I got nothing to do. I feel stagnant or something. I need a change, a real big change. That's why I'm thinking about the store, and talking to my guy about it. Talking about goals and stuff.

Beat.

ED: Did'ya notice the pizza place closed, there on the main drag? Great location, right off the highway, right into town. Everybody's gotta drive past there going in or out.

JEREMY: Ed—

ED: Have you heard from the lawyer? Been meaning to ask you about the reading.

JEREMY: Of the will? I don't think it's been scheduled.

ED: Why not?

JEREMY: He's busy until next week.

ED: He said that to you?

JEREMY: Yeah.

ED: When.

JEREMY: I forget.

ED: But you're leaving tomorrow.

JEREMY: We can do it over the phone. There's a thing called three-way calling. It exists.

ED: I hate lawyers. I hate them more over the phone. Annoying as hell and they charge you. It's like 500 bucks a phone call.

JEREMY: Sounds like you have a lot of experience with lawyers.

ED: I mean, 500 bucks to hear some guy's voice. I don't care how many years you spent at university, your voice isn't worth 500 bucks. I bet it costs *extra* for three-way calling. That's fancy. I mean, that's fancy shit.

Beat.

ED: So you don't have a copy.

JEREMY: Of the will?

ED: Yeah.

JEREMY: Why would I have a copy? Did you get a copy?

ED: Dad must have a copy somewhere, right?

JEREMY: I don't know.

ED: How do we know if we're doing it right?

JEREMY: Doing what right?

ED: Cleaning up. We're going through his stuff, what if he said: "Don't touch anything. Don't touch anything for a year."

JEREMY: Why would he say that?

ED: I don't know.

JEREMY: It's an unusual request, "don't touch anything for a year." I've never heard of that.

ED: Well, I don't know. What if.

JEREMY: Why a year?

ED: I don't know. But we should read the thing, make sure his wishes are being met. Make sure we're doing it right.

JEREMY: Everybody has to do this, Ed.

ED: What if he said, "Leave my stuff to charity?"

JEREMY: Dad. Charity?

ED: Let's find out.

JEREMY: No. I'd rather wait for the lawyer.

ED: How do we know he didn't divide up everything?

JEREMY: You think he divided his clothes, his articles of clothing specifically?

ED: How do you know he didn't?

JEREMY: It's a lot of stuff to divide.

ED: "To my eldest son, Ed, I leave my badass leather jacket."

JEREMY: You can have it.

ED: I just want to make sure we're *doing* it right.

JEREMY: If you really want to *do* something, you can sort through that box.

JEREMY goes into Dad's room. ED dumps everything into his pile.

ED: What are you looking for in there? You haven't made a pile yet.

JEREMY: I haven't found anything I want.

ED: There must be something.

JEREMY: Wouldn't mind my school stuff.

ED: What about something of Dad's? Don't you want anything of Dad's? (*beat*) All I remember about your school stuff was A+ staring me in the face all the time.

JEREMY: What do you mean, "staring you in the face"?

ED: I dunno. A+, that's what you got on your report cards.

JEREMY: Yeah, but Dad never *displayed* them, they were never staring you in the face. They weren't even hanging on the fridge. It's not my fault you flunked out, Ed.

ED: When did I blame you?

JEREMY: That's what you're suggesting: that my report cards made you feel bad, because they were "staring you in the face." There was no room on the fridge 'cause of your MVP awards.

ED: Those are framed, still hanging in the basement. In the gym, actually.

JEREMY: Your MVP awards are hanging in my room?

ED: It's the gym now, but yeah.

JEREMY: I have ribbons!

ED: What ribbons.

JEREMY: The science fair. I had four ribbons, all first place.

ED: I don't remember seeing those.

JEREMY: Exactly! Dad never displayed anything of mine. Nothing was staring you in the face!

ED: All right, already! I take it back, Christ.

Beat.

JEREMY: I'm actually looking for stuff of Mom's.

ED: Like what?

JEREMY: Her wedding ring. I was thinking—I had this crazy idea I'd give it to Amanda.

ED: I don't think he kept it.

JEREMY: (*surveying the piles*) It's just—didn't he keep *anything*? There's not even a picture. (*beat*) Do you remember her?

ED: No. Not really.

JEREMY: You were seven. You must remember something.

ED: Mom was…she smelled like vanilla. She stood by the window a lot, she said, "I'm just soaking up the sunlight."

JEREMY: Didn't Dad say that?

ED: He'd say that when he missed her. You could tell he was thinking about her. She and Dad danced for hours, sometimes all night. And when you were born, Mom: she'd hold you, and sing to you. She loved you a lot, she really did.

JEREMY is pleased. He goes into Dad's room.

ED: You know, it's weird.

JEREMY: What?

ED: The doctors said he had lots of time, Dad. Said he was doing real well. We were planning another trip, maybe go to Peru, hike the Inca Trail. And then he went to see and you and Amanda—he was feelin' great, doing real well. (*beat*) And then he got depressed. I couldn't even cheer him up.

JEREMY: With your stories, you mean?

ED: Yeah. Died a couple weeks after that.

Beat. JEREMY finds the will. He hides it, then re-enters with purpose.

JEREMY: Who was that guy at the funeral?

ED: What guy?

JEREMY: The guy you were talking to.

ED: When?

JEREMY: After the service. I didn't catch his name.

ED: What was he wearing?

JEREMY: Black.

ED: Everyone was wearing black.

JEREMY: He didn't stay for the reception.

ED: I dunno. Today was a blur. This whole week has been… I mean, shit. I left my bike downtown yesterday—my *bike.* I walked half an hour before realizing I was holding my helmet. And now my wallet, my keys… I didn't tell you I was moving.

JEREMY finds Dad's jacket and gives it to ED. ED smells it.

JEREMY: It was in the back of the closet.

ED: He was wearing this the day I left. The day he gave me his blessing.

JEREMY: His blessing?

ED: Sure. You know. The blessing. (*beat*) He didn't… When you left for university, when you left the house, he didn't give you the blessing?

JEREMY: …No.

ED: I told him I was leaving with Willy Mench. We had this plan to hitchhike across America, then all the way to Mexico. Packed up my stuff. Told Dad I was eighteen and I was gonna go make my way as a man. Not much warning about the whole thing, just decided to go. And Dad was never religious. Dad hated religion.

This story is true.

ED: We were right here, by the door. My backpack was here. And I put on my shoes. And he said: "Stand up straight." So I did. And he said: "You're taller than me now."

(*beat*) Which was strange 'cause Dad was tall.

Then he hugged me, one hand on my back—in between my shoulder blades, and the other hand on my forehead. I'll never forget this, 'cause at the time it was… I mean, Dad hates religion, right?—but he said:

"Walk tall, with a strong spirit in your chest. Be proud. If you stumble, pick yourself up. You've got my blessing, so let you be favoured from this day on." The blessing.

Beat.

ED: I was right up against his chest 'cause he was huggin' me kinda tight. He was wearing this jacket.

JEREMY is devastated.

ED: You okay?

JEREMY: Yeah.

ED: You got food poisoning?

JEREMY: No. I got rid of it all.

ED: Okay.

JEREMY: I was just thinking about Willy Mench.

ED: I think he's a history professor now.

JEREMY: That suits him.

ED: We split off after the first month. He stayed with his aunt and uncle in Virginia. I headed west. Ended up in L.A. You know the rest. (*beat*) You sure you're okay?

JEREMY: I can't find anything of Mom's.

ED: We should check the will and see what—

JEREMY: Why do you want to open it so badly, huh? Christ! The man just died, he's dead. Have some fucking decency.

ED: I want to make sure we're doing this right.

JEREMY: That's not why you want to open it.

ED: We're...moving his things, okay, we've...we've pulled out his room, we've *pulled out everything from his room,* do you understand what we're doing? We've uprooted his life, we're uprooting his whole fucking life and putting it in piles, we're putting it in *piles* and we don't know if that's what he wanted.

JEREMY: I promise he wanted this, okay.

ED: Did he tell you that? I want to honour what he said.

JEREMY: You want to see who gets the house, or the boat.

ED: Okay, look—I know some other people interested in the old pizza place. Some other business people. Great location, I could turn it into a store—but I gotta do it soon, before somebody else puts in an offer. (*beat*) Nobody can get any camping gear—and we're surrounded by national parks. There's not a single place in town that sells that stuff.

JEREMY: It's a good idea, Ed. It was a good idea ten years ago.

ED: I didn't have the money ten years ago.

JEREMY: Sure you did. Dad was willing to sign the house, the property against the loan but it never happened. You never made it happen.

ED: What are you saying? You saying I can't—what?

JEREMY: How much is the pizza place? How much is the lot?

ED: I haven't looked into it, yet.

JEREMY: This is exactly what I'm talking about—you never *finish* anything, Ed. You just talk big, you have all these ideas in your head, all these plans—but then you never do anything. You've been talking about the store for ten years.

ED: I wasn't ready. My guy—

JEREMY: I know what your therapist says.

ED: Counselor. He's a counselor.

JEREMY: Okay.

ED: He's more like a coach, really.

JEREMY: All right.

ED: And he tells stories of these guys, recovering addicts, who jump into something big, like starting their own business. And they can't handle the pressure. It sends them right back to using, 'cause it's the only way they know how to cope.

JEREMY: You were afraid Dad would find out.

ED: Maybe. So what if I was? (*beat*) The Johnsons sold their place and they got—

JEREMY: I don't care how much they got.

ED: Almost a million. A million dollars, Jer. And they don't even have waterfront. We've got waterfront property. If we sell the house—

JEREMY: Dad built this house. (*beat*) Where are you going to live? If we sell the house—where are you going to live?

ED: I told you. In town. And I'd start the business because I'd have the money to actually start it up.

JEREMY: We need to talk about that.

ED: You could pay off your condo.

JEREMY: I don't think we should sell the house.

ED: Why?

JEREMY: You're going to need somewhere to live.

ED: I can live anywhere I want. We're talking about 1.4 million dollars.

JEREMY: Where'd you get that number?

ED: It's been assessed.

JEREMY: You got the property assessed.

ED: It just happened.

JEREMY: It just *happened*?

ED: The real estate agent was next door, talking to the Johnsons—just listen, all right? She came over to give her condolences, because of Dad. And we got to talking about what I was gonna do, and I said I was thinking of moving on, and she did a free assessment—okay, *free*, no commitment on our part. It's a good idea to know how much your property is worth, anyway.

JEREMY: Who was the guy at the funeral?

ED: A guy from town. With a lot of money. And he, uh...

JEREMY: He wants to buy the place?

ED: Nothing is done, I mean, we can change our minds if we want.

JEREMY: We're not selling the house. You're going to need somewhere to live. You don't know what's going on.

ED: *You* don't know what's going on! You're in your own little universe where things begin and end in Toronto and that's the world. You haven't *been* here. You took off.

JEREMY: *I* took off. You were the one who left at eighteen to go on your big adventure—and we know how that turned out.

ED: You think Dad's been easy these past couple of years, huh? You think it's easy to look after a dying man—a man who knows he's gonna die—your own father! By the end, he couldn't put on his pants, okay? I had to help him get dressed. You live four hours away. Four hours, and you couldn't even drive up here to see him. I'm the one who lived here with him.

JEREMY: Where the fuck else were you gonna live? You don't have a job. You can't do anything — I'm amazed you organized this so far: an assessment, a real estate agent, a potential buyer. That's the most productive you've been in years.

ED: Are you finished?

JEREMY: You wanted to sell the house without asking me.

ED: Well, maybe I woulda talked to you about it, if you were around more often.

JEREMY: Maybe I would come home if I felt welcome. Ever since I stepped foot in this house, it's been the same since we were kids: Ed's a real man, Ed plays football, Ed has girls all over him.

ED: Yeah, well, you're patronizing.

JEREMY: Guess what, Ed! I *have* fucked a girl in the back of the car, and it was Amanda — and it was *my* car. (*beat*) Oh, and, by the way, that's a true story.

Beat.

JEREMY: If I drove up the highway to the restaurant, would there be a *Gwendolyn* working there?

ED: Yes.

JEREMY: I don't think so.

ED: Call the restaurant. She's working today: Gwendolyn. What's your problem?

JEREMY: What's my *problem*? You've never been to Peru! There were no hyenas, no food canister, no jungle — no adventure. You didn't lose a tooth in a bar fight. You never made it to Mexico. You were in L.A., smoking crack.

ED: I understand why you're angry, but —

JEREMY: No, you don't. (*beat*) I left. I went to university, and I used to call home while you were gone — I was getting the highest marks in the class, scholarships to fucking Harvard and all he could talk about was your great adventure.

You know how he'd answer? Huh? He'd be out of breath from running to the phone, "Ed? Is that you, Ed? Ed? Are you there, Ed?" All he could talk about: Ed's in Mexico, Ed's in Argentina, Ed just hiked the Inca trail and got attacked by hyenas!

Beat.

JEREMY: I… This is ridiculous. I can't believe anything you say. It's like, it's like you lied to yourself so many times that you actually believe it. You've replaced your actual memories with things that never happened. It *never happened.* (*beat*) Like today, like earlier today, you're willing to tell me about hyenas in Peru, when I know the truth: you were never there. Did you forget that?

ED: Those stories made Dad happy.

JEREMY: Because he thought they were *true.*

ED: He'd feel better when he retold 'em. He'd tell 'em to his friends and the doctors, the cute nurses he liked to flirt with. So what if they were lies?

JEREMY: So *what?*

ED: Yeah, so what? You're upset because Dad liked me better, and I fucked up.

JEREMY: You took *trips* together. You went "back" and "retraced your steps." The whole thing was a lie. The whole relationship.

ED: I confided in you 'cause I had to tell somebody and I couldn't — I couldn't tell Dad, all right? So I owe you for covering for me. So what do you want from me?

JEREMY: You could be the man Dad thought you were, at least.

ED: What's that supposed to mean?

JEREMY: You can stop lying.

ED: All right, fuck! I won't lie anymore.

JEREMY: Okay. You're not gonna lie — not to me.

ED: Okay. I promise. No more lies.

JEREMY: Where's Mom's wedding ring?

JEREMY grabs ED by the collar.

JEREMY: Don't look away. You're gonna look at me and you're gonna tell me the truth. Where is Mom's wedding ring?

ED: I sold it. (*quick beat*) 'Cause I had to — they were gonna kill me, Jer, they really were, this gang was gonna kill me, 'cause I owed them money. You don't mess with these guys. I had been dealing for 'em, right? in L.A., and I started taking some money off the top, you know, selling the stuff a couple bucks more expensive than it actually was, and then keeping it for myself — so I guess they thought I was stealing and they came after me. And that's why I left, Jer, I got outta there 'cause they were gonna kill me.

Pause.

JEREMY: That story doesn't even make sense, Ed. You stole Mom's wedding ring before you left this house. Before you knew any of those guys in L.A. Otherwise, how else would you have it? In L.A. (*beat*) Get out.

ED: You can't tell me what to do.

JEREMY: You're out of the will.

ED: What.

JEREMY: Dad disinherited you.

Beat.

ED: He gave me his blessing.

Beat. ED understands.

ED: You told him? You fucking told him! (*beat*) Why would you do that? Why would you *do* that? I've been clean, I've been clean since I came home — for ten fucking years I've been clean.

JEREMY: I couldn't let him die thinking it was the truth.

ED: Tell me what he said.

JEREMY: Forget it.

ED: You tell me I'm getting nothing and you want me to forget it?

JEREMY: You greedy —

ED grabs JEREMY by the neck.

ED: Tell me what he said.

JEREMY: He called you a fuck-up. He realized he spent his whole life on a fuck-up.

ED: I don't believe you. He gave me his blessing.

JEREMY: Open it.

JEREMY gets the will.

JEREMY: Open it. And then you can get out of my house.

ED is still thinking.

ED: When did you tell him?

JEREMY: When he came to visit me and Amanda. He told me about your trip to Mexico. "Ed took me to the place where he lost his tooth."

ED: So you *told* him?

JEREMY: I was going to let you live here, but now you just keep lying. With that fucking bear-canister story, and your girlfriend!

ED: Call the restaurant.

JEREMY: Dad's not here for you to lie to. You're not gonna lie to me, I'm not gonna be the replacement for that.

ED: When he came back from his visit, that's when he got sick again. It was like he gave up.

JEREMY: If Dad died unhappily, it's because of you, not me.

ED: You jealous, *selfish* —

JEREMY: I told the truth.

ED: It killed him to know I turned out like Mom.

Beat.

JEREMY: What.

ED: You want to know what I remember, huh? Mom was never here. She'd come and go: steal money from Dad. Her skin was lumpy, with bruises. Her skin was the wrong colour: grey. She was missing teeth.

JEREMY: She died of cancer.

ED: She overdosed.

Beat.

ED: She overdosed, Jer.

JEREMY: My whole life, my whole fucking life I thought she died of cancer.

ED: Isn't that better?

Beat.

JEREMY attacks. They fight.

GWEN enters, with a pizza box. Both men pause.

ED: Gwendolyn.

GWEN: (*surveying the damage*) What's… What happened?

ED: Let's go.

GWEN: Are you all right?

ED: I'm fine.

GWEN: You have a bruise—

ED: I'm fine.

GWEN: You must be Jeremy, I—(*to* ED) Should I wait outside, or—

ED: We're leaving.

GWEN: But—

ED: Let's go.

ED and GWEN exit.

Beat. Time passes.

JEREMY puts on the jacket. It's too big, as if it belongs to someone else.

JEREMY's phone rings.

JEREMY: Hi… Yeah… It was good as far as funerals go… Ed? Ed's good… We've been packing.

Beat.

JEREMY: Did I ever tell you about my father's leather jacket? He was wearing it the day I left. The day he gave me his blessing. (*beat*) Told him I was going to make my way as a man. So he stood in front of me, and said, "You're taller than me, now," which is funny because Dad was tall—but he said, "you're taller than me now."

The lights begin to fade on JEREMY.

JEREMY is alone.

JEREMY is alone.

JEREMY is alone.

The End

Bathsheba

by Jennifer Kearney

About the playwright

Ottawa-born performer and playwright Jennifer Kearney is a recent graduate of Concordia University's B.F.A. program in theatre and development, where she also studied playwriting under Kit Brennan. During her studies in Montreal, Jenn developed a passion for teaching theatre in university classrooms, high schools, and community centres. She has also been a performer with both Echo Playback Theatre and Promito Playback Theatre in Montreal. Jenn has performed in various theatres in Ottawa and Montreal and her recent performing credits include: *Differences/The Clash* (L'Aquarium et le Globe), *The Skriker* (The Skriker Collective), *The Vagina Monologues* (Concordia University), and *The Dictatorship of Debt* (SJC Loud Justice Theatre).

Characters

LIZ — a woman in her late twenties

Setting

A room with chairs and a chalkboard. On the board is 'Miss Liz' written in block letters, and the lines of the Hail Mary. On the walls are a window and a clock.

Lights up. LIZ *is moving distractedly around the room, setting up chairs. Once she's arranged them, she looks at the clock first, then around, as if to make sure no one's watching, then kneels on the floor, makes the sign of the cross and folds her hands, preparing to pray. Feeling suddenly ridiculous, she gets up and tries sitting in one of the chairs. She makes the sign of the cross again, folds her hands, sits a few moments in hesitation, then abandons the whole thing.*

She rearranges the room and paces a little, looks at the clock, then stops to face the empty chairs, practicing.

LIZ: Good morning, boys and girls, how are you on this beautiful—(*looks out the window and amends*)—snowy Sunday afternoon? Let's start off with the prayer we learned last week. Does anyone remember?

(*reading from the chalkboard behind her, as if leading children*) Hail Mary, full of grace. The Lord is with thee. Blessed are thou among women and blessed is the fruit of thy womb— Jesus. (*She stares at the words, then suddenly erases the whole board.*) Jesus, Liz. (*rewrites on the board: Miss Liz*)

(*After a moment, she turns and looks back at her imaginary class.*) Why don't we start with a story instead? Okay… A long, long time ago in Israel, there was a shepherd named David. He impressed everyone with his bravery and skill and he was so well loved that he eventually became king. Then, one night, David was in his palace when he looked out the window and saw a beautiful woman named Bathsheba. So he called Bathsheba to him and…

(*sighs*) God…

I can't do this.

LIZ *gets up and kneels back in the same spot as before, makes the sign of the cross and folds her hands.*

(*to God*) First of all, I've never been really good at this. (*indicating her folded hands*) Second of all, I realize I haven't done this in a while… Not really, not since Mom died. I mean, I've been faking it with the kids in here on Sundays, but I'm assuming You know that… The faking bit… (*Pauses to look around, to make sure no one is going to walk in on her.*)

I know they say not to bargain with You, but I'm desperate, and I need You to come down here, send a holy gamma ray, whatever works so I can get the words out; so that I can tell him. I'll do anything. I'll start being a good Catholic, or at least a better one. I'll give something to charity. I'll say the rosary. I'll stop watching porn…

We both know I don't like coming to You, but I'm running out of options and I don't think I can do this on my own anymore.

I don't know if this whole thing is some kind of punishment, or just Your sense of humour: having me down here on my knees, in the attic of the church I swore I was done with, with what isn't likely the immaculate conception on my hands. But I'm not laughing.

Her eyes drift back to the door, and she gets up and locks it. She looks from the door back to the spot where she was kneeling, hesitating to return, but she looks again at the clock, and makes up her mind. She takes one of the chairs instead of kneeling.

Mass will be over in forty minutes, give or take. Forty minutes, and three hours, and David's—*Father Monahan's*—flight leaves for Brazil. Twelve hours later they touch down in Sao Paulo. Another two until they reach the slums.

Pause.

Forty minutes and through that door come all the kids of St Benedict's church ready to diligently colour in whatever Disney-fied Bible scenes I hand them, but if I don't make it down to the rectory before that, if I don't talk to Father Monahan before the kids come in and he leaves... There won't be another chance.

Still she doesn't move to get up.

Normally, I'd say the impending wave of kids is the icing on the cake in terms of Your sick sense of humour, but I bet even You didn't see this one coming, eh? Me as a Sunday school teacher? Don't feel bad; me neither, not after I left the church after high school. But it's not like I could have said no. I don't think Mom's casket was even in the ground yet, and there they were, asking me to take her job. The Ladies' Auxiliary can close a mean deal: stockbrokers in another life, maybe.

Of course, Father Monahan's brand-new-priest enthusiasm didn't hurt either, talking about how he looked forward to working together, to being friends, *smiling*. After a childhood and a half of Father McNulty glaring down at me from the pulpit every Sunday, I kind of assumed things like not smiling were just part of the work ethic they drilled into them at the seminary.

(*assuming an authoritative male voice*) It is widely believed, my sons, that it takes forty seven muscles to frown and only seventeen to smile. Therefore, we must be hard-working Christians and continue the practice of glowering at our congregations.

It was kind of intimidating, actually, the new parish priest wanting to be friends. The first time he invited me out to talk about my plans for the Sunday classes, I think I pretty much fell off my chair when he asked if I wanted to meet for coffee instead of at the church.

(*as DAVID*) Why not?

(*as herself*) Are you allowed?

(*as DAVID*) To go to a coffee shop?

(*as herself*) Yes, obviously I think the Vatican believes the coffee bean to be a sinful creation of the devil and the shops where it is sold to be gateways to hell. No, I mean... You and a woman...out...alone... Which could be construed as...something... I don't know.

(*as DAVID*) A date?

(*to God*) He said it, not me.

And then he looked at me very matter-of-factly:

(*as* DAVID) God isn't a jealous girlfriend, Liz. He's not going to punish me because I go out...to a coffee shop with a female parishioner.

And that was that.

I remember sitting there waiting for him the next day. I kind of had this notion that he'd be wearing the full-on robes when he came in from the rain, all soaking wet and wild-looking like John the Baptist. But when he finally got there he wasn't even wearing the collar to give him away. He was strictly incognito. Trying to put me at ease, maybe.

Slipping into the memory, she turns one of the other chairs to face her.

(*as herself*) Hi, Father, how are you?

(*as* DAVID) You can call me David.

And this must be something new they're teaching them in the seminary, because I'm pretty sure my mother, God rest her soul, would have crucified me if I'd called Father McNulty "Ted."

(*to* DAVID *in her memory*) So you don't drink coffee?

He orders tea: herbal tea actually, no caffeine. I'm a week into my ill-conceived plan to quit smoking and I'm fully ready to murder innocent children and puppies for a cigarette, and this guy isn't even drinking coffee. He probably doesn't smoke, probably doesn't get road rage or get drunk. He's not allowed to have sex either, so I wonder if he—

(*to* DAVID) So then do you— Come here often?

Vastly inappropriate, Liz.

(*to God*) It's a good thing I don't go to confession anymore because there are some things I couldn't have imagined telling this celibate, thirty-year-old man.

Still can't.

Pause.

(*to God*) Him, or You.

Checks the clock.

I need to talk to him, though—Father Monahan...David—before it's too late. He deserves to know.

Which, of course, he absolutely can't. He has to go to Brazil and set up a school, and make people believe in things, and generally not be screwed up. I can't be selfish here... Kids in slums outrank me for being in general need, right?

Still, I tried last night at the potluck dinner. I got him alone for just a second in the kitchen, away from the church ladies. I'd spent almost an hour before that in the bathroom, in front of the mirror practicing, talking myself down, and back up again, and I swear to God—

I swear to You, I was ready.

(*pretending* DAVID *is in front of her*) Father Monahan, I had to tell you, because I know tomorrow is your last mass here before leaving for Sao Paulo... I wanted to talk to you, because this could be my last chance. (*pause*)

My last chance before your flight leaves tomorrow night. I know I've been avoiding you since, well... David, it's really important. (*screwing up her courage*) You need to know... You deserve to know... I have to tell you...

Have a safe flight.

Have a safe flight. That's what I said to him. There were so many things I should have said, many, many of them pertaining to the home pregnancy test kit sitting on the back of my toilet at home. But "Have a safe flight," that's what came out.

We used to be able to talk. Even when we were still strangers in the beginning, I used to look forward to seeing him, to telling him things, asking his advice, and it didn't feel like I was talking to a priest, which, thank God, or um, thank *You*...because You know, as a kid, I used to hate going to confession.

(*writes 'Confession' on the board. To her imaginary class:*) Confession, boys and girls, is the sacred sacrament where you tell a priest all of your sins and he asks God to forgive you. You go into the confessional booth, which is a tiny cramped box with some curtains and mesh, and you tell a complete stranger embarrassing and painful things about your life. Then he tells you how many Hail Marys and Our Fathers to say.

(*back to God*) But David and I used to talk, a lot. I always got the sense that it didn't matter what we were talking about, he just genuinely loved to listen. He wanted to know everything about me, and not just in a "does she have a criminal record, or is she qualified, or will we find her passed out in the sacristy plastered on sacramental wine" kind of way.

Shift back into memory.

(*as herself to* DAVID) My mom used to be the Sunday schoolteacher here before she got sick, so I guess I kind of got passed the torch. I actually hadn't planned on staying so long after the funeral, but back in great big Napanee, with a basic BA and no immediate prospects, a house to sell and a will to settle, I figured: why not stay on and take the job?

(*back in the present, to God*) Why not go back to a long dead relationship with a religious institution? The Catholic church was my rebound after being dumped by my long-term boyfriend and losing my mother. It was my refuge from the new emptiness in my mom's house. I wanted to be out of there, applying to teacher's college, travelling Asia, something other than where I was. But for some reason, I couldn't leave and the church became a kind of refuge from the emptiness.

(*to* DAVID*, back in her memories*) And anyway, I still haven't finished going through all of the stuff in my mom's house. I'm actually finding I'm less suited than I thought to the task of bagging and tagging the remnants of my childhood and my mother for Goodwill.

(*to* DAVID*; ploughing ahead*) But I really like the kids and they seem to be willing in most cases to listen to what I have to say about this guy from the Bible or his wife or the Pharisees. Probably a good deal of my delivery's helped by editing all of those "begats" out of the stories. And Jared begat Enoch and Enoch begat Methuselah, and Methuselah begat Lamech and

Lamech begat someone who invariably begat someone else, and so on and so forth. I think I'm actually learning to tell a passably good story.

David laughs. He's got a completely dorky laugh.

(*feeling encouraged. As herself*) What about you? How did you end up here?

(*as* DAVID) You mean, exotic and exciting Napanee? Or the priesthood?

(*as herself*) The second one.

(*as* DAVID) A lot of praying and a lot of thinking, I guess.

(*as herself*) No burning bush scenario?

(*as* DAVID, *laughing*) No, no burning bush, no heavenly signs. My father was very religious and he instilled it in me, growing up. I knew for sure that I wanted to help people…and I was always told my faith was a gift, so I thought it only made sense to find a way to share it. I had an uncle who joined the seminary after he finished college, and when I graduated, I was young and single and unattached, so I thought: Why not?

(*as herself in the present*) Why not run off and take a vow of celibacy at age twenty-three? Yeah, I can think of a few good reasons.

(*as herself to* DAVID) You took the priesthood for a test drive?

(*as* DAVID, *laughing*) I guess you could say that. (*becoming serious and earnest again*) And then it just felt right. I felt called.

(*to God*) Called: he felt called. Me, I just figured after my undergrad that I could probably hack it as a teacher and generally believe in my career path — after all, kids being literate is probably a good thing. This man, on the other hand, was completely and utterly devoted to what he felt he'd been called to do.

I'm sure You noticed that I actually started coming to church after that. I mean, apart from when I was teaching classes. In a weird way, this has become home, more so than the house I grew up in.

When I moved to Vancouver to go to school, the cramped dorms that smelled like old socks every day weren't exactly home either, but it was something better, I thought. It was freedom. (*pause*) And then I got the phone call in my last semester at UBC. Mom told me not to worry, that she wanted me to wait until I was finished my last exams before coming home.

I made it home two weeks before she died.

I should have come sooner. But I didn't think I had it in me to watch the slow deterioration of my mother who, when I was a kid, would make the thirty-minute walk to church every Sunday morning in heels, not a hair out of place, the middle of January be damned.

By the time I got back, that Mom wasn't the one I saw, and then the house wasn't really even our home anymore, once she was gone.

Pause.

But the church…it's exactly the way I remember: the wood panels, and the old leather-upholstered kneelers in the pews, and the musty smell of the missals. It's all whispers and Sunday shoes and candlelight and slightly grimed-over stained glass. I can practically hear my mother's voice again here.

She sang every Sunday.

Sings:

This little light of mine
I'm gonna let it shine.
This little light of mine
I'm gonna let it shine.
This little light of mine
I'm gonna let it shine...

And I sang too.

Sings:

Let it shine, let it shine, let it shine.

Until I was almost fourteen, and then I was embarrassed. I'd clam up and look straight ahead, pretending to be completely bored. But actually, I just wanted to listen to my mother sing.

Pause.

And then later I started to come here to listen to David. I guess I thought maybe something of his faith would rub off on me. That, and he kind of reminded me of my mom. Not just her unquestioning faith; the arguments between us, too, though David let me push him further than Mom:

(*as herself*) Come on! The Catholic Church's saviour is a man born of a virgin, who herself was "immaculately conceived." Whatever that means.

(*as* DAVID) It means it was a miracle. Mary was without sin from the very beginning. It means—

(*as herself*) It means clean, David, pristine, like everything else is dirty and unworthy.

(*as* DAVID) The Church doesn't forbid sex, Liz, it just asks for some responsibility!

(*as herself*) No, it asks you either to get married too young and ruin your life or go completely celibate and mess up your whole psychology and turn out like those perverted priests who end up screwing their altar boys!

Silence.

(*as herself*) Oh, David. Jesus, I'm— I didn't mean it like that. Or, okay, I probably did, but I didn't mean you. I mean you're not...you're not in that screwed-up category. Here's that category, and here's you. Not even close. I... I just meant... Shit.

I bought him tea and doughnuts next Sunday, my guilt-ridden apology gift, but he just looked at me totally bemused. I think I kept expecting him to get indignant about my lack of faith or the way I talked or something, but for some reason that didn't happen. Instead, he asked me to a movie. A film festival, actually, a Japanese film festival to which he already had tickets...

(*as herself*) I don't know, what if someone from church sees and thinks... something weird—

I told him, and he looked at me like I'd sprouted an extra head.

(*as* DAVID) Weird, like: look at those two people watching a movie in a public place? (*deadpan*) Oh, the scandal.

He took in my completely incredulous look and sighed.

(*as* DAVID) Fine, fine, yes, okay. But hear me out: I just want to have a normal night, watch some good samurai movies and have someone to talk to about them. Apart from seventy-five-year-old church ladies, I don't exactly have a lot of friends, since I left them all behind after seminary school. Honestly, I'd like to spend a night doing something besides sweeping the rectory and wondering how long it'll take me to turn into Father McNulty, asleep on the couch by nine, watching *Golden Girls* reruns. Come on. (*teasing*) I promise we won't get excommunicated.

I was ridiculously nervous. I hadn't been out with a guy, clergy or not, since Danny. Danny, the boyfriend I'd been with all through undergrad; Danny, who had the good taste to leave me a week after my mother's death. Maybe that's why I agreed to go with David: because I didn't feel any risk of anything on my end or his. Needless to say, I wasn't looking to hop right back in the saddle, and even less so with the parish priest.

I remember when I let slip to David the story, about my ex. I was in his office, in the rectory, organizing supplies for the Sunday school class.

(*as* DAVID) Liz, is everything okay?

I think I was going at the stapler a little too vehemently.

(*as herself to* DAVID, *irritably*) You taking confession right now?

(*as* DAVID) No… But I'd make an exception if you'd really *prefer* to go to one of the confessionals…

LIZ makes a show of pointedly ignoring DAVID and looking busy.

(*as* DAVID, *persisting*) Nice and dark, not a lot of elbow room…very appealing…

(*as herself*) It's nothing.

(*as* DAVID) The kind of nothing the parish is going to need a new stapler for…

(*as herself, sighs*) No offence, but I don't think you'd understand.

(*as* DAVID) There's always that possibility, but…if I can help, I want to, even if it's just to listen. I care about you, Liz, you know that.

(*as herself, reluctantly*) Danny called me from Vancouver. He said…a lot of things. And I said a lot of things. Most of which I'm thinking I can't repeat in a church. But basically, he's giving up. He broke it off. Apparently since Mom died, I'm too… "different."

(*in the present, to God*) I figured I was in for some scripture quoting or "pray to God for guidance." But I remember he just said:

(*as* DAVID) I'm sorry, Liz. Some people are just cowards.

That was it; simple. No pity, no platitudes. I admired that. I admired a lot about David. He believes, you know, and not just in God or in his calling to serve, but in goodness, real actual goodness, and that all it takes is the love of one person to make the world a less dark place.

(*transitioning back to memory. To* DAVID *in her memory:*) Brazil? How long would you be there?

(*as herself, to God*) We were out, five months later, on one of what became our many unsanctioned not-dates. We'd just gotten cones from Dairy Queen. Classically lame, but also kind of perfect.

(*as* DAVID) If they accept me and if we get that new deacon from Oakville… two years, I guess.

Two years.

And I realized in that moment, with the threat of him leaving for another continent, that it wasn't God, it wasn't the church, it wasn't my mother's faith I believed in. I believed in David. I felt renewed, I felt consoled, I felt at peace when I was around him. He listened, he supported me, and he offered me his whole self.

(*to God*) It wasn't You I was trying to get closer to at all. I didn't care what You thought. I cared what David thought, what David felt.

She turns and erases her name from the board.

(*as* DAVID) Liz?

(*as herself*) Don't go.

And the words were out before I really had any control over them.

(*as herself still*) I need you…

Pause.

(*as* DAVID) I need you, too.

LIZ *writes 'I need you' on the board.*

I think we tried to make small talk after that. But there was something in the way David looked at me, something about that admission that changed things from me being infatuated with a man who could never love me back, to words out of David's own mouth that he couldn't pretend hadn't spilled out. The realization scared us both, I think. Whatever we had been trying to deny was going on, was really going on. And what did that mean? Where the hell were we supposed to go from there?

They'll say I'm a slut, that I seduced him, a poor innocent man of the cloth. I thought about it then, still think about it now. If not a slut, then deranged. They'll whisper about how I'm some kind of stalker with a Daddy complex or a God complex or just an overactive imagination. If I don't get the dubious honour of at least being a Jezebel, then I'm stuck with "lonely and pathetic." And if they don't blame me, they'll call him a pervert. 'Well, of course," they'll say, "he's just another priest abusing his power. They were fresh out of altar boys, so Father found someone else's ass to — "

What about "They love each other"?

What about "Life happens"?

But in the week that followed my confession, denial came first, because it's easier. It's much, much easier to live safely, even if miserably.

LIZ *erases everything else on the board and writes: 'Doubting Thomas.'*

(*to her class*) There's an apostle in the Bible — Thomas — who, unlike the other disciples, can't believe that Jesus has risen from the dead. Even after they find the tomb empty, even after The Lord himself walks right up to Thomas, Christ has to make him touch the bloody holes in His body before the man will give over his belief. Thomas had the right idea.

At first we both chose denial. Some things are too much.

But some things you can't deny, not once someone comes and places your hands or your heart right into them.

LIZ erases 'Doubting Thomas.' Carefully writes 'David' on the board.

(*back to her imaginary class*) A long, long time ago in Israel, a shepherd named David proved his bravery and became king. When the giant Goliath challenged the Israelites to send out their champions to try to defeat him, they were all too afraid. But not David; he took only a sling and five small stones and defeated the giant. David could also make the most beautiful music, which was the only thing that could soothe King Saul, who had a very bad temper.

(*to God*) One night we were working late, David and I, getting Christmas Eve Mass organized. As we're coming back downstairs, there's this man, mid-forties, kind of hunched over in the pews. David hands me the keys and goes over to tell the guy we're closing up for the night. I'm imagining he came in off the streets to get warm or something, maybe fell asleep, but when David puts a hand on his arm, the guy jackknifes up faster than you can imagine and he's holding something and David takes a reflexive step back.

That's when I realize it's a gun.

This guy's been hanging out down here with a gun, waiting for what? Waiting for us to come down? I can feel my heart trying to claw its way up into my throat, and I'm far enough away that I can't hear what David's saying to the guy, but he's speaking in this calm, soft voice, like there isn't a total nut-job with a gun not a foot away from him. I can't go closer because the guy might just panic and get trigger-happy. I can't call out to David, I can't run for help. That's it.

But I'm standing there and I watch the guy get more and more wound up, and then he stands up and he's waving the gun around, yelling but slurring, so even now I can only make out a few things about his wife and his boss, but even if I could make it all out I doubt there's anything coherent going on there. David doesn't move, just keeps talking low and slow and calm, even as the guy's shouting over him. I'm sure in this moment we're all going to die and my heart and my brain are basically turning inside out.

And then a fire truck goes by outside, sirens blaring, and this guy with the gun in a church the night before Christmas Eve, he completely panics. He starts shouting at David that he called the cops and David's still trying to play it calm but I can't help myself, I yell:

It's a fire truck! It's just a fucking fire truck!

Silence.

It's like time freezes and it shuts the guy up. None of us are moving. We're just standing there in the half-lit church, this guy with his gun, me still clutching my cardboard box of art supplies for the kids, and David standing there palms upturned, non-threatening, but frozen like that.

And then it all happens at once. The guy drops the gun. David motions for me to go get help. I drop my box. Somehow, I remember how a phone works and I do finally call the cops and they come and they take the guy and David smiles sympathetically and squeezes his shoulder. And the cops question us. And David's shaking, like all that adrenaline was bottled up and held at bay and now it's engulfing him. And he tells me he's so glad I'm okay, doesn't know what he'd have done if I wasn't… And I take him for a drink to try to calm both our serrated nerves. And we have beers in a dingy bar like we're college kids. And then we're still too wired so we go for all-night breakfast. And then we go back to my place because neither of us wants to be alone. And then. And then. And then…

Pause.

(*to the class*) David was in his palace, when he looked out the window and saw a beautiful woman named Bathsheba. She was taking a bath on her rooftop above most prying eyes, except for the king's. So he called Bathsheba to him, and despite her being married to another man…they saw each other in secret. And soon after, she sent word to him that she was pregnant.

Pause.

She was carrying the child of the king who, against the law, against God himself, had taken her into his bed. Yes, the Almighty didn't like that too well, and the child, a son, died soon after he was born, and the rest of David's line was troubled and David himself punished for his indiscretion. King David fell out of favour with God because he dared to go after a woman not meant for him.

But what could he have done? Why would he go through all of that if it'd been as simple as going inside and taking his own, much colder bath that night? Why send down to her, why get her with child, why have her husband killed and risk the wrath of the Almighty if there was some way he could have stopped himself? A lesser man, playing the peeping Tom, or even taking their neighbour's wife for a spin, would hardly have earned themselves a personalized curse from God. David's main fault was being held up to a standard of perfection as king that most other men weren't accountable to, and when he fell from God's good graces, he downright plummeted.

Have mercy upon me, O God, according to Thy loving kindness: according to the multitude of Thy tender mercies.

(*to God*) I knew David felt guilty almost every morning. I knew he loved me, and he knew it as well, but I think the contradiction between loving me and loving You was impossible sometimes. It doesn't seem fair that that should have to be a choice though, that You and I should be mutually exclusive, does it?

There's a psalm that King David himself wrote, and I would hear him, David, my David, praying it sometimes, some mornings when he thought I was still asleep.

(*as* DAVID) *Have mercy upon me, O God, according to Thy loving kindness: according to the multitude of Thy tender mercies. Cast me not away from Thy presence: and take not Thy holy spirit from me. Restore unto me the joy of Thy salvation and uphold me. The sacrifices of God are a broken spirit: a broken and a contrite heart...*

(*as herself again*) I didn't have the same misgivings, especially not at first. I did feel guilty sometimes, but more in the anxious vein of: What if someone finds out? What if we get caught? If I didn't think about it too deeply, I could pretend it was like being back in high school, like being fifteen again and losing my virginity to Kyle Nichols behind the bleachers—a light, buzzing kind of guilt that never really went away.

(*as* DAVID) Liz?

Once again, I'm pulling the quilt up around me like I've never actually been this naked. I'm like Adam and Eve in the Garden of Eden putting fig leaves over themselves. Never mind the fact that they've been running around naked together all the livelong day already. Never mind that David and I just made love. I feel too naked suddenly.

(*as* DAVID) Liz, I need to tell you something.

Please don't. *Have mercy upon me O God, according to Thy loving kindness...* He needs to not be talking right now, because I've now remembered the second part of the story where I lost my virginity to Kyle Nichols behind the bleachers, the part where I go to the girls' bathroom and puke.

(*as* DAVID) My application got accepted to go to Brazil. They accepted me. I'm leaving in two weeks.

(*as herself in the present*) *The sacrifices of God are a broken spirit: a broken and a contrite heart.*

If he was going to go back to the role of self-sacrificing clergyman, I decided a vow of silence was the only answer. Maybe I'm just not ready to break the safety of that silence yet. I stopped seeing him, stopped speaking to him. I didn't return his calls and I took over planning all of my classes without any input from David. I wanted to start distancing myself right away. I told myself it would be easier. It's not.

I know medieval monks and nuns used to take vows of silence and would go days, weeks, months, years maybe, without speaking a word. But it feels like I have words and words and words building up behind my teeth, clenched with the sheer will of damming the tide. All of those words building up, pushing, pushing to be let out. I can imagine those medieval nuns, brimming to burst in a dark bare cell with nothing but a crucifix and a chamber pot beside the bed.

I have to tell him. I can't keep this in. (*to God*) Give me the strength to tell him. You will. You have to. Haven't I pleaded my case enough? He deserves to know this. We deserve to be able to love each other. I'm an okay person, a crappy Catholic but an okay person. But David, he believes in goodness, in love, in faith, and You're not the only one who can give that to him. He can have faith in me. He can have faith in us. He can choose me. The guilt will pass, and he'll still be the same old David. He'll still have faith and be the man I love. Even if he leaves the priesthood, even if he doesn't go to Brazil, and follow his calling or whatever, he can still be happy. I can make him happy…

Long pause.

Have mercy upon me, O God, according to Thy loving kindness: according to the multitude of Thy tender mercies.

Cast me not away from Thy presence: and take not Thy holy spirit from me.

Restore unto me the joy of Thy salvation and uphold me.

The sacrifices of God are a broken spirit: a broken and a contrite heart…

No more priesthood,

means no more church,

means no more faith:

means no more David.

A broken spirit.

He can't know.

Pause.

(*forcing a smile. To the imaginary class:*) Who can tell me what a martyr is?

There's a famous painting, of Saint Sebastian, who was a martyr. Does anyone know it? He's been struck by arrows. He's actually a human pincushion, but the painting is beautiful. Martyrdom is apparently beautiful. A saint, we believe, dies with a song of praise in his heart even with a sword straight through it, or an arrow.

Church bells. LIZ *goes and opens the door to let the children in.*

The End

The Stillbirth

by Kara Crabb

About the playwright

Kara Crabb is from Windsor, Ontario. She is a writer at *Vice* magazine. She lives in Montreal. *The Stillbirth* premiered in March 2010, at Concordia University's Winter SIPA/Short Works Festival (Student Initiated Production Assignments). Victor was played by Scott Humphrey; Chloe was played by Amy Kitz; it was directed by Kara Crabb; the set design was by Aaron Golish; and Norah Paton was the stage manager.

Characters

VICTOR — early 30s/late 20s
CHLOE — same age

Setting

In a small city in North America. 2010. An expensive restaurant, and a shitty gross alleyway.

Scene 1

VICTOR: (*To audience*) When I would entertain the idea of impregnating a woman — which wasn't often, actually, nor was it entertaining — I would get overwhelmed by this incredible sensation of disgust, and then I'd have to consciously refuse to acknowledge the likelihood of it ever happening to me. Obviously, that alone is not enough to prevent a child from…happening. They recommend, you know, birth control. I mean, I fear the continuation of my bloodline. This is rational; it is a rational fear. There's just no need for any more humans to be generated. In the grand scheme of things — the grandest scheme that I can imagine — who cares if we're here or not? The world would probably be a "better" place without us, anyway. I think population control is what environmentalists should be advocating. So, in addition to that, my parents are complete assholes, who are festering with swarms of hereditary diseases, really. What are we supposed to do? Take one for the team and don't have a kid. But. "But." There's always a "but." Procreation is designed to be accidental, I'm convinced. We're tricked into it, it's perfect.

There are only three types of animals that have sex for sheer pleasure — apparently — humans being one of them. Apes and dolphins are the others. They are the horniest animals and the smartest. That's the point: trickery. For instance, if dolphins weren't so horny all of the time, there probably wouldn't be any dolphins left, because they would just decide that they would rather travel around the world, or write a novel, or maybe just keep their vaginas intact — you know, the term "birth canal" is so repulsive. Sexual reproduction is a necessary accident. Consequence means nothing when she's next to you. On top of you. In and around you. The best part, or the worst part, I haven't decided yet, is that the outcome replaces everything that ever came before it. Then we're changed people.

I can't stop thinking about it. Where once my wife and I had seriously considered getting an, um, shma-shmor-tion, we are now trying to wrap our heads around the unpredictable termination of our unpredictable pregnancy. He somehow choked on his own umbilical cord, like a fucking idiot.

Scene 2

CHLOE and VICTOR are getting ready to go out.

CHLOE: Okay. There's this: up-do. Powerful, clean, sophisticated, but still feminine. Then there's this. Soft, full, delicate. You see the difference? What it does to my face? What do you think?

VICTOR: You look the exact same.

CHLOE: Really?

VICTOR: Yes.

CHLOE: It's too late now, I'll just keep it like this. Maybe we just shouldn't go. God! I know! Why do I care so much?

VICTOR: Your behaviour is unsettling.

CHLOE: Oh, my God. I look like a Victorian prostitute. But on, like, Christmas or something. Would a Victorian prostitute even celebrate Christmas?

VICTOR: Maybe they had block parties, just between the whores.

CHLOE: Should I wear different shoes? I shouldn't wear lipstick, that's it. Eh, Victor? Victor? It doesn't matter.

VICTOR: Chloe, would you like a compliment?

CHLOE: Yes.

VICTOR: You look exquisite. When we're in public and you go to hold my hand I feel rude because I feel I'm suddenly bragging.

CHLOE: (*laughs*) We should just stay in.

VICTOR: What?

CHLOE: (*mischievously hinting*) Maybe we should just stay in.

VICTOR: What, like sex?

CHLOE awkwardly nods her head.

VICTOR: We made reservations.

CHLOE: Of course, of course… It seems kind of crass to me, to go. It seems as if we're celebrating.

VICTOR: Excuse me?

CHLOE: Never mind. I don't know. Never mind.

VICTOR: What did you mean by that?

CHLOE: No, it's just, I mean, that we're healthy. We're moving on. We are alive. Do you think people think that we're insensitive?

VICTOR: What people, what are you talking about?

CHLOE: People say things, you know. Gossip.

VICTOR: Yeah…?

CHLOE: At work.

VICTOR: You heard people talking about you?

CHLOE: It was probably just my imagination. Do you think there will be anyone we know at the restaurant?

VICTOR: What, you don't want to go? We made reservations.

CHLOE: I want to go. Should we be acting sad?

VICTOR: We are sad.

CHLOE: Yes, I know, but.

VICTOR: Stop thinking so much.

CHLOE: It has been so long since I've felt, since I— There's nothing to be embarrassed about. I'm just making things complicated. I'm just paranoid. It's stupid.

VICTOR: Yeah, just take a breather.

CHLOE: Take the whole medicine cabinet.

Scene 3

CHLOE is sitting at table, drinking wine.

VICTOR: (*to audience*) It's interesting that absence can be so impactful. Maybe it's the only thing in life that truly is impactful. Is that crude? I don't think it is.

CHLOE: It is so quiet tonight.

VICTOR: It's just the things that people notice the most. Silences, and emptiness. Vacancies. It feels like foreshadowing.

CHLOE: It is Saturday. Why is no one here?

VICTOR: I know. I've never seen it like this before.

CHLOE: Is there something going on tonight?

VICTOR: Maybe Bono is in town?

CHLOE: God, what's the point? We are literally the only people here.

VICTOR: Hey, what are you drinking there? It looks to me that you're drinking out of a glass that's half-full.

CHLOE: Join me.

VICTOR: It's actually really weird to see you with that. I keep wanting to stop you.

CHLOE: Yeah, I'm flooding the sacred temple.

VICTOR: Jesus.

CHLOE: Are we staying here? Listen, I was thinking, and I want to be honest with you, Victor—I HAVE to be—so I'm just gonna say it: I've been feeling relieved. Really very much so relieved.

VICTOR: Me too.

CHLOE: Oh, good! I can't explain to you how terrified I was. And for the longest time I wasn't admitting it to MYSELF, let alone to anyone else. It's difficult now, even, to bring it up. But I just—I feel so heavy. Heavy and light. Heavy with guilt because I'm so light with relief? Does that make sense? I mean, like, maybe we really should be celebrating.

VICTOR: This *is* a much more pleasant setting than I imagined. I was expecting to see a gaggle of human beings waiting at the door. Just waiting. WAITING. It's absurd.

CHLOE: Ummmm?

VICTOR: Can you imagine living in a world where you didn't ever have to wait in some form of a line? How would you spend fifty percent of your day if not waiting in a line? You wouldn't know what to do with yourself.

CHLOE: (*drinking lots*) Yeah. Yeah. Well, maybe just bring a book with you.

VICTOR: If only it were that easy.

CHLOE: But it is that easy. My glass is looking regressively less full.

VICTOR: Oh, this should be interesting. Are you already buzzing?

CHLOE: Not really, I don't think my tolerance level is *that* low.

VICTOR: Of course, because you never did quit the drinking, did you?

CHLOE: You know very well I took good care of myself.

VICTOR: I was just kidding.

CHLOE: It's true though, I did take good care of myself.

VICTOR: I said I was just kidding.

CHLOE: I still have all of the vitamin supplements.

VICTOR: You have to start again, you know that?

CHLOE: Start what.

VICTOR: You have to ease your mind. It's just as important as taking care of your body. You need to relax.

CHLOE: That's what I've intended for the night. I really would like to have a nice evening outside of the house. Outside of familiarity... God, I'm exasperated! I wake up in the morning and I see my surroundings, I feel suffocated! (*checking menu*) How nice it is to be in a different setting. You can see the people on the street going about their own business.

VICTOR: You know Patrick?

CHLOE: Your co-worker?

VICTOR: I saw him eat an apple today. Have you ever really watched someone eat an apple?

CHLOE: You watched him eat an apple.

VICTOR: The sound! Oh, my God, the sound! And he's a fork-biter, too. Saw him eat his whole lunch. He chews with his mouth open. The whole package. It's disgusting. And I couldn't help but imagine his orgasm-face just looking the exact same way. (*imitates face*) Imagine that.

CHLOE: I'm sure.

VICTOR: Oh, I was so repulsed.

CHLOE: You must have some sort of complex.

VICTOR: When I watch the way *you* eat it never grosses me out.

CHLOE: (*genuine, glancing up from menu*) Thank you.

VICTOR: It's true.

CHLOE: Oh, Victor, listen to this, pan-seared scallops with orange-glazed smoked pork belly, and pomelo marmalade. It sounds amazing.

VICTOR: But you know, I hate seeing you with that wine glass. I want to whip it against the floor and watch it break. I can't help it.

CHLOE: Alaskan crab cake perfumed with coriander. My God. Sensational.

VICTOR: "Sensational." Yes, well, maybe it is too soon? Maybe there's another one in there, did you check?

CHLOE: Veal sweetbread and foie gras terrine with roasted hazelnuts. I'm getting that, I'm getting that.

VICTOR: You know, I would have named him Julio.

CHLOE: These are just hors d'oeuvres!

VICTOR: Chloe?

CHLOE: What are you going to have?

VICTOR: Spaghetti and meatballs, I don't know. I—

CHLOE: Boring, Victor. Really, there are so many interesting dishes here. I think the closest thing to spaghetti and meatballs is, like, quail-egg carbonara.

VICTOR: I don't care. Pick something out for me. I—

CHLOE: Pick something out for you? Haha! You know, I think we might be becoming a little too dependent on each other.

VICTOR: We're married.

CHLOE: So you trust my tastes, hmm?

VICTOR: Chloe, I've been having really weird dreams lately.

CHLOE: Nightmares?

VICTOR: I don't know if I would call them nightmares. But they do make me uneasy.

CHLOE: I know what you mean. How about the rare-roasted partridge with raspberry coulis?

VICTOR: I dream that I'm out of my body. Have you ever had a dream like that?

CHLOE: I usually don't remember my dreams.

VICTOR: These dreams of mine have been extremely vivid.

CHLOE: Maybe it's the baby. Trying to communicate with you.

VICTOR: A-Are you mocking me?

CHLOE: Well, that's what you wanted to hear, isn't it?

VICTOR: Pffffft. Whoa.

CHLOE: Oh, I'm sorry, I'm not trying to be cold, I'm sorry. Oh, I'm so sorry. That came out wrong.

VICTOR: It doesn't matter. I was just making conversation.

CHLOE: I'm sorry.

VICTOR: I know you don't think that it's spiritual.

CHLOE: I just wouldn't use that word to describe it. I think everything makes sense. I think it's, I think it's invisible stuff. More of a science than a mystique. Just a science, nothing grand or full of meaning. Maybe *I'll* get the rare-roasted partridge with raspberry coulis.

VICTOR: Nothing grand or full of meaning. Of course. "Naturally." Oh, what's the point? What's the point of all this?

CHLOE: There is no point, dear.

VICTOR: I don't know why I'm upset. I don't know what I want.

CHLOE: There *is* a lot to choose from.

VICTOR: I don't know what it's worth to us. The constant guilt. Paralyzed with decision-making. Or possibilities, rather!

CHLOE: The guilt! I know! It's torturing.

VICTOR: No matter what we choose there will always be the feeling of the death of some other possibility. Murdered by our choices.

CHLOE: Victor…

VICTOR: Ah! I sound crazy! I sound crazy! This is awful!

CHLOE: No, you don't. We just have a lot on our plates.

VICTOR: I'm obnoxious, with all of this gibberish.

CHLOE: Are you all right? We don't have to stay if you don't want to.

VICTOR: This is stupid. I'm a grown-ass man.

CHLOE: That's right, you're a grown man, therefore you are impenetrable.

VICTOR: Yeah. Let's just forget it. We'll just pour ourselves another drink and forget it.

CHLOE: Well. Don't drown your sorrows, though. We don't want to start any bad habits.

VICTOR: Oh, God.

Scene 4

VICTOR: (*to audience*) Oh, God. I know what it looks like. I know. And here's the thing: I don't want to be that guy stumbling into cafés with plastic bags on my feet, shouting about capitalism and Jesus. But I'm really starting to wonder how much that guy and I have in common… I've started developing nervous twitches, believe it or not. And I've started talking to myself. As if people are there listening… We've thought about going to therapy. And sure, that sounds great in theory. But there was a definitive moment in my youth when I decided I would never see a therapist again. I was thirteen and I was depressed and I was in the waiting room, on my sixth or seventh appointment with Dr. Schwartzman — this name will never escape me — right then, a doctor from down the hallway came bursting in, absolutely bawling, grabbed my chair, fell down on his knees and cried in my face: "DR. SCHWARTZMAN IS DEEAAD!" My therapist fucking killed himself. My psychologist shot himself in the cerebellum and now I can never trust another one ever again. If I go crazy, there won't be any chance of coming back. Those plastic bags will give me trench foot and they will stay there until even after I decompose. But I'm not going to go crazy. I won't turn into that guy.

Scene 5

CHLOE is drunk.

CHLOE: Took you long enough!

VICTOR: Those bathrooms are phenomenal, Chloe, you have to see them. *Luxury toilet paper.* Can you believe it? Made of one hundred percent virgin pulp for "maximum softness." That's what it said: "maximum softness." I took an entire roll. It's in my jacket.

CHLOE: I can't believe we made reservations at an empty restaurant. It's not fair.

VICTOR: Oh, it's such a tough world isn't it, Chloe?

CHLOE: It is a tough world.

VICTOR: And it's only going to get worse.

CHLOE: Not for us. We'll be dead before shit really hits the fan. With the bi-polar bears, icebergs — lettuce, you know, no more seeds to plant vegetables is what I mean. They said bananas are going extinct, remember? It's bullshit, I love bananas. I love bananas. I eat bananas like four — maybe five ti — FIVE TIMES a week.

VICTOR: You ought to make a complaint.

CHLOE: I should.

VICTOR: Send an email.

CHLOE: god@hotmail.com. No wait, gmail, gmail.

VICTOR: Absolutely. I mean I can't imagine a world without bananas.

CHLOE: Or imagination itself.

VICTOR: Or imagination itself. I know, you're right.

CHLOE: Oh, God, it's going to be so horrible.

VICTOR: In all fairness though, we deserve whatever's coming to us.

CHLOE: Don't pull that card. It's too easy. It's not even worth mentioning. Personally, I refuse to accept responsibility for — for — anything! I can't help what I do.

CHLOE accidentally knocks over her wine glass with an emphatic gesture. It spills on the tablecloth.

VICTOR: Did you want to use this toilet paper?

She pours salt on the stain.

CHLOE: Ah, that was a close one.

VICTOR: "Close."

CHLOE: Salt takes out the stain, did you know that? It's my trick.

VICTOR: Of course I know that, how could I forget the time you tore open a packet of salt —

CHLOE: Oh, yeahah.

VICTOR: And sprinkled it on my genitals?

CHLOE: On your pants, if you do recall.

VICTOR: While I was driving.

CHLOE: You made a mess.

VICTOR: We almost got in an accident.

CHLOE: But we didn't. And you liked it.

VICTOR: So that's — that's how you get stains out.

CHLOE: I could make a really wonderful housewife.

VICTOR: The sad part is that I wish you believed that.

CHLOE: Are you being nice to me?

VICTOR: I suppose.

CHLOE: What makes you think I don't believe it? Why would I say it if there wasn't a silver of truth. Sliver. (*hiccup*)

VICTOR: You can convince yourself of anything. It's endearing.

CHLOE: Don't re-instill that notion in me. It breaks my heart. It does.

VICTOR: I idolize you.

CHLOE: Don't bully me, Victor.

VICTOR: You haven't seen anything yet.

CHLOE: What do you want?

VICTOR: You know what I want. I want what any person wants. But the world won't give it to me.

CHLOE: It's not the world, it's just a matter of timing. Haha, everything is a matter of timing. It's um, it's nothing to be embarrassed about.

VICTOR: I'm not embarras—

CHLOE: Look at the stain!

VICTOR: Where?

CHLOE: Exactly.

VICTOR: I don't know what to believe.

CHLOE: Fuuhhh. I'm sick of all this tiptoeing around! We sound crazy. And I'm never distracted for long enough. I smile and then I realize where I am. I hate being nervous always.

VICTOR: You don't seem nervous to me at all.

CHLOE: You keep bringing me back to it, you asshole. Can't we rid ourselves of it, can we? When I'm awake, so awake, I feel like I'm standing on a stage in front of people, everyone's looking at me, I'm isolated, captured by a single spotlight. Or a desk lamp in a detective's room. Or in headlights, and I'm a deer. Or on a hospital bed, with doctors crowding around me. And I'm silenced by a mask, and my vision is blurring, and I'm scared but I can't help myself from feeling sleepy. And someone produces a sharp blade from their laboratory coat and it glistens "SHRING" and they're wearing a headband with another—LIGHT! and I can't see their face because *they're* wearing a mask too; and glasses, they're wearing GLASSES that only reflect, you can't see through them, you just see yourself. But I can't recognize myself, I just understand that that there, is me. And then the blade becomes motorized and it's coming closer, and I'm trying to protect my middle, and who is hiding beneath it, but all of my limbs are numb and I can't FEEL them to MOVE them. And it's all so bright, so, so bright, all I see is white even when I shut my eyes! We're both so nervous, but I have to fall asleep, I have to submit myself to what I don't want to know, and I leave him all alone. And I know that I won't remember at all. I won't remember exactly what we were like. I have experienced us so uniquely, so vividly, and now I'm detached, and it's all just fucking gone.

Pause. VICTOR *is looking around the room.*

CHLOE: I'm here, AREN'T I? I wanted a cure!

VICTOR: Chloe, you're wincing.

She lets out a tiny hysterical pout.

VICTOR: You look like a crumpled-up paper bag.

CHLOE: I don't want you to bring me back to this earth again. Please.

VICTOR: I'm not sure if I'm going to bring you back into public again.

CHLOE: It is within these moments of sobriety—

VICTOR: Sobriety.

CHLOE: That I hate to be an intelligent creature.

VICTOR: Oh, my God.

CHLOE: I hate what it is that, they say, separates us from animals. Memory, and knowing. I don't want to remember! I don't want to know! I find the separation to be — an impairment!

VICTOR: What is this really about?

CHLOE: Everyone knows about it. At work. The women. Silence when I enter the room. They won't smile or make eye contact. They cross sides of the hallway in order to avoid me. Wait until I leave the coffee machine.

VICTOR: You're not alone in this, Chloe, please.

CHLOE: I don't want to cry tonight. I don't want to cry tonight.

VICTOR: Grief is hard for people.

CHLOE: I hate it.

VICTOR: I love you.

CHLOE's emotions intensify.

VICTOR: Come on. You're okay. You're okay.

CHLOE: Oh. Oh. Onions, raw onions, chopped and diced.

VICTOR: No, come on, babe.

CHLOE: Stop, stop.

VICTOR hugs her, he kisses her. She sighs.

CHLOE: You know what we should dooo when we get hooome?

VICTOR: What?

CHLOE: Call up a therapist.

VICTOR: A-are you serious?

CHLOE: YES, I'm serious!

VICTOR: Why!

CHLOE: Oh, you're so difficult!

VICTOR: Do I have to explain this to you? Do you know what it requires to be a psychologist? Loose screws, my dear. Loose screws. You're better off talking to a garbage can.

CHLOE: A garbage can! You're just so smart, aren't you? You want to talk about feelings. I'm having nightmares, too.

VICTOR: We don't have to talk about feelings.

CHLOE: What do you want from me! Do you want me to become an emotional eater or something? Is that what you want? (*eating handfuls*)

VICTOR: I just don't see the point. At all.

CHLOE: It would be healthy.

VICTOR: I don't know, we could read self-help books instead, it's practically the same thing.

CHLOE: You have to forget about that stupid doctor.

VICTOR: Doctor Schwartzman.

CHLOE: You're so stubborn.

VICTOR: We should focus on something else. Something fun, creative. Stop dwelling. That's all it takes.

CHLOE: I never thought I was one to dwell.

VICTOR: Oh, you're a dweller.

CHLOE: I really don't think I am… You are! Your dwelling is preventing us from getting help.

VICTOR: I am doing you a favour.

CHLOE: (*threat*) Should we discuss this at home, Victor?

VICTOR: Hey. I think what we need is to get out in the world and experience something new.

CHLOE is rolling her eyes and shaking her head.

VICTOR: Come on, really, I mean it. Let's have some fun.

CHLOE: You want to do something. You want to start doing water aerobics together on the weekend or some shit?

VICTOR: Chloe. I want dessert. I have an idea. And I want champagne. The best champagne.

CHLOE: Oh?

VICTOR: Let's do something fun.

CHLOE: Dessert.

VICTOR: And champagne and—(*whispering*)—imagine running through the streets of the night.

CHLOE: (*whisper*) Yes.

VICTOR: (*whisper*) Like a wild panther.

CHLOE: Why are we whispering?

VICTOR: We're going to have FUN. How are you doing? Are you okay? You okay?

CHLOE: I'm okay, but—

VICTOR: Good, you're good. I fucking hate this restaurant.

CHLOE: You do?

VICTOR: We're going to have dessert and we're going to disappear.

CHLOE: Hahaha what do you want, to "dine n' dash"?

VICTOR just looks at her.

CHLOE: Pah!

VICTOR: Come on.

CHLOE: All right. Screw dessert.

VICTOR: Is anybody looking?

CHLOE: Probably.

They begin to put on their things casually and slowly leave the table arm in arm, maybe whistling. They slowly strut through what would be the door, and then they bolt. They run away holding hands until they feel they've cleared it. VICTOR is panting, out of breath. CHLOE laughs a little. They abruptly start making out and groping each other.

VICTOR: Let's make another little fuckin' baby.

CHLOE: We are in an alleyway.

VICTOR: So, good.

CHLOE: We've never done this outside before.

VICTOR: Julio is a myth!

CHLOE: Who's Julio?

VICTOR: Fiction.

CHLOE: Mmm, oh, Victor. Victor, stop, stop, stop. We are guaranteed to come out of here with chlamydia.

VICTOR: (*clapping his hands in song*) It's curable.

CHLOE: This is weird.

VICTOR: Ah, I feel so exhilarated!

CHLOE: Hey, look what I grabbed.

She produces a wine bottle from her coat.

VICTOR: Is this from the restaurant? Ha, how did you do that? I didn't even notice.

CHLOE: I had a pretty big shoplifting phase when I was fourteen.

VICTOR: That's awesome! Next time we should rob a bank!

CHLOE: I can't believe we just fucking ran! Oh, my God! I haven't felt so — so — sneaky in ages.

They start touching each other.

CHLOE: But I feel like I'm forgetting something.

VICTOR: I feel like I wanna split you in half with my dick.

They are kissing deeply for a moment and then CHLOE *pulls away, suddenly horrified.*

CHLOE: We had reservations.

VICTOR: What?

CHLOE: We had reservations.

VICTOR: We had reserve — WE HAD RESERVATIONS.

CHLOE: YOU'RE SUCH A DUMBASS.

VICTOR: Could we go to jail for something like this?

CHLOE: No!

VICTOR: So what happens?

CHLOE: (*thinking that is an absurd question*) I don't know.

VICTOR: So…

He leans to kiss her.

CHLOE: Oh, my God. We should go back.

VICTOR: "Back"?

CHLOE: To the restaurant.

VICTOR: But we ran so far!

CHLOE: You are out of shape. You're getting fat!

VICTOR: Huhhhwhat!

CHLOE: You wouldn't last one minute in water aerobics.

VICTOR: How dare you.

CHLOE: We have to go back.

VICTOR: No. No! Gosh darn it, no! We cannot sheepishly retract all of that passion! That youthfulness and virility! Be proud, Chloe!

CHLOE: "PROUD?"

VICTOR: What, are you afraid of getting sent to the principal's office?

CHLOE: Fuck off. We just stole from people.

VICTOR: God, don't call it "stealing." I hate that; what a fluffy manipulation of words that is. Plus, it's not like they don't "steal" from us. And what about that bottle of wine that you took?

CHLOE: That's different.

VICTOR: How is that different?

CHLOE: Do you want to know how I feel right now?

VICTOR: Oh, oh, how do you *feel*, Chloe?

CHLOE: I feel like I am married to a pubic louse on the scrotum that is our planet earth. That's how I feel right now.

VICTOR: I could do without this attempt at moralizing.

She opens her wine bottle. She starts to talk to a garbage can.

CHLOE: Hello, Mr. Therapist, I am on the verge of a massive bodily hiatus.

VICTOR: However!

CHLOE: I just want to die. I just wanna fuckin' end it right now.

VICTOR: HOWEVER, I agree that we should maybe do something about this situation on ha—

CHLOE: I feel like I'm going to start to kill people pretty soon.

VICTOR: LET ME FINISH.

CHLOE: Better yet, O Mr. Therapist, would you happen to know any divorce lawyers? Could you just direct me towards one right now? (*looking around the alleyway*)

VICTOR: Hahaha, divorce lawyer, that's a bold one, Chloe. And have you noticed that I'm right? That speaking to the garbage can is as equally progressive as speaking to a therapist?

CHLOE: What were you trying to accomplish? Who does this? We are not teenagers, we are not poor or desperate.

VICTOR: No. We are the latter, actually. Just because we're well off, in terms of the green, and the copper and nickel...doesn't change the fact that we are still oozing with desperation, in another realm, though. Can I propose a solution, please?

CHLOE: I don't know if I can handle listening to you speak any more.

VICTOR: We calm down and stop worrying about it, for one.

CHLOE: Pffft.

VICTOR: Yeah, listen: Tomorrow morning we call the restaurant, explain the situation, apologize to some people, give them our credit card number, whatever. It's really that simple. Then we'll just have a beautiful breakfast together, and maybe some afternoon delight.

CHLOE: More like Turkish delight.

VICTOR: That doesn't even make sense.

CHLOE: It makes sense in that I would rather eat the world's most unappealing snack than have sex with you right now.

VICTOR: God, I'm not the one who cares so much. I could give two shits if we're never allowed back at that restaurant.

CHLOE: Fine, we'll call them in the morning, I don't care. I just don't care anymore.

VICTOR: Okay, so when we explain our situation to them, it will obviously have to be much more creative. Example: "We were so intoxicated, perhaps because your waiters failed to stop serving us alcohol, and were taking so long with the bill, that by a restless and drunken decision to leave, we simply forgot to pay you. Sorry."

CHLOE: I want to see a therapist.

VICTOR: I'm sorry? I don't think I heard you properly.

CHLOE: We are NOT WELL. Why are we committing petty juvenile acts, why are we arguing in the middle of a disgusting alleyway, why are we going out for dinner, like a happy dating couple, ignorant to all of the terrible things that happen to you when you try to merge two people into one, person, who — who — AGH!

She throws the wine bottle and it smashes against a wall.

VICTOR: CALM DOWN. You know, they'll just give you all the wrong answers anyway. They'll tell you that you're subconsciously trying to alleviate some sort of emotional trauma, or something totally implausible like that!

CHLOE: I don't see why you're being such a little bitch about it. It would be healthy for us.

VICTOR: Because I have had a rough past with that kind of stuff.

CHLOE: Oh, really? DO YOU WANT TO TALK ABOUT IT?

VICTOR: Suck my ball sack, Chloe.

CHLOE: What ball sack?

VICTOR: Ha! You, of all people, have no right to denigrate my reproductive organs.

CHLOE: What does *that* mean?

VICTOR: You're the one with the Venus flytrap of a uterus. You've got a fucking black hole up there.

CHLOE: I'm leaving.

VICTOR: No, wait, I'm sorry! I didn't mean to say that!

CHLOE: You are so mean to me. You think that just because you're witty and you don't yell that it means you're not mean? You are mean.

VICTOR: No, I wasn't trying to hurt your feelings.

CHLOE: What were you "trying" to do?

VICTOR: I don't know!

CHLOE: Trying to make a point? Is that what you were doing?

VICTOR: No.

CHLOE: Well, you made your point! It wasn't my fault! So what if I wasn't meant to be a mother, at least I can be honest with myself! I'm not some pathetic — I'm not filled with some grand deception of hope! Oh, God. It's not my fault. Why don't you say something now, Victor? Say SOMETHING for once. Something beyond your "I don't knows" and your little jokes. You think you're so funny.

VICTOR: Okay. I'm sorry that I compared your uterus to a carnivorous plant.

CHLOE: FUCK OFF!

VICTOR: I'm trying to be sincere! I don't know where to begin with you anymore. You've become so sensitive!

CHLOE: No, Victor, you're just a goddamn idiot.

VICTOR: (*blurts out*) I wish you believed in something! That's — that's what I want to say! I wish you would believe in something: a mystique, not a science. Or I wish that you were *happy* believing in nothing. I wish you would abandon your sense of purpose! It's too strong. It's much too strong. It ruins everything, Chloe. Don't you see it? It ruins everything. You try to protect yourself from being hurt, you're so skeptical, you bring it upon yourself. You fuck everything up when you fear that there is no reward. Don't you see how crippling it is!

CHLOE: How can you still accuse me of this? You think I'm responsible for it? Because of my attitude? It doesn't work like that. How naive you are.

VICTOR: No, you're not listening. You're just getting defensive.

CHLOE: I feel like I'm being attacked. Over and over again.

VICTOR: Just forget it. I'm not blaming you for what happened. (*VICTOR is emotionally breaking down now.*) I would never, EVER. I love you, Chloe. We are in this together!

CHLOE: You don't think I'd be a good mother.

VICTOR: Oh, my God. *YOU* don't think that you'd be a good mother! And that's the point!

CHLOE: That is NOT true.

VICTOR: You just said that.

CHLOE: No, I said maybe I wasn't "meant to be" a mother. If you were listening, you would have known that.

VICTOR: What does that even mean! It sounds like a bad excuse. An excuse for what? For selfishness?

CHLOE: Yeah, I guess I'm just selfish, Victor.

CHLOE is crying.

CHLOE: Why are you so mad at me? I'm not a monster. I didn't mean for anything bad to happen.

VICTOR: You make me feel like I'm putting too much of myself on the line sometimes, because you — you don't want to appear vulnerable? What is it? I wanted this so badly. I know how shitty you feel, Chloe. You don't need to talk to a therapist, I'm right HERE. You need to talk to ME.

CHLOE: (*shocked realization*) I don't want to appear vulnerable.

VICTOR: Look at me.

CHLOE: Oh, Victor, I just want— Everything— It hurts. I am. Afraid. And it hurts so badly.

VICTOR: I know how much it hurts, believe me, I do.

CHLOE: Victor, it's so powerful, and that startles me. I'm really very startled by my capacity to…love. And yes, how vulnerable that makes me. I don't want to keep hurting. I don't want to get hurt.

VICTOR: I know. I know. You are so full of love. And that's a good thing. It's good.

CHLOE: You're just so okay with everything, with, with looking ahead. I'm not equipped with that underlying optimism… It seems naive? To me.

VICTOR: Naive because—

CHLOE: (*sobs*) Because creation is not harmonious in itself.

VICTOR: You can't carry those expectations.

CHLOE: I wish I didn't! I need help. I want to feel better, Victor! Better!

VICTOR: Okay. Okay then.

CHLOE: You understand?

VICTOR: Listen, I'll set up an appointment if that means that much to you. I'm sorry. But you have got to open up to me.

CHLOE: I will. I'm sorry. I'm so sorry.

VICTOR: I can't believe how much we wanted it. After everything.

CHLOE: That's all it does, is hurt.

They are grabbing onto each other tightly.

CHLOE: We are changed people. We have new territory. To protect.

VICTOR: I don't want to deny how much this means for us.

CHLOE: Neither do I!

VICTOR: I'm glad.

CHLOE: (*smiling weakly*) It's so fucking scary.

VICTOR: Yup.

CHLOE *laughs about it a little bit.*

VICTOR: I feel sick to my stomach.

CHLOE: I know, whenever I think of it.

VICTOR: I don't know if it's the alcohol, or, or objective truth.

CHLOE: Yeah, fuck, the world is spinning a little bit.

VICTOR: Yeah, it *ACTUALLY* is. Like in outer space, but also inside of my head. Inner space.

CHLOE: (*touching her stomach*) Everything is so round.

VICTOR: My stomach.

CHLOE: Are you okay?

VICTOR: I'll be fine.

CHLOE: I can't believe that just happened. What a strange night. Feel the air, how cool it is?

VICTOR vomits all over himself.

CHLOE: OH!

VICTOR: I am sick.

CHLOE: Your suit.

VICTOR: Fucking quail eggs.

CHLOE: Give me that toilet paper.

VICTOR: No, I don't want you to waste it on this. I'll just brush it off.

CHLOE: Ah, we have to get you home. Come on, we'll get a taxi.

VICTOR: I'll go topless. I'll go topless.

CHLOE: Yeah, maybe just leave the jacket part on.

VICTOR: We should go streaking.

CHLOE: Victor… You look beautiful.

VICTOR: Shut up.

CHLOE: I mean it. I love you. I want to make love to you RIGHT NOW.

She thinks it funny and he starts smiling devilishly.

VICTOR: Oh, yeah? Yeah?

He grabs her and kisses her all over her face.

CHLOE: Ahh! Stop! Ahh! TAXI! TAXI!

CHLOE exits.

VICTOR: Where once we had considered many things—

CHLOE: (*offstage*) VICTOR!

VICTOR: Now there is nothing to consider. Everything just perfectly is.

CHLOE: (*offstage*) Victor?

VICTOR: She said, "To be fair, we didn't really know him that well." And we laughed because it was true. We laughed because it was also a complete lie. We cried because. Because. Be cause… The very best things I know are without an identifiable cause, and so really I don't *know* them at all. I have them, I'm in them, I'm of them. I am lost, innocent. Am I making any sense? Well, it was here that I gave up my brain. It was giving me a headache. So it was here that I found out what to do. She said calmly and sweetly, "Let's just take our time." And yes, then the whole world appeared.

He runs after her, exiting.

The End

The Kharkiv Letters

by Alexa Gilker

About the playwright

Alexa Gilker works as a freelance writer based out of Victoria, BC, where she lives in a big orange house with four of her favourite women and a cat that isn't really theirs. She will soon be graduating with a B.F.A. in creative writing from the University of Victoria with a focus on poetry and playwriting. The story of *The Kharkiv Letters* was sparked from research on the many faces of human trafficking.

Characters

MASHA — 25, Strong-willed Ukrainian woman, blonde and beautiful
KATYA — 43, Masha's mother, once pretty, but roughened from a hard life
VLAD — 26, Masha's unemployed boyfriend, tall, skinny, wears a muscle shirt, leather jacket, and fake gold necklaces
VIKTOR — 40, Masha and Katya's landlord, too suave, too charming

Setting

Outside a rundown townhouse in the present day industrial city of Kharkiv, Ukraine, during an unusual summer heat wave.

Scene 1

Lights up on a street sidewalk. Centre stage is the front stoop of a rundown townhouse. There are three steps leading up to a front door; the door has a faded Ukrainian flag hanging above it. A mailbox beside the door has mail sticking out of the top. A street broom leans next to the door. On stage left is a group of overflowing trash cans.

VLAD stumbles onto stage from stage left, awkwardly carrying MASHA in his arms.

MASHA: Put me down! I'm not an animal!

VLAD: (*grunting*) It's romantic.

MASHA juts her elbow into his side, he drops her and keels over in pain. MASHA flops down onto the stoop.

MASHA: Gawd, it's hot out.

VLAD recovers but gets down on one knee in front of MASHA.

VLAD: Masha, darling—

MASHA: Oh, not today, Vlad.

VLAD: (*grandly*) For seven years, ever since high school—

MASHA: Get up before people see you!

VLAD: Masha, will you—

MASHA: I have told you for the millionth time not to propose to me on Mondays.

VLAD: It's Tuesday, baby.

MASHA: New rule. Tuesdays are out.

VLAD: But, baby, I love you. You're going to have to say yes to me one of these days, or I'm gonna find some other girl.

MASHA: You wouldn't dare.

VLAD: You know how many girls want this?

He gestures to his crotch. MASHA gets up to go inside.

VLAD: After my show last night I was beating the girls away, literally swatting them like this—

He swats her behind.

MASHA: Hey!

VLAD: Come on, baby. Marry me and all your dreams will come true.

MASHA: And then what, Vlad? Move into your shithole apartment with Alex and Yosyp? Leave Mama to support herself until she dies—

VLAD: We'll move out—

MASHA: How? You won't even take the job Alex scrounged up for you at the plant.

VLAD: The band's about to make it big, I've told you, I can't take time to fool around at the plant. I have to focus on my music.

MASHA: Oh, great. Well, you focus on your music and I'll focus on trying to find a job so Mama doesn't have to work herself to death and so you can *hoy* around like a *schlob* —

VLAD puts his arms around her, holds her to him.

VLAD: Let's go upstairs, hey?

MASHA: There's no air conditioning. It'll be a sauna in there.

VLAD: Baby, when are you gonna be mine? You know I'm crazy about you.

MASHA: I know.

VLAD: I'll give you whatever you want. I'll fix everything.

MASHA: My father used to say that. You're going to stop us from losing the apartment?

VLAD: Baby —

MASHA: 'Cause that's what going to happen, Vlad. If I can't find another job, soon. Can you fix that?

KATYA struggles up to the stoop with a bag from the pharmacy.

KATYA: (*to VLAD*) Make yourself useful, why don't you?

VLAD leaps up to help with the bags.

VLAD: Katya, baby, you're looking fine today.

KATYA: There's enough heat in the air without you opening your mouth today, Vlad. Phew! How is any decent woman supposed to keep her modesty on a day like today?

She ties her shirt up above her stomach while crossing herself.

MASHA: Did you rob the pharmacy today?

KATYA: I can't help that they all expire on the days I work. You're not going to believe what I got! Vitamins, some old anti-inflammatory pills, these weird little pills for tooth plaque —

VLAD: Did you get those ones for that little problem I asked you about?

KATYA pretends to look for them.

KATYA: Yes, I think —

She smacks him on the back of the head.

KATYA: *SCHLOB*! You think I'd steal for you?

VLAD: Well, you stole my heart.

MASHA: Honestly, Vlad, at least try to pretend you're in love with me, not her.

KATYA: Ha! You're not buttering me up to him, today. Not a chance.

KATYA notices the mail in the mailbox, rifles through it. VLAD rifles through the bag, pulls out a box of condoms.

VLAD: Oo, baby, guess what we're doing tonight?

MASHA: Looking for jobs?

VLAD: Why you got to be like that, baby?

KATYA: It worked! Our lives are saved! Thank St. Andrew!

MASHA: What's happened, Mama?

KATYA: What's happened is that I've saved our lives. I've saved *your* life, and here's the proof.

She shoves a letter into MASHA*'s face.* MASHA *grabs it from her hand.*

MASHA: Heavenly Hearts International Marriage Agency.

KATYA: That's just the agency it goes through. Read the return address.

MASHA: Jonah Harris, Quesnel, British Columbia, CANADA? What have you done?

KATYA: Your future husband! From Canada! Just think, my little Maria going off to the West, marrying a nice, rich Western man—

VLAD: Let me see that!

He yanks the letter from MASHA. KATYA *yanks it from him, hands it to* MASHA.

KATYA: Maybe even sending for old Katya when she's settled. I can quit the pharmacy. Oh, that reminds me, I brought you some new pills, they make your skin glow like a peach.

KATYA *digs in the bag for the pills.*

KATYA: Well, open it!

MASHA *tears the envelope open, pulls out a letter.*

MASHA: (*reading*) "Maria"—

VLAD: Maria? He uses *my* girlfriend's formal name?

MASHA: "I first want to tell you how beautiful you are in your profile picture." What profile?

KATYA: Your cousin Svetlana showed me how; I made a profile for you on the website—

MASHA: *What* website, Ma?

KATYA: Heavenly Hearts International Marriage Agency! Svetlana said all her friends do it and they get all kinds of letters, from the American men especially, who can't wait to find a beautiful, obedient, Ukrainian wife—

MASHA: *Obedient?*

VLAD: They don't know Masha very well.

KATYA: Oh, Masha, you will be so happy in Canada!

MASHA: No one is going to Canada, Ma. I've heard about these websites.

KATYA: Svetlana said—

MASHA: And you can't make decisions like that for me! I'm going to get a job soon and I'm going to school—

VLAD: And my band is about to explode—

KATYA: (*to* VLAD) Into rotten pieces of no-good, unemployed *bezlads* who ruin the lives of all the young woman around here!

MASHA: Mama, Vlad's band is getting pretty big.

VLAD: Thank you, baby.

KATYA: Pretty big like how Aneta Babacio is getting pretty big?

MASHA: You can't just sell me off to some rich —

KATYA: Masha, honey, you are getting so old. None of the other girls your age are single still —

VLAD: That's what I keep telling her.

KATYA: We are women. We need men.

VLAD: That's what I —

KATYA: (*to* VLAD) Can you even grow a beard?

MASHA: Ma, it's the twenty-first century. We can do this on our own.

KATYA: It's not about the century, it's about Ukraine. It's about Kharkiv. You see this street? You see all the women sitting out here like us? Who do you think is supporting them? We are all one pay cheque away from losing what little we have, Masha. The idea of women in this century is nice. But we are not yet those women here. Now, try these.

She tries to feed some pills into MASHA*'s mouth.*

MASHA: Ma! Stop it! I'm not a child.

KATYA: Your skin will be like peaches —

MASHA: Fine, then Vlad and I are getting married.

VLAD: We are?

MASHA: Well, eventually, yeah.

KATYA: Oh, Maria, don't tell me this —

MASHA: We are, we're getting married. Vlad proposed and I said…yes. Isn't that what you want?

VLAD: Oh, baby, we'll be so happy!

KATYA: But — but —

MASHA: If it's a man that will save me, then that's that, isn't it? I guess we can just tear this up.

VLAD *grabs the letter and envelope.*

KATYA: I meant —

MASHA: You meant what? You meant that you'd rather I sell myself to some man in Canada so we don't lose our house? Is that what you want?

KATYA: I want you to have a better life than I did.

VLAD: Hey, there's money in here!

He pulls out a hundred dollars.

KATYA: We're saved!

VLAD: How much is that?

KATYA: That's, I mean that's about a thousand *grivna.*

MASHA: We can't accept that.

KATYA: Are you crazy? You know we can't pay our rent this month.

MASHA: Rip it up, Vlad.

He hesitates. MASHA *grabs the money and the letter and tears them both in half.*

KATYA: NO!

VLAD: No!

MASHA: What? It was mine. I can do what I want with it.

She moves towards the door.

KATYA: It's a furnace in there.

MASHA: I have a job interview. I've got to change.

She exits into the townhouse.

VLAD: So…what do you think I should wear to the wedding?

KATYA: You think I'm going to let my daughter end up like me in five years when you get bored and leave her for some desperate younger woman? Well, I won't let it happen. Now get out of here. Go make trouble somewhere else.

VLAD: Katya, I love her.

KATYA: Shoo!

VLAD: Only because I want to go!

He exits. KATYA *waves to someone across the street.*

KATYA: Ai! Aneta! Did you hear what happened to Inna?

She wanders offstage. MASHA *comes back outside, dressed in nicer clothes for her job interview.* VIKTOR *enters silently, sneaks up behind her as she locks the door, and puts his arms around her waist.* MASHA *turns abruptly.*

MASHA: My mother is right there!

VIKTOR: It's about time we let her in on our little secret, don't you think?

MASHA: Don't say it like that, like it's good.

VIKTOR: Oh, you're going to hurt my feelings, Maria.

MASHA: DON'T call me that. I have to go.

VIKTOR: Where you gonna go without me?

MASHA: I have a job interview, and when I get this job, things stop with us, you got that? I'll pay you back.

VIKTOR: Do you know how many months you owe me?

MASHA: I'll pay you back, I said. Now, let go of me.

She tries to elbow past him, but he intercepts her.

VIKTOR: Masha, Masha. If the cow isn't milked, he's going to kick.

MASHA: Cows are female, Viktor.

VIKTOR: You said it, darling. Not me. Now, come on—

MASHA: I'm going to be late.

VIKTOR: (*yelling*) Oh, Katya!

MASHA: Shut up! What are you doing?

VIKTOR: Paying my end of the deal, fair and square.

MASHA: Please, please not today. Not now. Look, I've got—

She digs in her purse, pulls out the ripped pieces of money.

MASHA: This is American—

VIKTOR: *Was* American.

MASHA: It's still good, a bit of tape, it's a lot of money. This should cover this rent and the next.

VIKTOR: (*aggressively*)You little *sooka*. I'm not playing this game. Get in the house.

MASHA: Not today. I'll get this job. I'll get this money fixed. I'll—

She scoots away from his grip, runs offstage.

Lights fade.

Scene 2

KATYA sits on the stoop, writing a letter. MASHA enters from stage left, tripping over the garbage cans.

MASHA: *Hivno!* (*to offstage*) What are you looking at, hmm? You people just chuck your garbage all over the street now? Is there no pride in us anymore?

KATYA: Watch your mouth. No one wants a girl with dirty lips.

MASHA: Have you even gone inside yet?

KATYA: Too hot. I'd die on the stairs.

MASHA crumples onto the stoop, puts her head in her hands. Her cellphone rings.

MASHA: *Privet?* (*pause*) I'm not in the mood for this, Vlad. (*pause*) Ugh, fine. I'm wearing my work clothes for the job interview. (*pause*) No, the long skirt. (*pause*) That's disgusting.

She hangs up on him.

KATYA: So...how did it go?

MASHA: Why are you even asking?

KATYA: What happened?

MASHA: Nothing happened. There are ten billion women in this city without a job, that's what happened.

KATYA: Did you tell him you could cook, too?

MASHA: Yes, I told him that.

KATYA: And that you are reliable? Did you give him your references?

MASHA: I did all that, Ma. They hired some girl with a college degree.

KATYA: For waitressing you need a college degree?

MASHA: That's the job market, Ma. That's the best she can do, too. Svetlana said there's a plant looking for a night cleaner. I'll apply there tomorrow.

KATYA: Rent is due tomorrow.

MASHA: I paid Viktor.

KATYA: Well, what about next month? (*beat*) We could have used that money.

MASHA: I made a decision. I'm not giving up, yet, why are you? (*beat*) Who are you writing to?

KATYA: Your husband.

MASHA: What?

She grabs the paper from her mother.

MASHA: "My dearest American love—" Ma!

KATYA: It's a little romance, that never killed anyone.

MASHA: I don't want romance with this man.

KATYA: Not even—

MASHA: Not even to get money from him.

She reads from the paper.

MASHA: "... I want to have lots of children and only desire to be obedient to a good husband." How can you write these things?

KATYA: You think your mother can't be sexy anymore?

MASHA: Sexy! Ma, this isn't who I am, this isn't who I want to be. You want me to fly away to Canada and get married so I can spend my life in some man's house, cooking him dinner and lowering my eyes?

KATYA: Well, what would you say to him, then?

MASHA: Well, for starters, I'd tell him a thing or two about the Ukraine; our beautiful country isn't just ripe for plucking wives from.

KATYA hands MASHA the piece of paper and pen.

KATYA: And what else?

MASHA: I'd say...

KATYA: Write! Write!

MASHA begins to write.

MASHA: I'd say, "Dear Mr Big-Shot Canadian. I want you to know that I love my country, and I have no desire to leave it. I'm looking for a man who is a real man, who wants a partner in his wife, not a slave— "

VLAD sneaks up the street behind her.

MASHA: "A man who is serious about making a difference in this world— "

VLAD throws his his hands over her eyes.

VLAD: Guess who!

MASHA screams.

MASHA: What are you—

VLAD: I called you just to throw you off, so you wouldn't suspect me.

KATYA: Ai, this crazy *shlob* wants to murder me with fright. As if I'm not sweating enough already.

VLAD yanks the letter out of MASHA's hand.

VLAD: What's this?

MASHA: Don't!

VLAD: You're writing the American? What about this morning?

MASHA: No, Mama was writing him back, pretending to be me. Listen to what she said, though:

She reads KATYA*'s letter.*

MASHA: "I want nothing else but to be a good mother to your children." Can you believe that?

VLAD: No, you'd be a terrible mother.

MASHA: No, I wouldn't.

VLAD: It's okay, though, babe. I don't care. Rock stars don't have kids anyway. But Katya, an arrow in my heart.

KATYA: Forgive me for trying so hard to make a better life for my daughter even though she decides to throw her life away with the likes of *bezlads* like you.

MASHA: Anyway, I'm writing him back.

VLAD: To ask for more money?

MASHA: No! I have to tell him this is wrong. This is the reason why Ukraine is in such a mess right now, people thinking we're something we're not. I don't care who this man is, I'm sick of the way—

She begins to write again.

MASHA: "For starters, I'm not Russian, I'm Ukrainian. They are separate countries!" He probably thinks we're all blonde, too.

VLAD: You're hardly a natural blonde, babe.

KATYA: Oh, don't be mad. Trust me. This is all in your best interest. In the next letter I was planning to tell him about your love of books. Men love an intelligent woman.

VLAD: Hey, babe, when you send that, can you stick in a copy of my demo?

MASHA: What?

VLAD: In case he knows Bono or someone. Bono's from there, you know. This could be a really big break for me.

MASHA: This isn't about you. This is about reclaiming the dignity of Ukrainian women.

VLAD: Babe, let's think about the future here. If you love me, you will put a copy of my demo in the letter.

MASHA: The extra postage will be way too expensive.

VLAD: Fame has its price.

He digs a demo out of his back pocket.

MASHA: That can't be comfortable.

VLAD: You never know when you might run into someone with a lot of power. I heard of this guy who met the head of a big Ukrainian label when he was in the urinal, he just pulled out a demo and stuck it in the man's jacket pocket for him. I mean, he couldn't even say no because he had no hands free to—

MASHA: Okay, okay, give it to me.

KATYA: Oh, it's so exciting, I wonder what he'll write back. Maybe he'll send a gift, oh! Or a ring!

MASHA: I don't think he'll want to send a ring after he reads this.

VLAD: Make sure you put the return address, though. Maybe you should put my address in case Bono writes back.

MASHA: I'm not going to put your address on it.

VLAD: Compromise. We'll put both.

MASHA: There is nothing to compromise!

VLAD: Sheesh, calm down, it was just a suggestion.

KATYA reaches into her bag of pills.

KATYA: You should take one of these. Aneta takes them to calm her down, a very anxious woman. So much worrying about things she can't change.

MASHA: Aw, Ma, your pills are melting in the bag. I don't know what you think we're going to be doing with all of these. I'm not taking them, and you certainly can't take twenty pills every day.

KATYA: I got them for the neighbours.

MASHA: Who?

KATYA: Oh, a little for everyone. Volha got some for her allergies, wool of all things. Inna got some for her husband's sex drive; she'll just slip them in his morning coffee, then BAM.

MASHA: Do you really think you should experiment with expired pills on your friends?

KATYA: Who's experimenting? Tonia from the front counter's been doing this for years, the experiment is over. How do you think she gets all those bottles of Chernigovskaya that her husband drinks away? It's not from her pay cheque, let me tell you.

MASHA: So she takes all the expired pills home and exchanges them with her friends for vodka?

KATYA: It's the only way to stop her husband from drinking away their rent money.

MASHA: You should sell these, Mama. You must have a thousand *grivna* just in this bag.

KATYA: I wouldn't make my friends pay for something I got free.

MASHA: They're not free, though. The pharmacy paid for them. Mama, this is brilliant. This is what we'll do! We'll sell the expired pills you bring home. If we sell them for less than the pharmacy, everyone will get a good deal. We'll *have* to be successful.

KATYA: I wouldn't know the first thing about a business. We women should stick to what we know.

MASHA: Don't you see? We could really make money from this. We could be independent. Vlad, are you listening to this? Mama and I are going to start a business. You could do the delivering.

VLAD: I've got my band.

MASHA: This isn't a question.

KATYA: I'm not working with him.

MASHA: You want to lug around bags of pills in this heat? (*beat*) I didn't think so. Here's what we're going to do —

VIKTOR saunters up to the porch.

VIKTOR: Katya, you're looking more beautiful every day.

KATYA: Oh, Viktor, you gave me a fright. How are you, love?

VIKTOR: Much better now that I'm with you.

KATYA: Oh...

VLAD: Viktor, buddy, the best news today!

VIKTOR: You've grown chest hair?

VLAD: Have I?

VIKTOR: A rhetorical question.

VLAD: Masha and I are getting married!

VIKTOR: What.

KATYA: Hmph.

MASHA: No, that's not true.

VLAD: Masha.

MASHA: Vlad's just excited. His band is getting really big right now.

VLAD: No, this morning —

VIKTOR: So you'll be moving out, I assume.

VLAD: I'm going to get us a place over by —

MASHA: No, we're not. I'm not going anywhere. Please, Viktor —

VIKTOR: A lot of rent unpaid on this place.

VLAD: I'll cover it. I mean, with the band —

VIKTOR: I'm not sure you have the right type of payment.

MASHA: Please, Viktor —

VLAD: Masha, what's wrong with you?

MASHA: Nothing, I just — we were just joking around this morning.

VLAD: Joking around?

KATYA: Don't you worry about our Masha. She's a stubborn one when it comes to romance.

VIKTOR: I'm sure that's not always the case.

Long awkward pause.

VIKTOR: Well. I should be going, I've got collections to do all down this block still. Oh, Katya, that reminds me. Your rent hasn't come in yet this month.

KATYA: Hasn't it? Masha, you said you paid.

MASHA: No, I—

VIKTOR: She was mistaken. Masha. Katya. Hope you survive the heatwave.

He exits. VLAD starts to walk away as well.

MASHA: Where are you going?

VLAD: I told you. I've got band practice.

MASHA: Right now?

VLAD: Soon. Later.

MASHA: What are you mad at?

VLAD: I'm not mad.

MASHA: Vlad.

VLAD: What do you think, Masha? In case you'd forgotten, you said yes to me this morning.

MASHA: I can't plan a wedding when I'm about to be kicked out of my apartment.

VLAD: Fine, you're right. It's fine.

MASHA: Vlad, you don't understand.

VLAD: It's fine, Masha. I'll just wait around forever for you to make up your mind, you know.

He exits.

KATYA: What do you see in that *schlob?*

MASHA: He loves me.

KATYA: That's not what I asked.

MASHA: I've known him my whole life.

KATYA: *That's* his redeeming quality?

MASHA: Ma.

KATYA: It's a fair question!

MASHA: I guess… I guess I love him.

KATYA: If that's true, why don't you marry the poor boy already and stop torturing him?

MASHA: Because I'm not like you! I don't have to marry to support myself. I want to figure out my life on my own first, go to school maybe. We're in love. He'll wait for me.

KATYA: Love doesn't pay the rent. And neither do you, apparently.

MASHA: I know, I'm sorry. I will. Things just got away from me. (*beat*) How often do you work?

KATYA: That depends. I work my butt off around the house 24/7.

MASHA: You work three days a week, don't you? So if you bring home expired pills every time, say there's about a thousand *grivna* a bag, that's three thousand a week.

KATYA: Really?

MASHA: *Yes,* Ma, I'm telling you. We could do this. We *have* to do this. Let's make a list.

She pulls out pill bottles and holds them up.

MASHA: Who's this one for?

KATYA: Anti-depressants for Aneta Babacio.

MASHA: Really?

KATYA: Ate herself away when her husband left.

MASHA: And the little blue pills?

KATYA: Alec Czonko's stomach ulcer.

MASHA pulls out the condoms.

KATYA: Svetlana Deckniak.

MASHA: Ma! Condoms expire for a reason!

KATYA: Ah, it wouldn't be the end of the world if that girl got pregnant. Might tame her a little. Hand me that pen.

MASHA: We can do this, Ma.

KATYA: I'll finish this. You go mail your letter.

KATYA hands MASHA the letter to the Canadian.

MASHA: It's more like your letter.

KATYA: Go! I want it to get into today's post.

MASHA gets up, takes the letter.

MASHA: (*laughing*) That's fine, I'd look forward to seeing his response after where I told him to go.

KATYA: We'll see.

MASHA exits offstage. KATYA fans herself in the heat.

Lights fade.

Scene 3

Lights up on the front stoop. A bouquet of flowers sits on the top step. An EVICTION NOTICE is on the door. MASHA walks up to the house, sees the flowers, picks them up and reads the card.

She sees the eviction notice, drops the flowers, tears the notice off the door. She runs offstage with the notice in hand.

VLAD walks up to the house, picks up the flowers, knocks on the door. No answer. He sits on the top step, looks at the note on the bouquet.

VLAD: Ugh! That *blyat*! Thinks he can steal my girlfriend with his stupid American money. How did he get these all the way here?

He crumples the note up and tosses it onto the step. Pauses.

VLAD: (*singing, not bad*) *Hey, man, think you can steal my girlfriend.*

He taps a beat on the step.

VLAD: (*singing*) *Think you can...who do you think—*

MASHA enters the street. VLAD leaps up from the stairs.

VLAD: Hi.

MASHA: What are you doing here? It's been two weeks.

VLAD: I...got you some flowers.

MASHA: Oh, really.

VLAD: Yeah.

MASHA: So these aren't from the agency on behalf of my Canadian guy?

VLAD: Listen, I... I'm sorry. I shouldn't have said those things. Or...whatever I said that made you mad. (*pause*) And I just came by to tell you that my band got signed.

MASHA: What?

VLAD: Yeah. Yeah, well, that's why I've been busy. This local label rep was at that last show. It's not huge but, they're going to pay for us to get some real studio time and—

MASHA: Congratulations.

VLAD: You mean it? You're happy for me?

MASHA: If they're going to pay you to record, that's kind of like a job, right?

VLAD: I guess.

MASHA: So maybe you could start to pay me back for all the food you've eaten, or maybe you can help me—oh, I don't know—not get evicted!

VLAD: Yeah, yeah, the only thing is, the thing is—

MASHA: Of course. The catch.

VLAD: Masha, I'm trying.

MASHA: What is it?

VLAD: Part of the contract for the band is that we have to go on tour, so people know who we are, to get known, you know?

MASHA: Well...for how long?

VLAD: I don't know. Six months? It's hard to say. And the thing is, I just, I need a bit of a loan.

MASHA: Here we go.

VLAD: But baby, baby, here's the thing. I convinced them to let you come with us! We need someone in the bus who can, like, cook and do some errands and stuff. It'd be great, you and me and the band. You could see me play every night. Then you could get rid of your place for a bit—

MASHA: Get *rid* of it? Are you even listening?

VLAD: — could save some rent money —

MASHA: You want me to drive around on a bus with you and cook your meals and, I don't know, wash your laundry, without getting a job or going to school…for six months?

VLAD: Well…yeah. It's — we'd be together.

MASHA: And where do you think Ma's going to live now?

VLAD: She has a job, all the women on this block take care of themselves, why can't she?

MASHA: Did you ever wonder how they 'take care of themselves,' Vlad? Ever wonder how they do it without jobs, without husbands? We all manage mysteriously, somehow?

VLAD: This opportunity's not going to wait around for me forever.

Silence.

VLAD: Let's get married. We'll get married and then — it'll be like a honeymoon.

MASHA: Yeah, you, me, Alex and Yosyp.

VLAD: We'll see the country! That's better than school. You'll learn street smarts. We're not from Moscow, Masha. We don't get to go to school and get good jobs and fly to the West. We'll be here our whole lives like everyone else in Kharkiv, scraping for cash to pay the big guys. Let's have some fun before all that, hey?

MASHA: I can't believe that.

VLAD: I promise it will be fun. We'll drive —

MASHA: No, I mean. Vlad. If I let myself believe that we'll never be anything better than we are now, than our parents were…things can change. Vladimir. Things have to change. The new president said —

VLAD: Oh, not you, too. You don't believe that shit? Presidents have been making promises to our country for years and years, Masha. Nothing's going to change. People like us don't change. We can't afford to.

The door flies open and KATYA *stands inside.*

KATYA: What are you standing out there for, girl? Come inside!

VLAD: Hey! I knocked on the door but no one answered.

KATYA: The day has come!

She whips an envelope out of her pocket. MASHA *takes it.*

MASHA: It's already been opened.

KATYA: I got nervous, but I only took a tiny peek at the first line, and, Masha, it's not bad.

MASHA *pulls the letter out.*

MASHA: (*reading*) "My dearest Maria, I am so excited to receive a letter back from you."

VLAD: What did he say about me?

KATYA: Oh, the romance has begun!

MASHA: "Thank you so much for your honesty. You sound like you really know what you want out of life."

VLAD cranes to look at the letter over her shoulder.

VLAD: I think your thumb is covering my name.

MASHA: "I myself am still trying to figure that out."

VLAD: Maybe he sent me a letter to my house, since we gave him both addresses.

KATYA: (*to* VLAD) What are you doing on my doorstep? Did anyone invite you here?

VLAD: Masha did.

KATYA grabs the broom from beside the door, shoos it toward VLAD.

KATYA: (*to* VLAD) Get out of here, go back to your *bezlad* friends—

VLAD slips the broom from her hands, uses it as a microphone. MASHA continues reading the letter.

VLAD: (*singing*) *Oh, Katya, babyyy—*

KATYA: Stop that.

He sings her towards the house.

VLAD: (*singing*) *You don't look a day over sixteen—*

KATYA: Don't you try to butter me up—

VLAD: (*singing*) *Don't hate me, babyy—*

MASHA: Oh, my gawd.

The other two stop. MASHA shakes a piece of paper out of the envelope.

KATYA: What?

MASHA: He sent me a plane ticket.

VLAD: To America?

KATYA: Canada.

VLAD: What's the difference anyway.

MASHA: He said I can use it whenever I want and he'll pay for everything.

VLAD: Like a prostitute.

MASHA: It's not like that.

VLAD: I'll kill him! Who does he think he is?

KATYA: Oh, Masha, you'll be married in Canada!

MASHA: It wouldn't be for good right away, he just wants me to visit and see his country and where he lives.

VLAD: I'll rip his American balls off!

KATYA: So violent! You want to be with such a violent man, Masha?

MASHA: Ma, what do you expect poor Vlad to do here? He's my fiancé!

KATYA: Oh, sure, on the outside you're angry and I'm the bad one, but inside you're smiling, you're happy to be on the verge of freedom.

Pause.

VLAD: Masha? Are you smiling inside?

MASHA: Vlad—

VLAD: Are you? (*beat*) Rip the ticket up.

MASHA: I...it's very expensive.

VLAD: Give it to me!

He lunges for it, she leaps back.

MASHA: I'll just send it back to him.

VLAD: You want to go!

MASHA: No I don't!

VLAD: Yes you do! You do! You think he's better than me, that he'll rescue you from all this? You think some American cowboy'll pick you up from the airport on a horse and ride you off into the sunset where you'll have money and, and nice clothes and...but he won't love you like I do, Masha! You think about that. He only wants you because he thinks you're desperate. He wants a servant. Fine. Is that what you want?

MASHA: Of course not!

VLAD: Then marry me! Marry me tomorrow, before I leave. Can you do that?

MASHA: Vlad.

VLAD: That's what I thought. What would put it off this time? You'd wait to see if your little pill scheme would work out, and if not, you'll think about marrying me? I can't wait around to find out if you're ready for me to save you or not, Masha. This other guy can have the honour, now. Go ahead and write your letter.

MASHA: It's not like that! I just wanted to tell him about us, show him that he's wrong about the women here.

VLAD: Is he? Is he wrong? What does he think, he thinks you're desperate? That you think you deserve more than everyone else in this country? How is he wrong about that? He's not wrong about you. You'll sell yourself as his slave just for a chance to be rich—

KATYA picks up the broom and smacks VLAD on the head with it.

VLAD: Ow!

KATYA: You get out!

MASHA: Mama!

KATYA: Out! Don't you come back to my house ever again!

VLAD: Masha!

MASHA: ...Good luck on your tour. I hope you get famous.

VLAD: Please.

She is silent. He exits.

KATYA: It's better this way.

MASHA: He loves me for who I am, Ma. Which is a lot more than I can say for this guy.

KATYA: Will that matter when you're like me in ten years? Your father loved me, too, at first. I didn't always look like this, breasts hanging down to my knees. I was quite the knockout, but ten years of scrubbing floors at the industrial plants so we could live and feed you and guess what, he doesn't love me so much anymore. You think in ten years Vlad won't be after some younger woman, too? You think he won't leave? Love isn't all you think it is, Masha. It's not all books and talking and rock stars. Men like this — one of Svetlana's friends married one in England, she said her bathroom is the size of our apartment. She won't ever work a day in her life. She won't ever worry that her kids will starve. That's love, Maria. That's what love is.

MASHA: We've been evicted.

KATYA: What? How?

MASHA: We can't pay our rent. What did you expect?

KATYA: But Viktor said —

MASHA: I sleep with Viktor so we don't have to pay.

KATYA: But I have a job.

MASHA: You barely make enough to pay for groceries. Where did you think the rest was coming from?

KATYA: Oh, my Maria —

MASHA: So you're the genuis, what do we do now?

KATYA: Write him a letter.

MASHA: I can't. He'll be moving around a lot.

KATYA: Not Vlad, ai. I'd be surprised if that *bezlad* can read. The Canadian. Is it so crazy to think that you could fall in love with someone who could support you? Someone who is trying to understand you, to know you?

MASHA: He's trying to buy a wife, Ma.

KATYA: He is lonely, just like me. Did you even read his letter? He lives in the middle of nowhere, no women around, and he is shy. Lots of other men in his town have brought wives there, too. You could make him so happy, and he could save us.

MASHA: Vlad's right!

KATYA: He wouldn't know 'right' if it hit him over the head with a broom.

MASHA: He is, Mama. That's against everything I stand for. It's the easy way out.

KATYA: What's wrong with that? There's nothing wrong with taking a shortcut if you find it.

MASHA: We could make some honest money this week because of my business plan. We're going to be okay.

KATYA: Honest? What happens when we get caught? Hmm? You want to sneak around on the black market for the rest of our lives? That's no way to live. That's not what I raised you for. You have to use the ticket, Masha. Just go. You want to.

MASHA: And leave you here to fend for yourself? I'll never do that.

KATYA: Don't you understand, I don't want this for you. I want you to go more than anything. Listen to me, Masha. You have a golden opportunity, the golden ticket is staring you in the face.

Pause.

MASHA: Fine. I'll ask him to come here.

KATYA: Here! To Kharkiv? He's not going to want to stay in our filthy city, stinking smog from the plants pouring into the sky every minute.

MASHA: If he wants a wife so badly, he will.

KATYA: What good will that do us?

MASHA: It's something to do.

KATYA: And what if he says no?

MASHA: Then it looks like we're on our own again, Ma. Me and you.

Pause.

KATYA: This heatwave is going to kill me.

MASHA: It's supposed to break next week. Nothing to do but bear it 'til then.

KATYA: Seems like years away, right now. Like years.

Lights fade.

The End

Mrs. Ferguson's Bed

by Sherryl Melnyk

About the playwright

Sherryl Melnyk's play *Millicent's Pothole* has recently taken first place in the Playwrights' Guild of Canada's Post-Secondary Playwriting Competition. *Millicent's Pothole* was also a finalist in the 2009 BC National Playwriting Competition and will be produced by the Revelstoke Theatre Company in 2012. *Even The Walls Have Eyes* was a co-winner in the From The Cradle to Stage playwriting competition and was produced by the Walterdale Playhouse in Edmonton. Her play *Mrs. Ferguson's Bed* was produced at FemFest in Winnipeg by Sarasvati Productions and *Outnumbered* was produced by Soulocentric Productions in Calgary. She has also published an essay entitled "Landscape My Body," and a documentary for CBC radio called "Mom Leaves Home." She has an M.A. in English literature and is currently a Ph.D. student at the University of Calgary in the Interdisciplinary Graduate Program. Sherryl grew up on a farm in Manitoba with an eclectic family who has unwittingly provided much fodder for her writing. She lives with her poorly trained but greatly loved pug Sasha.

Characters

VIOLET is a 73-year-old woman, conservatively dressed, wearing a flower print dress and a hat that matches. She is carrying a purse and holding a Bible.

Setting

A folding chair that VIOLET carries on stage.

VIOLET: Well. Irwin. Here I am. (*Settles down into the chair. Straightens her dress.*) Quiet today, isn't it? Saturdays are usually busy around here. Strings of cars everywhere. No one ever seems to notice me anymore, though. Feels like I'm a ghost sometimes. You can believe I used to get noticed, though. Plenty. (*nods her head, reminiscing*) Yes. Plenty. I would get noticed by people…men even. Handsome men. Don't look surprised. True as me sitting myself right here in front of you.

Pause.

Like the time I walked into church and Doc Baker stared at my legs. I had nice legs back then. He wasn't the only one, Doc Baker. There were others who glanced over the tops of their hymn books at me. Like…oh, what's his name…you know the man I'm thinking of…this is silly…the taxidermist… John… Shephard. Yes. Well, he used to stare at me, too. I did have the most amazing legs, even if you never said it. I used to do those deep knee bend things. One squat for every clothes pin I'd clip to the line. That's four squats per sheet. Two for pants. Up and down. Up and down. One for a pair of panties. Don't look at me like that, Irwin. God knows women wear panties. Kept my thighs from wiggling around like that head cheese you used to crave after working yourself into a tizzy writing late into the night. Guess you never had the time to notice my legs.

Pause.

No sense beating around the bush. I might as well come clean and tell you why I'm here this week, and it's more than just for a little visit and a chat like usual. Considerably more, you might say.

Pause. VIOLET is nervous. She's having trouble getting out what she wants to say to Irwin. She starts pulling at the sleeve of her dress. Then she rolls the sleeve up and shows Irwin her arms as a means of biding her time.

Look here, still have lovely arms, too. (*leans in close, like she's telling a secret*) Hymn books gave me tight arms. Didn't know that, did you? All these many years and there's lots you don't know about me. Well, I'll tell you right now, since I do all the talking these days and you do all the listening. Nice change, isn't it? I'd walk up and down the pews after church picking up those hymn books doing exercises to keep my arms nice and tight—hymn book arm curls—that's what I called them. Ridiculous, I suppose. Rose O'Connor, you remember her? Dead now. Angina, or was it a stroke? No…no, I'm sure it was a heart attack. Well, it doesn't matter now, won't bring her back. She caught me doing those curls and I told her all about it and showed her my arms and that's how we became friends. We would have stayed friends too if we hadn't moved again. I know you don't want to hear about how much I hated moving every few years. Heard it all before, heard it all before, as you say.

Pause.

Gosh, you'd think chatting with my husband about this would be easier… I mean, we've been married fifty-four years in May.

Pause.

Guess you never had the time to notice my arms. Don't worry, I know you were a busy man. I'm not here to start a fight. I'm just saying, you never had the time to notice how nice I kept my arms. It's a simple black and white statement. Don't mean a thing by it. Not a thing. No point in getting all worked up the way you like to.

Pause. VIOLET digs in her purse and pulls out a driver's license.

Looky here. (*shakes it in the air*) My driver's license! It has a picture of me and everything. I wore lipstick and a smudge of eyeshadow — shady blue — that's the colour. Eyeshadow isn't a sin, Irwin. The young man who gave me the driver's test said I did fine. Just fine. Maybe a little slow around the corners, but he didn't deduct any points for that because he said I was a good, cautious driver, and who doesn't appreciate a cautious driver on the road these days. Let me tell you, though, right at the end of the test a yellow light snuck up on me right out of nowhere without a lick of warning… (*Violet stares at the license and shakes her head at it in disbelief.*) Never would have believed it. Never.

Puts her driver's license away.

Look at me. I haven't even given you this week's present. No need to thank me. (*holds a Bible up*) Looky here — gold around the edges. I know you don't like extravagance, but it didn't cost a fortune. I bought it last week after I went to the Co-op for coffee. Can you imagine, just like that, without a second thought in my head, I grabbed my new license and drove myself to the Co-op? Yes, sir, I did. Coffee and a big slice of apple pie and ice cream at the Co-op. I don't have to tell you that the pie wasn't nearly half as good as mine — they don't use Granny apples, which is the secret — but it was something just to get out there, driving myself down the streets, making my way to the Co-op for some coffee and apple pie. Anyway, I bought this here Bible at a little shop called Christians Galore, right on the same block. Don't you love that name: Christians Galore? Like you couldn't swing a dead cat without hitting a Christian. (*chuckles at her little joke. Pause.*)

Not used to saying much and now look at me…can't seem to shut myself up…but I… I can't seem to get out what I come to say…like it's stuck in my throat…

Pause.

Do you like the Bible, Irwin? I roughed it up a bit for you. But it *is* brand new. I stepped on it a couple of times and threw it down the church stairs after the service on Sunday. Then I let it ride around all week in my trunk next to the extra tire you always kept full up with air just in case. That young man with the purple hair who works at the Shell station across from Gernick's Bakery checked it and didn't even charge me anything extra. "Fine," he said, "tire's just fine, ma'am." I know you don't like that stuff: purple hair and pierced eyebrows and a diamond stud through the belly button. Where's it all going to end? is what you're thinking. But he's a polite young man. You'd think it'd sting when he talks, but he's a chatty little fellow every time I stop in to fill up. It doesn't cost anything extra to keep the top half of the tank full. Well, that young man always says, "Yes, ma'am" this and "No, ma'am" that, so I got up my nerve and I asked him straight out if the holes in his face hurt. In a real chipper way, like the question wasn't any kind of big deal, he said, "Not a bit, ma'am." So I asked him, if he took the earring out of his lip, could he whistle through that little hole, and he stared at me for a long time like I was a nutty old lady but all he said was, "No, ma'am." Guess he didn't see it was a joke but I laughed about it the whole drive home and I thought, Irwin's wrong about what God has to say about kids and purple hair and the tattoos they're all getting now. I know you don't see it, Irwin, but I think God's got bigger things to worry about like…oh, I don't know…like if that kid with the pierced lip is safe when he gets home from that job he's working so hard to keep. Well… enough of that. I know how you don't like when people disagree with you. I'm just giving my opinion. Even if it's wrong.

Pause.

I am here for a reason and it's more than just to give you that gold Bible. Which is beautiful, you have to admit. Nothing wrong with appreciating the beautiful things the Lord showers down on us. Think about that for a couple of days and you might just come to the same conclusion, despite all your years of keeping our money hid away in the bank. Let me tell you, Irwin, that keeping a sack of money locked away in a bank isn't near as much fun as having coffee and apple pie at the Co-op. Or as much fun as driving myself over to visit Nelly Wilson, and she lives clear across town at the Oakville Manor. And before you even ask, I'll tell you straight out that, no, she isn't a Christian and well… I like her anyway. I met her at the Co-op and she told me I better just get myself in my car and drive over to her place for a game of two-handed bridge, and I did just that without giving it another thought. We've decided to play every Tuesday afternoon and next week she's inviting two other ladies and, no, I'm not even going to ask them if they're Christians or Muslims or Hindus or what's the other one called…oh, yes, Buddhas. We're just going to play cards and it isn't going to matter a whit what they think about God or the devil or the price of tomatoes. Simple as that.

Pause.

My goodness, look at me, I'm all twisted up. I just can't seem to say what I come to…

Pause.

On my way home from Nelly's house, I stopped in at Wal-Mart and bought an air freshener and hung it from the rear-view mirror. Looks like a strawberry. Smells like a strawberry. Not fresh ones right from the garden. But still, it does smell a bit like straw… (*frustrated with herself*) Gosh, never mind about all that. That's not why I'm here. Strange, though. Doing those things for myself now—the tire and getting gas and such. Don't think I'm complaining about having to check the spare tire. I'm not. I'm getting used to it. I mean, it's been a couple of years now. I'm just saying, I got awful used to you doing those kinds of things for me. You always liked to keep everything in order—a perfect straight line is the way God likes it—that's what you'd say, Irwin—neat and tidy in a perfect straight line…

Pause.

I know it worries you — what people say — that's why I roughed that Bible up. You wouldn't want people thinking you were a newbie Christian and just got the thing. People love to talk, as you say. You've been around the Christian block, so to speak. Earned some respect. See how I put those little yellow sticky papers in there for you too? Makes it look like you've marked all the important spots. I stopped at the 7-11 on my way here today to get them. That's what cost a fortune. $3.23 in stickies so no one looks sideways at you.

(*leans forward like she's sharing a secret*) Put extra ones in the Old Testament. (*shakes her head*) No one reads the Old Testament anymore. Lazy, that's what they are. Plain lazy. 'Course I don't read the Old Testament either. But that's because it's too violent. I've always hated violence and I'm dead sure the Lord would agree with that one.

Pause.

I better get to it before I lose my nerve and I'll have to go through this whole miserable song and dance with you again next week, just like I did last week and the week before that. Miserable, that's what this is, miserable. Drive all the way over here and...

Pause.

This isn't the easiest thing I've ever told you but...but life is full of bumps. Yes, that's how we can think of this, a speed bump on the road of life. I know what they're like to try and drive over without banging up the bottom of the car — now that I've got my license. But this would be considerably bigger than the speed bumps in the Co-op parking lot...more like, oh, I don't know...the monster ones they've got at Wal-Mart so folks don't go speeding through there and kill one of their customers carrying stuff to their car.

Pause.

I figured our chat would be a lot easier than this, but it feels like the thing is lodged here in my throat, strangling me. Like a pair of hands, Irwin, strangling me. Honestly...

Pause.

Look here...we got ourselves a new minister. Young one. Barely in his forties. Bald as the day is long. Got himself a whole brood of kids — some adopted, some not, all different colours and sizes sitting up at the front of the church, snuggled up to his wife. She's got her hands full, believe me: rocks one back and forth; hushes another; tries to keep the two-year-old from racing up to the front of the church and jumping up on his daddy; all while the baby grabs a feather out of some lady's hat and one pokes his brother in the eye. My goodness! They've really livened up the place, Irwin — the bunch of them. Anyway, with all that commotion it's hard to concentrate on what that preacher is trying to say but...well, he likes to talk about everyday stuff like...oh, I don't know...how frustrating life can be if you get a flat tire and you've got a screaming baby in the back seat, for example. Or what it feels like when the kitchen tap drips and drips and drips 'til it pretty near drives you half crazy but your husband won't fix it 'cause he says he's too busy. Then that young minister talks about how cutting yourself a nice fat slice of apple pie can make everything seem okay for a little bit — even though it's loaded with calories and you're trying to stay slim and trim. You see, he thinks God doesn't expect anyone to be perfect. No sir. He says God just wants a person to enjoy the day he gave you without having a dark cloud of guilt and anger following a person around everywhere they go. Anyway…you get my meaning, he preaches about everyday kinds of stuff that can weigh a person down over the years. But there's no need to get worked up, Irwin, his sermons aren't half near as good as yours. Everyone knows that you could get that whole congregation sitting straight up stiff as a board when you started talking about Jesus and how little we deserve considering what we give back and how much he gave up and all that. But still, that young preacher talks about how God wants us to live life and enjoy every minute. I know it sounds strange to you 'cause you were always waiting for death and the glory that comes after that, but this young guy says he doesn't buy that story. Anyway… that was when I decided I'd tell you the whole thing I've got to say straight out.

Pause. Takes a cloth hanky out of her purse and wipes her forehead and neck.

Maybe it's the heat that's strangling me. Feels like I can't breathe.

Pause.

Remember when we lived in that little town…the one with the church that didn't have a single stained glass window in it? Not a one. What on earth was the name of that…it had those mice that would scurry up and down the church aisles. How a person is supposed to talk to God when they're worried their feet'll get trampled… (*shakes her head*) Now that I'm being honest with you, Irwin, I can tell you I always wanted to grab a Bible off the pew and smash one of those miserable little mice. Of course, it's not the kind of thing a minister's wife would do…but I thought about it. A lot. *Every* Sunday I dug my nails into that damn Bible so my hand wouldn't up and do it before I even had a chance to stop…

Pause.

But I didn't. Did I? Even when you told me to pack up the station wagon *again* — that it was time to move to a new horrid little town to do God's work. Not *even* then did I pick up that Bible and…

Pause.

Killarney. Yes, it was Killarney with all those dreadful mice. Do you remember it? What am I saying? Of course you remember it. We lived there for eight years. Well, it was right there in that horrid little town with no stained glass windows and mice everywhere that… I…well…fell in love with Doc Baker. There, I've said it. You're shocked, of course, but I needed to come right out and lay it flat on the table so you could see it. It wasn't my fault, really. I mean, he was such a kind man. It happened that time he gave me those pills. Remember the ones? Of course you do. Don't be ridiculous. The ones that calmed me down. They made me dizzy, too, like I was spinning round and round in slow motion.

Pause.

He had such kind eyes, Doc Baker. He took my hand real soft that day and said, "It can't be easy being the preacher's wife." And I started to cry 'cause no one ever noticed that before. Cried flat out right there in his office. And I didn't care one bit that I blubbered and sniffled or what he might think of me. It just poured out like I'd never cried before. Know what, Irwin? He didn't even try to stop me. Or tell me to stop being ridiculous, that the people in the waiting room might be able to hear me make a fool of myself, and that I was embarrassing him with all my drama...imagine... I didn't even feel stupid. Then things tumbled out of me. Like I didn't have any control over my mouth. And even before I could stop myself, I told him about the blood. Doc Baker kept nodding and squeezed my fingers and I just kept going until the whole thing came out. How it happened the night you were at the hospital holding Mrs. Ferguson's hand when she died. Do you remember her, Irwin? I guess not. Why would you? There were so many over the years. All of them wanted someone to listen because their father just died. Or they couldn't pay the mortgage. Or needed you to pray for their daughter who was paralyzed in a car accident. Or they just got diagnosed with cancer, the rare kind that isn't curable. And the ones with depression and lousy marriages and kids on some kind of drugs or their father was a drunk. They were an army, Irwin, all those people. An army all fighting to keep you away from me.

Pause.

But *I* needed you that night you were at Mrs. Ferguson's bed when she died. I begged you to come home, Irwin. You told me to stop being selfish. Calm down. I was being ridiculous. And to quit being so foolish. That all my drama was giving you a headache. To think of Mrs. Ferguson and what it might be like for her, taking those last few breaths. And what about her two young daughters crying and her husband who was losing his wife after six years of marriage. To stop embarrassing you with all these calls. But that night, it wasn't like all the other times I called you, crying. It was different because I needed help cleaning up the blood.

Pause.

I didn't know there could be so much blood in my little body, Irwin. Of course, a woman gets used to a little blood. But...nothing like this. Nothing. I kept wiping round and round thinking, my God, how can I still be alive? How could a person lose so much blood and still be kicking? It kept dripping out like I was some kind of tap that couldn't get turned off. Then it hit me hard because I hadn't realized it right off and I thought, my God, there's a... baby in here somewhere, what if I...what if I wash him away? What if I don't notice him because there's so much blood? What if he gets soaked up in the rag because I can't...

(*VIOLET begins crying. She is reliving the past.*) Help me find my baby. Where are you, Irwin? Where are you? Hurry! Hurry! Help me find my baby. I need you. I need help. Come home and help me. There's so much blood. Help me find my baby before it's too late. I need help. Where are you? Don't let my baby die alone on the bathroom floor. Our baby needs you. He's dying, he's dying in all this blood. Where are you? He's dying right here in front of me. Tell your God to help my baby.

Pause. VIOLET *takes a minute to compose herself.*

I sat there, hunched over and I watched that blood trickle out of my body until a tiny lump slid out real soft and easy as a purr. I stared at it for awhile like a slice of my own body had fallen clean off and I didn't understand how to put it back because...well, how was I going to live without it? Then I lay down in that blood and curled myself around him. See, I wanted to die right alongside of that baby who wasn't ever going to come back to life. Not for me. Not for you, Irwin. (*angry*) Not even for your God.

Pause.

That was when Doc Baker patted the examining table and told me to hop up here and that I'd be fine. "Just fine. You're a young woman, Violet," he said. "There'll be other chances." But I never gave you another chance to have a baby with me, Irwin, 'cause it wasn't you who had to find the Javex bottle and clean up the blood. And it wasn't you who had to flush my baby down the toilet. You were sitting at Mrs. Ferguson's bed, holding *her* hand. When you got home that night, Irwin, everything in the bathroom was neat and tidy in a perfect straight line. Just how you like. And that's how it stayed all these many years.

Pause.

I didn't tell you about it because you didn't deserve to know. Black and white, simple as that. You probably never noticed, but after that, I left the phone plugged in and pulled the curtains open wide so people would know you were home. That army of people could have you, Irwin, 'cause I didn't want you anymore.

Pause.

After Doc Baker examined me, I blew my nose and it honked and we both started laughing. That was when I fell in love with him. We were laughing and his blue eyes went soapy and he held my hand real soft and he said, "You'll be fine, Violet, just fine." I never went back to his office after that. But I would wait for him to come into the church and find a seat. Then I'd pick a spot where I could watch him. I'd pretend that it was me when he'd put his arm across the back of the pew and twist a piece of his wife's hair around his finger. Or it was me when he'd pick up the glove that she'd dropped, sliding on her coat.

Pause.

It was years after that when I caught Doc Baker looking at my legs. Just...just that one time. I started crying right there in the church. Do you remember the time I ran out of the church crying, Irwin? I was sobbing and trying to catch my breath and tears were running down my cheeks. When you got home you demanded an explanation for all my drama and for embarrassing you in front of the whole congregation. I said that you had just given the best sermon I'd ever heard and I was overcome with emotion. Then...well, I worked up my nerve and I was going to tell you the truth but...but you grabbed your brief case and yanked that speech out and you said, "Which part, Violet? Which part set you off?" You talked about making a difference, how you were showing people the right path — you could see it in their faces staring up at you. But I was crying because Doc Baker had looked at my legs and it was too late. I had closed up years before that. Closed up tight.

Pause.

Closed up until that young preacher talked about how God wants us to live every minute and enjoy the sunshine and the apple pie at the Co-op and even that flat tire and especially yellow and pink tulips. And I thought about that night on the bathroom floor and my baby slipping out of my body and Mrs. Ferguson and her crying husband and how I'd wasted so many years waiting for a preacher to say something *worth* listening to. And here it finally is, something I can hold on to. Something that makes sense in my bones.

Pause.

Now that we're talking straight to each other, steady yourself, 'cause another speed bump's creeping up on us…

Pause.

A gentleman moved in across the back alley and, well…he taped a handful of yellow and pink tulips to my door. 'Course they were stuck there with silver duct tape but I got the meaning. I knew it was him 'cause his whole backyard is covered in tulips like a rainbow blanket; like he doesn't know a person could plant something different. And… I…been baking apple pies every week, wanting to set a nice warm one on his front step. But I need to get things straight with you first before I start passing out apple pie. I'm not letting another chance pass me by and he won't wait on me forever.

Pause.

I'll set the Bible right beside the daisies I left you last week. But this Bible is the last present I'm bringing, 'cause pretending you're alive isn't helping anyone. And, just so you know, I won't be back to clean up the leaves and such off your headstone neither. No, sir. I don't *need you* to be mad at anymore. I'm saying goodbye to that baby I never got to hold, and I'm saying goodbye to you too, Irwin.

VIOLET stands and folds up her chair and walks away. Lights down.

The End

The Motherhouse

by Tamara Lagrandeur

About the playwright

Tamara Lagrandeur is a Montreal-based writer who studied playwriting at Concordia University. Originally from Knowlton, Quebec, Tamara's interests include sketch-comedy, travelling with the smallest piece of luggage while maintaining a high number of outfit options, and yelling at the Brome Lake ducks...for therapeutic reasons. Achievements include co-writing and acting in *Post-Modern Family: A Sketch-Comedy Show*, being bilingual (although her parents should receive some of the credit for this) and running the 10k marathon (this may have been a dream). *The Motherhouse* was originally presented in November 2010 for Concordia's Winter SIPA/Short Works Festival (Student Initiated Production Assignments). Amanda McQueen, a Concordia Theatre Performance graduate, performed Sister Constance McMullen, Jonathon Stradeski designed set and costume, Kyle Purves co-directed and Laura MacDonald was the stage manager. Somehow all of these people agreed and were not tricked into remounting the show for Montreal's Fringe Festival in 2011, with the addition of Jess Fildes as the "other" stage manager.

Characters

SISTER MCMULLEN — age 91

Setting

Sister McMullen's room in the Grey Nuns' Motherhouse, located in downtown Montreal. It is a very plainly decorated room with a single bed, nightstand, small desk and chair. There is a cross hung above the bed and religious pictures on the walls.

Scene 1

SISTER MCMULLEN is dressed in very conservative clothes with a small wooden cross around her neck. Apart from a slightly hunched back, she seems younger than her age and she is still very energetic. She paces around the room as fast as her ninety-one-year-old body allows her. She seems furious. She has a letter in her hand. She occasionally looks up and mumbles, as if speaking to God directly.

SISTER MCMULLEN:

They thought we would die off!

Pause, then continues to pace.

They thought it would only be a matter of time, a couple of years at most, before every last Grey Nun would either be in a hospital or buried six feet under!

(*sarcastically*) Or standing guard with Our Father above, as they say here. They speak as though nuns have reserved box seats up there… I mean, it's heaven; everyone is in the nosebleeds!

No, they never thought we would last this long. But what did they expect from nuns? We light candles for the good Lord but we don't burn them at both ends! I mean, they really should have foreseen this, especially now, with the emphasis on finding the right recipe to live longer. They all swear by ginkgo-biloba or protein shakes! Well, I have been drinking the same shake for the last seventy years. I call it the triple-threat: obedience, poverty and chastity! How is that for longevity!

She looks at the letter in her hand.

I still can't believe this!

She reads from the letter.

'Dear residing holy woman.'

She looks up.

Residing holy woman… Someone decided to get creative!

She reads from the letter.

Anyway, 'dear residing holy woman, as you are surely aware, Concordia University made the acquisition of the Grey Nuns' Motherhouse in 2004.'

She looks up.

I always did find that 'Motherhouse' made us sound like something out of the *Twilight Zone.*

She motions as if she is speaking into a walkie-talkie.

Captain, we have made contact with the Motherhouse of holy women, prepare the missiles!

She reads from the letter.

'It was the university's plan to use the site to house the Fine Arts department.'

She looks up.

Well, at least it's not the school of business. They are not close to God.

She reads from the letter.

'It was agreed that the process of moving the remaining occupants would be gradual, starting in 2007 and ending in 2022. However, as it is clearly stated in the legal document annexed to the 2004 contract, under clause A1.8, then revised in 2005 under clause A2.7, special clause B7.655 permits, under exceptional circumstances, that the occupants be moved to another location with two weeks' notice. It is our regret to inform you that we have reached the exceptional circumstances that demand that you vacate the premises within the next two weeks.'

She looks up.

Now, I have said it before and I will say it again: fine print is the work of Satan! The walls of hell are lined with it! And the lawyers who write it into contracts are forced to explain it to deaf businessmen, for all eternity! And here comes the best part…

She reads from the letter.

'All remaining occupants of the Motherhouse will be moved to a lovely and quiet convent located in the beautiful Eastern Townships.'

She looks up and laughs.

The Eastern Townships! Do they even know how insulting that is to an urban, sophisticated Sister like myself? I've seen battered women, drug addicts, the mentally ill, teen pregnancies; I've helped the whole lot of them! Who are we going to help in the Eastern Townships, people who have been attacked by bears? Depressed birdwatchers? Lord, give me strength!

She paces around the room.

Well, fine print or not, they said we would be allowed to stay until 2022… And I've put in too much preparation to be kicked out now!

I remember the day the order announced we were selling the Motherhouse to that university as if it was yesterday. That night, when I prayed my rosary… I grasped those little beads and…well, I prayed. But I also promised myself that I was going to live to see the day in 2022 when they would ride in with their flying cars and kick me out. The only thing that could stand in my way was death. And let me tell you this, when you step into the ring with the Grim Reaper, you know he's going to win in the end. The only thing you can do is hope that he gets to that ring as late as possible. If you're lucky, maybe he'll get his cloak caught in a door, or maybe he'll have misplaced his scythe…

Knowing that death is my ultimate opponent, I started preparing the very next day. It's no easy task to plan to live to be one hundred and three years old. The first step was to make sure that my body is getting plenty of vitamins and minerals.

She bends down as if telling a secret.

The other nuns around here call me 'the shopkeeper,' and let's just say I'm not dealing antiques. Centrum silver, vitamin D, cod liver oil, you name it, I have it. And take it; the doctor says I have the blood of a Chinese Olympic gymnast!

I also need to make sure that my mind doesn't slowly fall into the grip of senility. That is where my little Japanese friend came in. You may know him as Sudoku. I've been completing five expert-level puzzles every day for the last six years. My mind is as sharp as the nails they used on Jesus' cross!

And now, just like that, they want to hurry up the process and get rid of us. Well, the other nuns might be really happy about the Eastern Townships and its beautiful scenery and lakes and…ducks. But I'm not. This Motherhouse is my home and has been for the last seventy years. All I ask for is another twelve years. Give an old nun a chance to achieve her goal. Probably her last one…

Pause.

No, you know what? It takes more than fine print to kick Sister Constance McMullen out of her house! As God is my witness, I refuse to go down quietly! That's right, I'm a Sister with a plan, mister! While all the other nuns have been packing, I've been coming up with a scheme for retaliation! People may think it's unholy to retaliate against authority, but do you know what is really unholy? Kicking a bunch of old nuns out of their house! It's a time like this that makes me miss my wimple. They wouldn't be able to kick out nuns in their wimples.

Now, I've been thinking about this plan while reading that letter so I haven't worked out all the kinks yet. I believe at this point my best course of action is to let it stew for a while. And I'm ninety-one years old, so I'll take a nap on it!

Blackout.

Scene 2

SISTER MCMULLEN comes in pulling a cart full of what seems to be normal books. But actually, these books are Bibles. There is also a plastic bag on top of the Bibles but we cannot see what is in the bag. She stops and rubs her back and arms as if it has been a trying endeavour.

The nap was just what I needed. I've come up with a genius plan. If they want to get me out of this room, they'll have to carry me out. Not too hard of a task, they'll think. After all, I'm ninety-one and svelte. I can say without bragging, I'm a very svelte woman. So that's when I started thinking; if I were to, say, handcuff myself to the nightstand, I would be much heavier. Then, they would either have to go get some kind of big tool to cut the handcuffs, or they would have to carry me out still handcuffed to the nightstand. Of course they couldn't just break them, they couldn't risk hurting a sweet and delicate old nun like myself.

She walks over to the nightstand and, without any effort, lifts a corner of it up.

Unfortunately, I forgot that the Motherhouse has been trying to cut costs. First thing the new Mother Superior did when she was appointed was to auction off our real furniture! I used to have a nightstand made out of wood! With a quarter of the money they made at the auction, they went and bought us some nice cardboard furniture at IKEA!

She looks away from the audience.

(*angry*) Thank you!

Anyway, that's why all those Bibles are there.

She points to the cart filled with Bibles.

I borrowed them from the other Sisters' rooms. They're so excited about moving I could have asked for their right kidney and they would have given it to me! I told Mother Superior that I was borrowing the other Sisters' Bibles to write in the best memory I had of them in the Motherhouse, like some kind of high school yearbook.

She looks at the audience and contorts her face in a way that's saying 'as if I would ever do that.'

So with all these Bibles inside it, that nightstand will be much heavier. Proof that it's not always a bad thing to let religion weigh you down! And, I'll make sure they can't easily remove them from the nightstand. Maybe I'll use some of that, what's it called? Duck tape? I don't like ducks. They make me think of the Eastern Townships.

SISTER MCMULLEN goes over to the cart full of Bibles.

Of course, the first Bible that should be placed inside this self-sacrificing nightstand is my own.

She picks up a very neat-looking Bible and shows it off. She shows both covers, the sides, then the spine, looking particularly proud of this last part. She flips through the pages, showing that there is nothing written inside.

Now, you can tell a lot about a nun from her Bible. Look at this, no dog ears, no tears, look at how clean this is. It's pristine. Almost like the day my first Mother Superior gave it to me, in 1940, at the young age of twenty-one.

She takes the stance of a very proud woman. Her face becomes more severe, she lifts her chin up and raises an eyebrow. She speaks very clearly and loudly.

Sister Constance McMullen, let this be the Bible to guide you, to teach you and direct you in your sisterhood. Today, you begin your life of service, and promise to serve the poor in the name of our Lord. Today, you become a Sister of Charity, also to be known as a Grey Nun, in remembrance of our founding Mother, Marguerite d'Youville. Wear your grey habit proudly in her memory. Know, Sister McMullen, that you pledge to have a life of sacrifice and hardship; a life free of riches, personal liberties and carnal indulgence.

She moves as to mimic her young self. She just looks at the audience, eyes wide open in fear and confusion. After a moment, she finally speaks. Her voice breaks, it is younger and more high-pitched. She doesn't speak very loudly, almost whispers.

Mother Superior Tremblay…thank you.

She returns to her own Sister McMullen stance.

I felt a shiver go down my spine while she was speaking to me. Perhaps because it was such an uplifting speech! It's interesting that she omitted to explain why we were called the Grey Nuns. Our dear founding mother, Marguerite d'Youville, was a fierce woman who had a strong will, a pure heart…and a bootlegging husband! The French Canadians of the time, they would say that when people were intoxicated, they were grey. So they were basically calling the Grey Nuns the drunk nuns! (*laughing*) Have you ever seen a drunk nun? (*bends down as if telling a secret*) The secret is eggnog!

Short pause.

Good Lord, where was I? Oh, yes, a Bible can really tell you about the owner. Well, mine says that I'm very neat, very organized, and I know how to treasure my few personal belongings. And now, it's going in the nightstand.

She places the Bible in the little drawer of the nightstand. Then goes back to the cart, takes a few others and places them in the nightstand as well. She picks one up in particular and looks at it. It is worn and used, almost mangled. She touches the spine and shakes her head; it is cracked. She flips the pages in front of the audience to show that some passages are underlined and some pages have folded corners.

Well, well, if it isn't the Bible of little Miss Sister Lemaire. Look at this, look at all that writing and highlighting… This is downright graffiti! Jesus wouldn't approve of this! So I wonder what this says about Sister Lemaire. Perhaps that she is not organized… Or a bit messy… (*yells*) Or, if at one point in your life you decide to borrow the Motherhouse Buick LeSabre to drive a teenager home one day, she'll tell on you!

She gasps, realizing that she has said something that she probably should have not. She grasps her mouth with her eyes wide open. She makes the sign of the cross.

Pause.

Perhaps that happened. Oh, golly, I'm in the Motherhouse; I can't lie here! All right, that happened. There was just such a nice boy at the school where we were volunteering… He was cute as a bug's ear and he wasn't feeling well one day. He couldn't reach his mother, so I offered to drive him home. And I still don't see what the problem is! I mean the boy was fifteen years old and plenty able to take care of himself at home alone, and he really was sick. It's not as if I had been cooking up some gin in the bathtub, unlike someone's husband.

She looks up, as if she's looking at Marguerite D'Youville.

Anyway, when I got back, Mother Superior was waiting in the parking lot for me.

She once again takes the stance of Mother Superior Tremblay and imitates her voice. Mother Superior Tremblay seems very angry but is trying to restrain herself.

Are you aware that you have taken the Motherhouse's Vista Cruiser without authorization?

She raises a finger as if to prevent someone from talking.

That you have put yourself, that boy and my congregation in jeopardy for not having followed the school's procedures? That you could have gotten into an accident on the road and hurt yourself and the student? That you are guilty of insubordination by not asking my permission to use the Motherhouse's vehicle? Sister McMullen, you have been with the Sisters of Charity for over twenty years, surely you know the rules by now? What do you have to say for yourself?

She takes her usual stance but without the bend in her back. Her voice sounds younger as well.

Mother Superior Tremblay, I am sorry…that you know nothing about cars, because that is not a Vista Cruiser, it's a Buick LeSabre! So, there.

She takes her present stance and voice.

She made me dig out wicks that had been lost in the wax in every one of the two hundred and forty-five candles in the Church. Do you know what that will do to your skin? (*shakes the Bible in her hand*) All because little Miss Perfect here ran and told the Mother Superior the minute she saw me drive away. I can imagine her face, her… (*holding back what she really wants to say*) Her subtle beauty.

She takes a stance with her hands together and makes a face like a mouse.

Mother Superior Tremblay, Sister McMullen just drove away with the Motherhouse Vista Cruiser and her hands were not in the ten and two position on the steering wheel. Oh, and there was a student in the car with her, a male student!

Returns to her own stance.

You know why there's so much writing in her Bible? She highlights the passages that she finds most inspirational, to remember to quote them to people when they ask for advice. She also writes in the margins which situations will most benefit from the underlined passage. In a single page, you may come across in the margin: problem with co-worker, jealous neighbour or defective coffee maker. Dear Lord, give me patience! (*She pinches the part of her nose between her eyes.*)

It's true, though, with the past years' sharp decrease in interest in religion, it's surprising the number of people who will ask a nun for advice in the street. People see that little cross around your neck, long skirt and orthopedic shoes, and will tell you their lives! I started thinking about getting some business cards made: Sister Constance McMullen, professional holy woman. Anyway, I can never really remember any good passages of the Bible, so I just recite some Céline Dion song titles. People don't even notice! Someone will ask, 'What am I supposed to do if I think my wife is cheating on me?' I just answer, 'Oh, yes, it's all coming back to me now… There was a night when I felt alone so I drove all night. And found that a new day has come… Because of the power of love. So tell your wife, if you asked me to and because you loved me… I'm alive. And that's the way it is.' And that somehow gives them the answer they were looking for. People don't want to hear that old Bible language anyway. They want something they can relate to. And I'm almost sure that if the Bible had been written now, it would sound like a Celine Dion song.

She looks at the Bible in her hand.

Well, Sister Lemaire, I shall consider this indirect help as a sincere apology for having told on me forty years ago.

She places the Bible in the nightstand. She then returns to the cart and takes another Bible. She shows it to the audience. The pages are all orange.

See this, the pages are all orange. Do you know what this means? Orange pages in a Bible means you've got yourself a Sister who indulges in the Cheetos!

She puts the Bible in the nightstand, then goes to the chair and sits down.

That's a lot of work! I'm already tired!

She looks at the desk.

Oh, yes, I have another Bible here! Probably the most important.

She opens the desk drawer and takes out a Bible.

Dear Janie's Bible! Jane Lavoie, my best friend. She was my neighbour when I was a kid. We would put ladybugs in our mothers' lemonades in the summer. It was so funny until my mom swallowed one and never made lemonade again. I suspect she still made it for herself sometimes, but she would always finish it before we came home from school. I would open the door in the kitchen and would see an empty lemonade jug just sitting on the counter. Reminding me.

Short pause.

The Lavoies were a nice French-Canadian family. Jane had an older brother, Gilles, a striking young lad he was. Like a non-smoking Marlboro man. You could say that Gilles was my beau when I was a young lady. I was eighteen and he was nineteen. I remember during the summer, he would wash the rich neighbour's Ford Coupe. He would put on his father's sunglasses and roll up his sleeves. I would watch him all afternoon, just waiting for that moment when he would stop, turn around, wave and smile. Like this. (*She stands with her back to the audience, turns around, waves and smiles.*) The sun would hit his beautiful blond hair and he looked like…an angel, a waving, smiling angel! Oh, and sometimes, he would invite me to sit with him in the car while it was drying off. We would just sit there, not knowing what to say to each other… So he would tell me about cars. For an hour, all he would talk about was cars… What type of car he was going to buy later on when he got a good job, which car was the fastest, the best tires for a car… Then, when he was twenty, the neighbour let him borrow his…car, and he got into an accident…and he passed away.

Pause. She looks through the Bible nervously. She finds a photograph between the pages.

Oh, look, here's a photograph of us on the day we joined the Grey Nuns. Jane was so proud; her face was glowing. She was one of those people who wanted to help the entire world. When she was young, she had pictures of all the different saints and she would play with them like they were action figures. She always wanted to be a nun. After Gilles died, she started looking into joining the Grey Nuns. I didn't really know what to do with my life at that point… And I was so heartbroken over Gilles… So I decided to follow her. I can still see that big aisle we walked down on the day of the final vow ceremony. As we were walking down, one behind the other, like penguins, Mother Superior was reciting a prayer in Latin.

She takes the stance of Mother Superior.

Pater, qui es in caelis, sanctificetur Nomen tuum
Adveniat regnum tuum. Fiat voluntas tua, sicut in caelo et in terra.
Panem nostrum quotidianum da nobis hodie, et dimitte nobis...

She takes her young stance and has her hands together in front of her.

I looked around and everyone was so serious. I looked back at my parents and my mother had tears in her eyes. Jane gave me the thumbs up. Mother Superior's voice was resonating in the big church and it was as if it was the voice of Mary herself... And the sun was shining through the stained glass windows... And with every step, I just kept telling myself—(*slowly*)—I... am...so...itchy!

She takes her current stance.

It's true! I wasn't used to the habit yet and I was itchy all over!

The first few years were good. Jane would keep me out of trouble.

She looks at the audience with a smile on her face.

This may surprise you, but I like to play little pranks on people from time to time. I played my first prank on Sister Lemaire. I slipped a note in her Bible telling her that she had to wear her rosary around her head... And I signed it, "Yours truly, Jesus." Then I added: "P.S. My name is actually pronounced Hesus with a soft J." That was Jane's idea! For two days Sister Lemaire went around with her rosary around her head, saying that she had received the order from Hesus himself! Mother Superior knew it was me, so Jane spoke to her and I got a lighter punishment. Everyone loved Jane. Even Mother Superior Tremblay couldn't resist her. But then, at only twenty-nine, she was diagnosed with cancer and died later that year. Her parents asked me to speak at her funeral. They said they were so lucky that they had a nun to pray for their two children...

Pause. She looks at the Bible in her hand.

Well, Jane, sixty-two years later, you're still helping me!

She places the Bible in the nightstand. She then sits on the chair.

I deserve a little break, after all that hard work! Oh, I know, I still have to see...

She goes to the cart and takes the plastic bag. She goes back to the chair.

This is one of the most important parts of my plan.

She reaches into the bag and takes out a pair of handcuffs.

You should have seen their faces when I walked into that store of things related to the physical act of love; coitus. It was like when those people looked up and saw Sally Field flying, in the 1967 hit television show, *The Flying Nun*.

She looks at the audience, eyes wide open in disbelief.

They were all there just staring at me, so I said, 'Help an old Sister with a pair of handcuffs, won't you, dear? The good Lord will repay you twofold!' It didn't take a minute and I had paid and was walking out the door with my purchase in hand. I tell you, they were nice people. I would recommend that, what do they call it on the streets — oh, yes, I would recommend that intercourse shop to any one of the Sisters here!

Laughs.

Well, let's see if these work properly…

She gets up and goes over to the nightstand and puts one of the handcuffs around her wrist and the other around the nightstand's drawer handle.

Yes, I think this is going to be perfect!

She looks into the bag for the key.

Wait a minute, I thought they put the key inside the bag… Maybe I put it in my pocket…

Looks nervously in her pockets but does not find it.

Okay, just don't panic, Constance, everything is fine. This was the plan all along. To tie yourself to this nightstand in retaliation against being forced out of the Motherhouse.

Pause.

I just wish that I could have put more Bibles in the nightstand to weigh it down. And I wish I could have gone to the bathroom before. And gotten a glass of water… And maybe a snack. And closed the window in the hall in case a flock of migrating ducks fly in and next thing I know I'm Tippi Hedren in Hitchcock's *The Birds*. (*waves her arms as if swatting away birds*)

Is it just me or does it feel like that handcuff is around my neck and it's getting tighter and tighter with every second…

She grasps her neck and seems to have trouble breathing.

Help! Help! There's no one out there. They're probably all outside enjoying their last days in the city…

Well, there's just one thing left to do.

She makes the sign of the cross and gets down on her knees. She tries to put her hands together in the prayer position, but one of them is handcuffed, so after struggling for a moment, she finally puts only one hand in front of herself. She looks awkward.

Good Lord above… (*She looks up and gives a weak smile.*)

I know that I'm not always the model Sister here. I break the rules and complain about the food. But I promise, if You get me out of these handcuffs, I'll be better. I won't whine about the food… Okay, maybe instead of complaining, I'll go on the interwebs and goggle some recipes they could try… Okay, I'll even offer to stir the stew from time to time!

She looks around. Nothing happens.

Good Lord above, if You get me out of these handcuffs, I'll promise to stop skipping beads when praying the rosary.

She looks around and again nothing happens.

All right, I've been holding back, I know! Please, good Lord, get me out of these handcuffs and I promise I will reread the Bible and highlight the passages that I could tell people instead of song titles! I'll learn them by heart… And my heart will go on?

She waits. But nothing happens.

Good Lord, You test me! This might be blasphemy, but it seems like You've taken so much away from me and I've given so much to You! I've given You my entire life! I'm ninety-one years old! I'll never marry, never have children, never own a house, only be a nun! I've had the chance to help so many in my life, and for that I am grateful… But isn't it enough? Enough to at least release me from these handcuffs and let me use the washroom?

She waits again and looks around. Nothing. She puts her hand down.

What do You want from me? I've got nothing left!

Pause. She gets up.

I guess I knew it would come down to this in the end. Me, handcuffed to a flimsy piece of furniture, and You, up there… Sneering.

What do You want me to say? That I'm a bad nun? So maybe I wasn't like Jane, I didn't grow up dreaming of the day I'd be wearing the habit! So maybe at first, I thought that it would be temporary, that I would try it out! We didn't have psychology degrees back then to help us figure out what we actually wanted to do! And so what if I've been praying for the ability to fly since '67!

Maybe I could have done something else with my life after a few years, but with Janie gone… It was like I had no choice, I had to keep going… But this was her dream, her desire, not mine. Yeah, I said it! Is that what You want, honesty? Is that what I need to do so You'll get me out of these handcuffs?

All right, well, how is this; I've been holding on to that date in 2022 because it's the only thing that has kept me alive! I've handcuffed myself to my nightstand because I'm terrified of life outside this Motherhouse! I've been fighting to stay but actually I've been waiting for the courage to leave! I don't want to move out of the city and I'm tired of other people making decisions for me. I became Sister Constance McMullen when I was so young… I do think I've helped the community with the Order, but now I have to help myself. Is ninety-one too old to do that? I guess I'm going to find out…

She looks up.

You didn't see that one coming, did You? Dear Lord, what am I saying? Of course You did! I'm the one who's been surprised… But I understand now… I've been waiting for You to get me out of my handcuffs for seventy years. It's about time I got myself out.

She makes a swift movement with her handcuffed hand and breaks the chain between the cuffs. She looks at her arm in disbelief. She looks up and seems to be saying something. She looks at the audience, eyes wide open.

I'm so glad I didn't buy the more expensive pair!

The End

Information on Producing

To obtain permission for professional and amateur productions of any of the plays in this volume, contact the publisher:

Signature Editions
P.O. Box 206, RPO Corydon, Winnipeg, MB R3M 3S7
www.signature-editions.com
signature@allstream.net

or:

Kiss Me Outside the Box, Carmen Cartterfield, carmen.cartter@gmail.com

Mature Young Adults, Wesley J. Colford, wesleycolford@hotmail.com

Waterfront: The Blessing, Leah Jane Esau, leah.esau@utoronto.ca

Red, Jordan Hall, c/o Playwrights Guild of Canada, info@playwrightsguild.ca

The Motherhouse, Tamara Lagrandeur, tamaralagrandeur@gmail.com

Mrs. Ferguson's Bed, Sherryl Melnyk, slmelnyk@hotmail.com

Crazy Love, David Sklar, dsklar25@gmail.com

Third Person, Brandon Wicke, brandon.wicke@gmail.com

Eco-Audit

Printing this book using Rolland 55 Enviro White instead of virgin fibres paper saved the following resources:

Trees	Solid Waste	Water	Air Emissions
3	149kg	9,839 L	387 kg